PET
Preliminary English Test

Practice
Tests ▶ Plus

Includes 2004 exam specifications

Louise Hashemi
Barbara Thomas

Longman
www.longman.com

Contents

TEST 2

Exam Overview

PAPER 1 Reading and Writing

(1 hour 30 minutes)

Reading Parts 1–5

Part 1
Five short texts (signs, notes, messages, e-mails, notes, postcards, etc.) each with a three-option multiple-choice question.

Part 2
Five short texts which describe a person or group of people to match to eight short texts.

Part 3
One longer factual text with ten correct/incorrect questions.

Part 4
One longer text giving opinions or attitudes with five four-option multiple-choice questions.

Part 5
One factual or narrative cloze text with ten four-option multiple-choice questions.

Writing Parts 1–3

Part 1
Five sentence transformations all related to a common theme.

Part 2
One short communicative message, e.g. postcard, e-mail, note, etc. of 35–45 words.

Part 3
Either an informal letter or a story of about 100 words.

PAPER 2 Listening

(about 30 minutes)

Part 1
Seven short monologues or dialogues each with a three-option multiple-choice question based on pictures.

Part 2
One longer monologue or interview with six three-option multiple-choice questions.

Part 3
One longer monologue with six questions completing gaps in notes.

Part 4
One longer informal dialogue with six correct/incorrect questions.

PAPER 3 Speaking

(10–12 minutes for two candidates together)

Part 1
The examiner asks each candidate questions in turn about personal information, present situation, past experiences and future plans. (2–3 minutes)

Part 2
The candidates discuss pictures together, using language to make and respond to suggestions, make recommendations, and agree or disagree. (2–3 minutes)

Part 3
Each candidate talks on his/her own about one of a pair of photographs for up to one minute. (3 minutes)

Part 4
The candidates and the examiner discuss a subject related to Part 3. (3 minutes)

PAPER 1   Reading and Writing Test   (1 hour 30 minutes)

Reading Part 1

 Strategy

1 Read the instructions to the Exam Task on the opposite page.

1 How many questions do you have to answer?

2 What do you have to decide?

3 Where do you mark your answers?

2 Look at the example.

1 What kind of text is this?

a) a message on a board   b) a sign   c) a label

2 Where might you see it?

3 The correct answer is **A**. Let's decide why.

Look at **A**. Underline the words which mean *It is forbidden*.

Underline the words which mean *from this room*.

Underline the words which mean *without permission*.

4 Why is **B** wrong? Is the sign about using the computers in this room?

5 Why is **C** wrong? Is the sign about moving computers into this room?

> •• *Exam tip!* ••••••••••••••••••••••
> When choosing the correct explanation for
> each text, look at each option A–C and decide
> if it means the same thing as the text.
> ••••••••••••••••••••••••••••••••••••

3 Look at Question 1.

1 What kind of text is this?

a) an e-mail b) a phone message
c) a Post-it note

2 Will Katie pay for Emily's ticket?

3 Does Katie have a student card?

4 What does Katie advise Emily to do? Why?

5 Will Katie and Emily buy their tickets on the train?

6 Where will they meet?

7 Look at **A**, **B** and **C**. Which one means the same as the message? Mark it. What words in the message tell you? Underline them.

8 Look at the other sentences. Decide why they are wrong.

4 Look at Questions 2–5.

For each question:

• decide what kind of text it is

• choose the correct answer

• mark the answer on your answer sheet.

> •• *Exam tip!* ••••••••••••••••••••••
> If you prefer, you can mark your answers on
> the paper and copy them onto the answer sheet
> when you have finished this part.
> ••••••••••••••••••••••••••••••••••••

Part 1

Questions 1–5

Look at the text in each question.
What does it say?
Mark the correct letter **A**, **B** or **C** on your answer sheet.

Example:

0

> **IT IS FORBIDDEN TO MOVE COMPUTERS FROM THIS ROOM WITHOUT PERMISSION FROM THE HEADTEACHER**

A   You mustn't take the computers out of this room without asking the headteacher.

B   You should check with the headteacher before using the computers in this room.

C   You must ask the headteacher for permission to move computers into this room.

Answer:

0	A	B	C
	▬	☐	☐

1

To	Emily
From	Katie

> If you bring your student card tomorrow, your train ticket will cost less. I've found my card. See you in queue at ticket office.

A   Katie will buy Emily's train ticket for her.

B   Emily's train ticket will be cheaper than Katie's.

C   Katie will meet Emily before they get on the train.

2

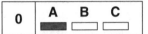

> **LOCKERS IN THIS AREA ARE RESERVED FOR USE BY VISITING TEAM ONLY**

A   Anyone who takes part in a swimming competition may use these lockers.

B   Swimmers from visiting teams needn't pay to use lockers.

C   Members of the local swimming team can't use these lockers.

3

> Paola
>
> Do you want to go to the concert with James tonight? Ring him before six to tell him. He'll go with someone else if he doesn't hear from you by then.   Tim

A   Paola won't be able to go to the concert unless she phones James by six.

B   James wants Paola to find someone to go to the concert with him.

C   James can no longer go to the concert with Paola at six.

[Turn over

4

E X I T
THIS DOOR MAY ONLY BE USED BY STAFF AFTER 5 P.M.

A You must ask a member of staff to unlock this door.

B People who work here must leave the building by 5 p.m.

C You may use this door in the evening if you work here.

5

> Chris____
>
> I've written this letter to Sam, but I can't find his address. Have you got it? If not, can you ring Mum and ask her? Then please post it.
>
> Sarah

Chris should

A phone Sam if he doesn't know the address.

B send the letter when he has found out the address.

C ask Mum to write the address and send the letter.

Language practice: Reading Part 1

1 Grammar: modal verbs (*may, must/ mustn't, should/shouldn't, needn't*)

> Modal verbs often appear in Reading Part 1, so it is important to understand what they mean. Modal verbs are also tested in Writing Part 1.

a) Find and underline examples of the modal verbs *may, must/mustn't, should/shouldn't, needn't* in the Exam Task on pages 7–8.

b) Look at the meanings of the verbs below.

- **It is forbidden to** move the computers.
  You must not move the computers.
- Anyone who takes part in a swimming competition **may** use these lockers.
  Anyone who takes part in a swimming competition **is allowed/permitted to** use these lockers.
- People who work here **must** leave by 5 p.m.
  It is necessary/essential that people who work here leave by 5 p.m.
- Swimmers from visiting teams **needn't** pay to use lockers.
  It isn't necessary for swimmers from visiting teams to pay to use lockers.
- Chris **should** phone Sam.
  Chris **is advised to** phone Sam.

c) Complete the second sentence so that it means the same as the first. Use one of the verbs in the box.

| may   must   mustn't   should   shouldn't |
| needn't   ~~should~~ |

0 I advise you to catch the early train.
You ......should...... catch the early train.

1 It is essential to check in your luggage an hour before your flight.
You .... check in your luggage an hour before your flight.

2 Smoking is forbidden in the youth hostel.
You .... smoke in the youth hostel.

3 It isn't necessary to take your own towel to that swimming pool.
You .... take your own towel to that swimming pool.

4 Customers are advised to check their change before leaving the shop.
You .... check your change before leaving the shop.

5 Visitors are permitted to use the school canteen.
Visitors .... use the school canteen.

6 Students are advised not to leave all their revision until the day before the exam.
Students .... leave all their revision until the day before the exam.

2 Writing: words left out

> Words like *the* and *a(n)*, pronouns (*I*, *you*, etc.) and parts of verbs (*is*, *are*, etc.) are often left out in messages, signs and notices.

Read the texts below and find places where words are missing. Write them in to make full sentences.

1

IN EMERGENCY USE
TELEPHONE IN HALL TO
CALL HOSTEL MANAGER

2

Fraser. Don't forget to take towel with you to football practice tonight.   Dad

3

READ INSTRUCTIONS
BEFORE EQUIPMENT IS
SWITCHED ON

4

Having lovely time in Spain. Weather wonderful.

5

If receipt needed,
ask assistant when paying.

3 Grammar: *if/unless* sentences (real situations)

> In Part 1, you often see sentences with *if* or *unless* giving information, advice or instructions.

a) Look at the following sentences. What is the verb tense in each part? What does *unless* mean?

1 If you bring your student card, the ticket will cost less.
2 He'll go with someone else if he doesn't hear from you.
3 He'll go with someone else unless he hears from you.

b) Match the sentence halves.

1 If you miss your appointment, ...b....
2 We'll be home by lunchtime   ....
3 If they invite us to stay with them, ...
4 I'll have time to talk to you   ....
5 If you aren't outside the restaurant, ...
6 I'll collect them from the station   ....

a) if you come back later.
b) you'll have to pay £10.
c) I'll go inside.
d) if they need a lift.
e) unless the traffic is very heavy.
f) we'll accept.

c) Now complete the following sentences with your own ideas.

1 I'll go to the cinema at the weekend if ....
....
2 Unless you help me with my homework, ...
....
3 I'll lend you this CD if ....
....
4 If we finish lessons early, ...
....
5 If I stay up late tonight, ...
....

d) Read your answers out. Did anyone have the same answers?

▶ **Strategy**

1 Read the instructions to the Exam Task opposite.

1 How many questions are there?
2 What do all the people want?
3 What are the descriptions about?
4 How many descriptions are there?
5 What do you have to decide?
6 Where do you mark your answers?

2 Look at the pictures.

Each question describes a different person or group of people. What kind of people do the pictures show?

3 Look at Questions 6–10.

a) **All the people are looking for something different. Look at the underlined parts of Question 6. What is important for Felipe and Gabriela?**

1 Where should the hotel be?
2 Are they alone?
3 What do they want to do?
4 Where will they eat?

b) **Now underline the important parts of Questions 7–10.**

4 Look at texts A–H to find the important information.

a) **Look at Question 6 again.**
1 Which hotels are near the city centre?
2 Which ONE of the hotels is best for Felipe and Gabriela? (Remember: they want to walk around the city centre!)

b) **Check your answer.**
• Is the hotel near the railway station?
• Do Felipe and Gabriela want to eat at the hotel?
• Is the hotel suitable for the baby?

c) **Mark the letter (A, B, C, etc.) by Question 6 on your answer sheet.**

d) **Look at the important points you underlined for Questions 7–10. Use them to decide which hotels are the most suitable for the other people. Mark your answers on your answer sheet.**

• • **Exam tip!** • • • • • • • • • • • • • • • • • • •
You must have a different answer for each
question. You cannot use the same hotel twice.
• •

Part 2

Questions 6–10

The people below all want to find somewhere to stay.
On the opposite page there are descriptions of eight hotels.
Decide which hotel would be the most suitable for the following people.
For questions **6–10**, mark the correct letter **(A–H)** on your answer sheet.

6

Felipe and Gabriela want to spend the weekend <u>in the city centre near the railway station</u> with their <u>one-year-old son</u>. They want to be <u>able to walk everywhere</u>. They plan to <u>eat in restaurants</u>.

7

Giorgos wants to be able to swim, but is not interested in other sports. He'd like to spend the weekend somewhere quiet in the country. The hotel must have a car park.

8

Monica would like to stay somewhere in the countryside where there are organised activities so that she can meet other people. As she has some work to do, e-mail facilities must be available.

9

Julia and Robert are travelling by car and want to park at their hotel. They don't want to be further than ten kilometres from the city. They want to swim every day and have dinner at the hotel.

10

Adam and Barbara need to stay somewhere in the city which provides lunch and dinner and has a car park. Their three children all enjoy sport.

A   **The Star Hotel** is a five-minute drive from the city centre, and all rooms have their own television and telephone. Guests can eat all their meals here – breakfast, lunch and dinner. The hotel has its own large car park. There is a gym and two tennis courts. Entertainment is available at weekends.

B   **York House** is between two farms. The hotel arranges dances and other events which you can attend if you wish, or you can walk in the gardens and enjoy the scenery. It is especially popular with people travelling alone and also has a fully equipped business room and internet café. All meals are available on request.

C   **The Grange Hotel** is outside the city, but hotel staff can collect you from the station and arrange trips in the area by coach. It is close to all the main roads and has a large car park. Although only breakfast is served, there are two good restaurants nearby. Fax, e-mail and photocopying are available.

D   **Rosewood Guesthouse** is about one kilometre from the city centre. It is easy to reach the city's shopping and entertainment areas or drive into the surrounding countryside. There is a swimming pool in the next street. Dinner is available if booked in advance, and there is a large car park.

E   **The Blue Lion Hotel** is on the south side of the city and is just a short taxi ride from the railway station and places of interest. Breakfast only is provided. Events such as talks and shows are organised every evening and are popular both with local people as well as the hotel's guests. Free parking is available in nearby streets.

F   Twenty kilometres from the city, in the middle of the hills, **Blantyre Manor** was previously a family home. It is a peaceful place to spend a few days, with very good sports facilities including golf, tennis and a swimming pool. There is a restaurant serving breakfast, lunch and dinner, and plenty of car-parking space.

G   **Victoria House** is a family hotel five minutes' walk from the railway and tram station and close to all the city's facilities. It is in the city centre near the shopping mall, where a range of restaurants is available. No car parking or meals except breakfast. Bicycles can be hired from reception.

H   Just five kilometres from the city centre, **The Spring Park Motel** is very near the motorway with plenty of parking space, so it is convenient for drivers, although it is in the countryside. Meals are not available, but only two kilometres along the motorway there is an excellent café where breakfast, lunch and dinner are available.

1 Vocabulary: hotel facilities

Match the words and phrases in the box with the hotel signs below.

restaurant   gym   swimming pool
telephone in room   car park   golf
bicycles for hire   lift   television in room
entertainment   garden   city centre – 3kms
railway station – 5 mins   tennis courts

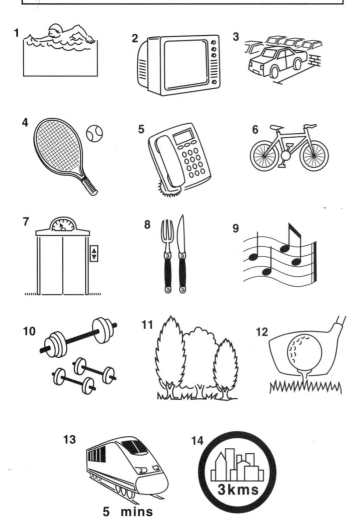

2 Grammar: linking words

There are several different ways to connect ideas in a sentence.
1   The words *because*, *as* and *since* answer the question *Why?*
   As she has some work to do, e-mail facilities must be available.

2   The words *but*, *although* and *while* introduce a contrasting idea.
   Giorgos wants to be able to swim, but is not interested in other sports.
   Although only breakfast is served, there are two good restaurants nearby.
3   The word *so* introduces a result.
   Felipe and Gabriela have a one-year-old son, so they need a family hotel.

a) Read the sentences below and choose the correct word for each space.

0   The Grange Hotel only serves breakfast .... there are two good restaurants nearby.
   A so   B because   C but ⟨circled⟩

1   It is popular with visitors travelling by car .... it is close to all the main roads.
   A but   B since   C although

2   The Spring Park Hotel is very near the motorway .... it is convenient for drivers.
   A so   B since   C but

3   .... the restaurant is very small, it serves excellent meals.
   A Although   B But   C Because

4   This hotel is near the airport .... a lot of business travellers stay there.
   A while   B because   C so

5   The hotel is closed in January .... the owners go on holiday.
   A but   B because   C although

6   The Blue Lion Hotel has talks and shows, ... York House has dances.
   A so   B while   C because

b) Join these sentences using linking words from above.

1   Parking is available in the street. It is sometimes difficult to find a space.

   ....

2   The rooms at the front are very popular. They have lovely views of the sea.

   ....

3   I like to eat dinner in my hotel. I choose hotels which have a restaurant.

   ....

4   Hotels usually offer lunch and dinner. Guesthouses often serve only breakfast.

   ....

3 Vocabulary: prepositions

> Prepositions are important in Reading Part 2 and are often tested in Reading Part 5, Writing Part 1 and Listening Part 1.

a) **Complete each sentence with a preposition from the box. They are all used in the same way in the texts about hotels on page 11.**

between	~~close~~	from	in (x3)	near
of (x2)	on	with		

0 My house is ..close.. to the shops, so it's very convenient.

1 It's .... the north side .... the town.

2 It's also .... a big park, where I can play tennis with my friends.

3 My best friend lives .... the next street to me, so she often comes to my house.

4 My school is .... the sports hall and the theatre.

5 I go to school by bus, and it's about ten minutes' walk .... the bus station to the school.

6 There are many places .... interest .... my town.

7 The sports centre is very popular .... young people.

8 My parents would prefer to live .... the countryside.

b) **Rewrite the sentences in your notebook so they are true for you.**

4 Grammar: present perfect and past simple

a) **Read the postcard and answer the questions.**

Hi Peter

I'm having a great time. We're staying at a super hotel in the middle of the hills. There's lots to do here. We've been here for a week, and I've played tennis and swum every day since we arrived. I've also ridden a moped twice! It's the first time I've ever ridden a moped. Two days ago we went to the nearby town to do some sightseeing. Tomorrow we're going on a coach trip to see some caves.

See you soon.   Barbara

1 How long has Barbara been at the hotel?

2 How often has she played tennis? swum?

3 How many times has she ridden a moped?

4 Has she ever ridden a moped before?

5 When did she go sightseeing?

b) **Match the sentence halves 1, 2 and 3 with the correct ending a), b) or c).**

1 We use *for*   ....

2 We use *since*   ....

3 We use *ago*   ....

a) when we mention the time something started.

b) to say how far back in time something happened.

c) to talk about a period of time.

c) **Complete the second sentence so that it means the same as the first, using no more than three words.**

0 It's a long time since I wrote to my penfriend.
I ......haven't written...... to my penfriend for a long time.

1 We haven't stayed in this hotel before.
This is the first time that .... in this hotel.

2 We arrived here a week ago.
We .... here for a week.

3 This is the first time I've ever ridden a horse.
I .... a horse before.

4 I haven't played tennis for a long time.
It's a long time since .... tennis.

5 The last time I had a holiday was two years ago.
I .... a holiday for two years.

5 Speaking: your experiences

Work with a partner. Ask and answer these questions.

1 Have you ever stayed in a hotel?

2 What is the best hotel you have ever stayed in? Where was it? What facilities did it have?

3 Where do you usually go on holiday?

4 Have you ever been to Scotland? Australia? France? When did you go there? Why did you go?

5 Have you ever ridden a moped? gone sailing? When was the first time you did it?

6 What do you like doing best on holiday? Why?

Reading Part 3

1 Read the instructions to the Exam Task opposite.

1 How many sentences are there?
2 What are the sentences about?
3 What do you have to read?
4 What do you have to decide?
5 When do you mark A on your answer sheet?
6 When do you mark B on your answer sheet?

2 Read Sentences 11–20 to get a good idea what the text is about.

Match the sentences to the following topics.

a) places to stay 17
b) how the day is organised ....
c) cancellations ....
d) what happens if it rains ....
e) what you need to take ....
f) when to pay ....
g) when they are open ....
h) staff qualifications ....
i) method of payment ....
j) who the courses are suitable for ....

3 Read the text to find the information you need.

For each sentence (11–20), mark the part of the text where you think the answer is. The first two are done for you.

4 Look at the sentences again.

• Compare them with your underlined text.
• Decide whether the sentence is correct or incorrect.
• Mark your answer on your answer sheet.

> •• **Exam tip!** ••••••••••••••••••••••
> You don't need to understand every word in the text to answer the questions. Some parts of the text aren't tested, so don't worry about them.

Part 3

Questions 11–20

Look at the sentences below about a company which organises sports camps.
Read the text on the opposite page to decide if each sentence is correct or incorrect.
If it is correct, mark **A** on your answer sheet.
If it is not correct, mark **B** on your answer sheet.

11 Some centres are open all winter.

12 The activities available depend on the weather.

13 Action Sports Camps courses are unsuitable for people who are excellent at sport.

14 You need to have your own sports equipment.

15 Children and adults spend some time together each day.

16 Some of the staff are unqualified.

17 Action Sports Camps only recommend accommodation of a high quality.

18 You have to pay the total fee one month after you book.

19 Action Sports Camps charge you more if you pay with your credit card.

20 If you cancel three weeks before your camp, you will get half your money back.

Action Sports Camps

Action Sports Camps provide activity holidays for children aged over five and adults. We offer training in over twenty sports at ten different centres throughout the UK. All the centres are open from April until October, and some open during the winter for weekend courses. The sports offered differ from one centre to another, so if you want to do something in particular, you should check our colour brochure.

The camps are not just limited to outdoor sports – we cover a wide range of indoor activities as well. So if the rain comes, the camps continue, although you may have to take off your football boots and pick up a squash racket instead. With the experience we've gained over the years, we put together the right mix of sport and activities providing sport for all, not just for those who are brilliant at athletics. It is unnecessary to bring any equipment because it is all provided.

We work in small groups, children working with others of their own age, but we do all come together for social activities and meals. So different members of a family can make their own individual choices, but they get a chance to exchange their experiences later on.

Our centres offer first-class accommodation, food and facilities – and the staff are first-class too. Qualified teachers or professionals receive training from us, and many work with us year after year. We always employ qualified staff for activities such as swimming, trampolining and gymnastics, but some of the assistants organising the children's games are students, many of whom came to the camp themselves when they were younger.

At most of our centres, accommodation is in a hostel or tents. It is not possible for us to arrange other accommodation, but we can send you a list of what is available in the area. Most of the places are recommended to us, but not all, so we are not responsible for the quality of the accommodation on this list. Luxury accommodation is not available near our camps.

To book a place at a sports camp, complete the form and send it with a cheque for the deposit to the address below. The rest of the fee can be paid at any time, but we must receive it at least one month before your camp. Please note, to keep costs down, you are charged 2.5% extra by us if you pay with your credit card. You will receive a letter of confirmation within ten days of sending your form. Cancellations made up to a month before the camp are refunded in full apart from a 5% administration fee. Fifty per cent of the fee is refunded if a cancellation is made up to two weeks before the date of the camp. After that, no refunds can be given.

1 Vocabulary: negative adjectives

a) Look at Sentence 13 from page 14.

Action Sports Camps courses are unsuitable for people who are excellent at sports.

Unsuitable means the same as *not suitable.*

So, *Courses are* **unsuitable** *for …*
= *Courses* **aren't suitable** *for …*

b) Rewrite these sentences using the negative form of the underlined adjective. You will need to use: *im-*, *in-* and *un-*.

0 It isn't <u>necessary</u> to bring equipment.
   <u>It's unnecessary to bring equipment.</u>

1 Some of the staff aren't <u>qualified</u>.
   ....

2 It isn't <u>possible</u> for us to arrange other accommodation.
   ....

3 Luxury accommodation isn't <u>available</u> near our camps.
   ....

4 Some of the other guests weren't <u>tidy</u> people.
   ....

5 It isn't <u>safe</u> to go on a boat if you can't swim.
   ....

6 His answer wasn't <u>correct</u>.
   ....

2 Vocabulary: words with similar meanings

> In Part 3, the sentences often contain words and phrases which are different from those in the text but which have similar meanings.

a) Look at the words in bold in Sentence 20. They mean the same as one word in the text.

Sentence 20: *If you* **cancel** *three weeks before your camp, you will get half your money back.*

Text: ***Cancellations*** *made up to a month before the camp are refunded …*

b) Use a word or phrase from the box to replace one word in each Sentence 1–8 without changing the meaning.

> advises   book   closed   employees   fill in
> less expensive   not allowed   ~~pleasant~~
> take back

                pleasant

0 There are several <u>nice</u> parks in the city.

1 The schools are shut at weekends.

2 All the staff had a pay rise last month.

3 Don't forget to return your library book when you're in town.

4 The concert is going to be very popular so we should reserve seats.

5 The CDs in the supermarket are cheaper than the ones in the music shop.

6 Drivers are forbidden to stop on the motorway.

7 Please complete this form using a pencil, not a pen.

8 The college recommends that students should apply early for popular courses.

3 Grammar: the passive

a) Look at Sentence 19 from page 14. How do we form the passive?

Sentence 19: *Action Sports Camps charge you more if you pay with your credit card.*

Text: *You are charged 2.5% extra by us if you pay with your credit card.*

b) Rewrite these sentences using the words given.

0 This pop festival was recommended to me by my brother.
   My brother <u>recommended this pop festival to me</u> .

1 Bands from all over the world are invited.
   The organisers ....

2 Every year the festival is attended by at least 10,000 people.
   At least 10,000 people ....

3 Tickets are sold at our local music shop.

Our local music shop ....

4 But I was given a ticket by my friend.

But my friend ....

5 I was also offered a lift in his car.

He also ....

c) Now rewrite these sentences using the words given. Put the verb into the passive and decide if you need to use *by*.

1 A man told us where to put our tent.

We ....

2 The campsite owner provided water for cooking.

Water for cooking ....

3 It rained, but the bad weather didn't spoil our weekend.

It rained, but our weekend ....

4 The organisers asked us to take all our rubbish away with us.

We ....

5 The people in the next tent woke us up too early.

We ....

4 Vocabulary: sports

a) Put the letters in the right order and label the pictures. Write on the line provided.

| sentin blate   signial   gwsndifuni   bliégnmi |
| lblyavléló   erohs-idgnri |

1 ....

2 ....

3 ....

4 ....

5 ....

6 ....

b) Match one piece of equipment from the box to each sport pictured in Exercise 4a and write it on the line provided.

| boat   rope   board   bat   net   hat |

c) You are going on an activity holiday. Which three of the sports in the pictures would you choose to do on holiday? Why?

> I'd choose sailing, because I've never done it before.

5 Speaking: your experiences

a) Look at the table below. Tick the boxes to show which of these adjectives you could use to describe staff, accommodation, activities and weather. The first one is done for you.

	staff	accommodation	activities	weather
boring	✓		✓	
cold				
comfortable				
warm				
helpful				
interesting				
rainy				
sunny				
friendly				

b) Which of the adjectives above can you make negative by using *un-*? Write them here.

....

....

c) Now work with a partner. You both recently went on a different activity holiday. Compare your experiences. Use the language in the table above to help you.

Student A: You had a great time.

> The activities were really interesting. You could go sailing and climbing.

Student B: Your camp was awful.

> At my camp, the activities were boring.

Strategy

1 Read the instructions to the Exam Task opposite.

1 What do you have to read?
2 What do you have to do?
3 Where do you mark your answers?

2 Read the text quickly to get a good idea of what it is about.

1 What sort of work does the writer do?
2 Where does he work?
3 Does he want to change his life?

3 Read Questions 21–25.

> It is important to understand the questions before reading the text in more detail. This exercise will help you to think about the questions.

<u>Underline</u> the best word or phrase to complete each sentence.

1 Question 21 asks about *when/why/where* the writer wrote the text. (This is always a general question.)
2 Question 22 asks about the writer's *feelings/plans/knowledge*. (This is always a question about detail or opinion.)
3 Question 23 asks about the writer's *pictures/conversations/thoughts*. (This is always a question about detail or opinion.)
4 Question 24 asks about what the writer *hopes to do/usually does/used to do*. (This is always a question about detail or opinion.)
5 Question 25 asks about what the writer *will do/might do/has done*. (This is always a general question.)

4 Read the text and answer Questions 21–25.

• Read the text again more carefully.
• Choose the correct answer for each question.
• Mark your answers on your answer sheet.

•• *Exam tip!* ••••••••••••••••••••
Questions 21 and 25 are always about the whole text. Don't try to answer them by looking at the beginning and end of the text only!
••••••••••••••••••••••••••••••

Part 4

Questions 21–25

Read the text and questions below.
For each question, mark the correct letter
A, **B**, **C** or **D** on your answer sheet.

The Artist

People think being an artist must be a wonderful way to earn one's living. And of course, there are lots of great things about working for oneself, at home alone, even in a cold studio like mine. What I really like is that nobody tells me what time to start in the morning. I like to paint as soon as I wake up, which is always early, but isn't the same time every day. And nobody tells me what to wear, or whether I can take the afternoon off and go to a football match.

But then, I have no one to chat with when I'm bored, no one to discuss last night's match with during the office lunch hour. Sure, I can spend the afternoon doing something I enjoy like cycling or gardening if I choose. But the work will still be there when I do finally get back home.

Unfortunately, working at home means that people can always find me, whether I'm bored or not, and once I've answered the doorbell, it's too late – my thoughts have been interrupted. No one would dream of calling in if I worked in an office, but I find myself listening to friends' troubles. As they talk, my ideas disappear and I feel increasingly stressed thinking of my work waiting to be done.

However, when I hear the traffic news on the radio, and imagine my friends sitting miserably in their cars in a jam, feeling bored, or waiting unhappily for an overcrowded tram in the rain, I realise that I really haven't got much to complain about. I find a CD which will start me thinking, turn it up really loudly and begin another picture.

21 What is the writer trying to do in the text?

  A encourage readers to work at home

  B explain why he has changed his job

  C describe his working life

  D say how he would like to work

22 What does the writer like about his life?

  A He has plenty of opportunities for sport.

  B He is his own boss.

  C He needn't work in the morning.

  D He has a comfortable place to work.

23 What does the writer imagine he might do with colleagues?

  A have meals in restaurants

  B go to the swimming pool

  C spend time in the countryside

  D talk about sport

24 The writer plays loud music because

  A the traffic outside is noisy.

  B it helps him to have ideas.

  C it prevents him from feeling bored.

  D he dislikes listening to the radio.

25 Which of these notices would be most useful for the writer to put on his door?

A

> I'm working – please don't disturb

B

> Please call at my office for an appointment

C

> **Please knock before entering**

D

> **NO VISITORS ALLOWED DURING OFFICE HOURS**

1 Language focus: feelings

In the text on page 18, the writer says what he likes and dislikes about his life. Which of these phrases from the text are about feeling good (+) and which are about feeling bad (–)?

0 a wonderful way to earn one's living ......+......

1 lots of great things ....

2 What I really like is ....

3 when I'm bored ....

4 doing something I enjoy ....

5 Unfortunately ....

6 it's too late ....

7 I feel increasingly stressed ....

8 sitting miserably ....

9 waiting unhappily ....

10 I haven't got much to complain about ....

2 Grammar: expressions with *-ing*

Here are some more ways you can say what you think or feel. They can all be followed by the *-ing* form of the verb. Complete the sentences with information about yourself.

1 I really like ....
....

2 I don't enjoy ....
....

3 I often spend the evening ....
....

4 I'm looking forward to ....
....

5 I hate ....
....

6 I'm bored with ....
....

7 I sometimes worry about ....
....

8 I'm quite keen on ....
....

9 I really dislike ....
....

10 I feel very happy about ....
....

3 Functions: giving opinions

▶▶ Extra Language for the Speaking Test, Section 16, page 161

a) Read these conversations. Who do you agree with?

1

Ann: I really like reading novels. What about you?

Jon: I like doing that too.

Sam: Do you really? I don't! I prefer watching football on TV.

2

Mary: I don't enjoy doing tests.

Peter: No, neither do I.

Jane: I do. I'm good at tests.

3

Joe: I hate getting up early.

Bob: So do I.

Kate: Me too.

4

Micky: I really enjoy playing computer games. Do you?

Shirley: Not much. But I like watching films.

Micky: Yes, I do too.

b) Work with a partner. Compare the things you wrote in Exercise 2. Use the language in Exercise 3a.

c) Tell the class which things you and your partner agree about and which you disagree about.

Gabriella really likes swimming, but I don't/ and so do I.

Nick doesn't enjoy doing maths, and neither do I/ but I do.

4 Vocabulary: jobs

> In the exam, you often have to read, write or speak about jobs.

a) Write the names of the jobs under the pictures.

1

2

....

3

4

....

5

6

....

b) Match each job 1–6 with a verb and a noun from the box. Use them to write a sentence about the job.

Verbs
cook ~~deliver~~ design play serve score
Nouns
buildings records customers goals ~~parcels~~ meals

1 A postman/woman .....*delivers parcels*..............
2 A shop assistant ....
3 A disc jockey ....
4 A chef ....
5 A footballer ....
6 An architect ....

c) Can you make sentences about these jobs?

actor pilot manager dentist detective doctor farmer firefighter hairdresser journalist lawyer librarian nurse police officer model bank clerk

5 Speaking: jobs

a) Discuss these questions.

1 Have you got a job or are you a student?
2 What job do you do?/What job would you like to do? Why?

b) Work with a partner.

Student A: Choose a job from Exercise 4. Don't tell your partner which one. Imagine what you do every day.

Student B: You have to find out what job your partner does. Think of some questions to ask. You can use the ideas below to help you. How quickly can you guess your partner's job?

- what time/get up?
- how many hours/spend at work?
- best/worst thing about/job?
- wear/uniform?
- travel?
- well/badly paid?

What time do you get up?

I get up very early, at about five o'clock.

c) Now change roles.

▶ Strategy

1 Read the instructions to the Exam Task on the opposite page.

1 What do you have to read?

2 What do you have to choose?

3 Where do you mark your answers?

2 Look at the title of the text and make guesses about the text.

Can you guess what you will learn about the book? Tick three questions you think you will find answers to.

1 When was it written? ☐

2 Is it fiction or non-fiction? ☐

3 How many pages does it have? ☐

4 Why does the reviewer like it? ☐

5 Are there any pictures in it? ☐

6 What is it about? ☐

3 Read the text quickly and check your guesses.

Don't worry about the numbered spaces for now. Which of your guesses were correct?

4 Look at the example (0) and read the first sentence of the text carefully.

1 What is the answer to the example?

2 Why are the other answers not possible?

5 Look at Questions 26–35 and choose the answers for the ones you are certain about.

For each question:

- read the whole of the sentence which contains the space

- write the word you choose in the space – it may help you to understand the text.

> **•• Exam tip! ••••••••••••••••••••••**
> Look carefully at the words after each space as well as the words before it. The word you need must fit the grammar of the space as well as the meaning.

6 Go back and guess the other answers.

7 Check your work.

When you have finished, read the text again all the way through. Do your answers make sense?

8 Mark your answers on your answer sheet.

Check that you have put them in the right place.

Speaking Part 1, Exam Task (page 45)

Student A, ask your partner these questions.

1 What's your name?

2 Where do you live?

3 What part of the city is that in?

4 Where do you usually go shopping?

5 Which shop is your favourite?

6 Which road is that in?

7 Can you spell the name of the road for me, please?

Part 5

Questions 26–35

Read the text below and choose the correct word for each space.
For each question, mark the correct letter **A**, **B**, **C** or **D** on your answer sheet.

Example:

0   **A** enjoyed   **B** pleased   **C** amused   **D** delighted

Answer: 0 | A | B | C | D |
              | ■ | ☐ | ☐ | ☐ |

A BOOK I RECOMMEND

I found *Escape from Time* by Andy Treen very exciting and I really (**0**) .... reading it. It's a story (**26**) .... a boy called Troy who goes on a journey to (**27**) .... for his friend Zyra. It wasn't what I had expected, although I am interested (**28**) .... science fiction. I thought this story would be like films I had seen, but I (**29**) .... after a few pages that it was (**30**) .... interesting than a film.

Troy goes to many places and times. He (**31**) .... his knowledge with different (**32**) .... of people and learns new skills from them. Then he moves on. The last part of the book (**33**) .... the meeting between Troy and Zyra when they are both caught by some space criminals from the future. But that's enough information from me (**34**) .... I don't want to spoil it for you. It's really quite (**35**) .... , too, with some excellent jokes about time travel in it.

26	**A** from	**B** about	**C** on	**D** with
27	**A** ask	**B** follow	**C** look	**D** find
28	**A** by	**B** with	**C** of	**D** in
29	**A** explained	**B** realised	**C** showed	**D** believed
30	**A** even	**B** more	**C** much	**D** too
31	**A** divides	**B** joins	**C** shares	**D** adds
32	**A** kinds	**B** variety	**C** range	**D** qualities
33	**A** shows	**B** discovers	**C** describes	**D** says
34	**A** when	**B** because	**C** if	**D** unless
35	**A** funny	**B** sad	**C** shocking	**D** frightening

1 Vocabulary: similar meanings

Part 5 tests words which look similar or have similar meanings.

Questions 30, 31, 32 and the example on page 23 all contain words with similar meanings, but only one word is right.
Read these sentences. Choose the word which best fits each space. You can use your dictionary to help you.

0 This story is about a murder. It's too .... for small children.

A fearful   B nervous   C afraid   (D frightening)

1 This old book belongs to my father. He says it's interesting, but it's very boring, in my ....

A opinion   B thought   C idea   D feeling

2 There weren't enough computers for everyone in the class to have one, so they had to .... with each other.

A divide   B join   C add   D share

3 Good dictionaries aren't cheap. How much did you .... on your new one?

A spend   B buy   C charge   D pay

4 I enjoy reading all kinds of stories. We have to learn a lot of facts at school, so I read .... when I want a change.

A novel   B thriller   C fiction   D adventure

5 I work hard every day, so I need a change in the evening. Going to the cinema with friends is a great way to ....

A rest   B relax   C enjoy   D entertain

6 Teaching isn't as easy as it looks. You have to do a .... course before you can work as a teacher.

A study   B training   C learning   D practice

7 I promised to phone my friend tonight, so I mustn't forget. Please .... me to phone him tonight.

A remember   B revise   C report   D remind

8 Our teacher encouraged us to study at home. She .... us to read more books.

A told   B talked   C said   D spoke

9 My sister enjoys travelling round different countries. She is going on a .... of Scotland this summer.

A journey   B voyage   C tour   D trip

10 You had to wait for us, so you're annoyed. We're late because the train was cancelled, it's not our ....

A problem   B mistake   C fault   D cause

2 Grammar: comparative forms

Reading Part 5 and Writing Part 1 often test ways of making comparisons.

a) Look at these ways of making comparisons. Complete each sentence with the correct word.

1 My new music teacher is friendlier .... my last one.

2 I love going to the cinema. I wish I could go .... often.

3 The film about the robbery wasn't .... exciting .... the book.

4 Paul's new motorbike was .... expensive .... mine because it has a smaller engine.

5 She doesn't like Chinese food as .... as I do.

b) Complete these sentences so that they mean the same as the ones above, using no more than three words.

1 My previous music teacher was .... my new one.

2 I can't go to the cinema .... I'd like to.

3 The book about the robbery was .... the film.

4 My motorbike was .... Paul's because it has a bigger engine.

5 I like Chinese food .... she does.

3 Grammar: too/very/enough; so/such ... that

These words are used to say how much?

a) Complete the sentences with too, very or enough.

1 The test was .... difficult, but I passed it.

2 The test was .... difficult, and I failed.

3 This suitcase is .... small for all the clothes I want to take.

4 The swimming pool isn't big .... for international competitions.

5 I haven't got .... money to buy a new coat.

b) Match the sentence halves.

1 It's so hot in here that ....
2 The programme was so boring that ....
3 My cousin walks so fast that ....
4 It was such hot weather that ....
5 She is such a bossy person that ....

a) I have to run when I'm with her.
b) nobody wants to be friends with her.
c) we couldn't study.
d) I feel very sleepy.
e) I switched it off.

c) Complete the second sentence so that it means the same as the first, using no more than three words.

1 That bike is too expensive for me to buy.
   I haven't got .... to buy that bike.
2 The film was very good, and I'd like to see it again.
   The film was .... that I'd like to see it again.
3 The students made such a lot of noise. They had to leave the café.
   The students were .... that they had to leave the café.
4 This coat is very warm. I don't want to wear it in the summer.
   This coat is .... to wear in the summer.
5 The music is very quiet. I can't hear it.
   The music isn't .... for me to hear it.

4 Vocabulary: books

a) Look at these kinds of books. For each one, decide if it is fiction or non-fiction. Write F or NF next to each book.

0 a science-fiction story   F
1 a cookery book   ....
2 a romantic novel   ....
3 a book about sport   ....
4 a travel book   ....
5 a historical novel   ....
6 a book about animals   ....
7 a horror story   ....
8 a history book   ....
9 a detective story   ....

b) Work with a partner. Can you guess what types of books these are?

 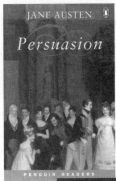  

> **Useful language**
> It could be …/It's probably … because …
> I think it might be …
> I don't think it's … because …

5 Speaking: books and magazines

a) Think about the following questions. When you are ready, discuss the questions with a partner.

1 What kind of books do you have to read? Why?
2 Do you prefer reading books or magazines? Why?
3 Do you ever read books or magazines about films?

> **Useful language**
> For school, I have to read books about …
> I prefer reading …
> I'm not very keen on …
> I'm very interested in …
> I enjoy finding out about …
> I like the kind of magazines which …

b) Think about a book you have read recently. Ask and answer questions about each other's book. Use these questions to help you.

- What sort of book is it?
- What is it about?
- Why did you choose it?
- What did you like about it?
- What didn't you like about it?

Strategy

1 Read the instructions to the Exam Task below.

1 How many sentences are there?
2 What are the sentences about?
3 What do you have to do?
4 How many words can you use?
5 Where do you write your answers?
6 How much do you write there?
7 Where can you do your rough work?

2 Compare the two sentences in the example.

1 Read the first sentence. What information does it give you about the guesthouse?
2 Now read the second sentence. Does it give you the same information as the first sentence?

3 Answer Question 1.

1 Read the first sentence. What information does it give you about the guesthouse?
2 Now read the beginning and end of the second sentence. How does it begin? How does it end?
3 How can you complete it? Write your answer.

4 Check your answer.

• Does your sentence give the same information as the first sentence?
• Is the grammar correct?
• How many words have you used?

5 Answer the other questions in the same way.

Write the answers to Questions 2–5 on your answer sheet.

Remember: you can write your answers on the exam paper first if you wish and then copy them.

• • **Exam tip!** • • • • • • • • • • • • • • • •
In this part of the exam, you will lose marks if your grammar is not correct. If you are not sure about your answer, write it on the exam paper first and read it carefully before you copy it onto your answer sheet.
• •

Part 1

Questions 1–5

Here are some sentences about a guesthouse. For each question, complete the second sentence so that it means the same as the first. **Use no more than three words.**
Write only the missing words on your answer sheet.
You may use this page for any rough work.

Example:

0 There is a games room in this guesthouse.

This guesthouse .... a games room.

Answer:

0	has

1 The guesthouse is called 'Sunshine Cottage'.

The name .... is 'Sunshine Cottage'.

2 I haven't stayed here before.

This is the first time that .... here.

3 I was told about it by my sister.

My sister .... about it.

4 It is essential to book your room in advance.

You .... your room in advance.

5 My room is bigger than my friend's room.

My friend's room isn't .... my room.

1 Grammar: matching patterns

In Part 1, the same grammar patterns are often tested. It is a good idea to study these patterns so that you can recognise them.

a) Read the twelve sentences below. Find the six pairs which have similar meanings.

1 Her name is Jane. ....7....
2 I was told the news by Jane. ....
3 It was essential to talk to Jane about the news. ....
4 I haven't met Jane before. ....
5 I had to talk to Jane about the news. ....
6 Jane is taller than me. ....
7 She is called Jane. ....1....
8 Jane told me about the news. ....
9 This is the first time I've met Jane. ....
10 There are twenty people in Jane's class. ....
11 I'm not as tall as Jane. ....
12 Jane's class has twenty students. ....

b) Match each pair of sentences above with these patterns.

0   ... is called ... ➜ ... name is ...   .1.... and ....7....

a) It was + adjective ➜ modal verb .... and ....
b) I haven't ... before ➜ This is the first time ... . and ....
c) comparison .... and ....
d) active verb ➜ passive verb .... and ....
e) there is/are ➜ has/have .... and ....

c) Complete the second sentence so that it means the same as the first, using no more than three words.

1 It isn't necessary to pay if you are a student.
You .... if you are a student.
2 Alana was given a moped by her parents.
Alana's parents .... a moped.
3 It's a good idea to rest until your leg is better.
You .... until your leg is better.

4 This is the first time I've been to a nightclub.
I .... to a nightclub before.
5 There are lots of CDs in the library.
The library .... lots of CDs.
6 The bus was delayed by an accident.
An accident .... the bus.
7 The name of the singer was Dermot.
The singer .... Dermot.
8 There aren't any good clothes shops in this town.
This town .... any good clothes shops.
9 My new computer is smaller and lighter than my old one.
My old computer was bigger and .... than my new one.
10 This book is more interesting than that one.
That book isn't .... that one.

2 Correcting mistakes

Read these pairs of sentences. There is a mistake in the second sentence of each pair. Can you correct it?

0 He is called Robert.
                is
His name ~~called~~ Robert.

1 This car is too small for my family.

This car isn't enough big for my family.

2 That factory is owned by my uncle.

My uncle is owned that factory.

3 The town has several pleasant parks.

There is several pleasant parks in the town.

4 I haven't visited an internet café before.

This is the first time I'm visiting an internet café.

5 It isn't necessary to book a ticket for this show.

You mustn't book a ticket for this show.

Writing Part 2

 Strategy

1 Read the instructions to the Exam Task opposite.

1 What are you going to write?
2 Who are you writing to?
3 How many things must you write about?
4 How many words must you write?
5 Where do you write your answer?

2 Planning your answer

Before you begin to write, look at the words in the instructions. Mark the words that tell you what information you should include. Think about what extra information you can add.

1 What has your friend invited you to do?
2 When?
3 How will you start your e-mail?
4 Why can't you go?
5 Where will you suggest meeting? When?

3 Writing your answer

Read the e-mails A, B and C opposite.

1 Which is the best answer to the task? Why?
2 What is wrong with the other two answers?

4 Checking and correcting your work

a) Read this e-mail. It has eight grammar mistakes. Find and <u>underline</u> the mistakes.

Dear Sylvie
Thank you for asking me coming with you to the city centre on Tuesday. I sorry, but I can't come because I go to the dentist this afternoon. What about we meet on another time? Do you like to go the Friday afternoon?

b) Work with a partner and compare the mistakes you found. Correct the mistakes together.

Part 2

Question 6

An English friend of yours called Charlie has invited you to go clubbing next Saturday, but you can't go.

Write an e-mail to Charlie. In your e-mail, you should

• thank him for inviting you
• tell him you can't go
• suggest meeting another time.

Write **35–45 words** on your answer sheet.

A

Dear Charlie

I'm inviting you to go clubbing with me next Saturday. I hope you can come, but please tell me if you can't. If I don't see you on Saturday, we could meet another day. Are you free on Friday?

Sara

B

Dear Charlie

Thank you for inviting me to go clubbing with you next Saturday. I'm sorry, but I can't go because I'm going to Edinburgh for the weekend with my cousins. I'd like to see you next week. Are you free on Monday evening?

Ivana

C

Dear Charlie

I can't come clubbing with you on Saturday. Can we meet another time? I am free on Tuesday. We could go to a café.

Patricia

1 Grammar: future plans

> In Part 2, you often write about plans. It is important to use the correct tense forms.

a) Read Sentences 1–4 and match the verb forms to the descriptions in the box.

1 We're visiting France next summer.
2 The football match starts at 3 p.m.
3 I'm going to cook a meal for my friend tonight.
4 I'll have a coffee, please.

> A We use **present simple** for fixed events in a timetable.
>
> B We use **present continuous** or *going to* for personal plans.
>
> C We use *will* when we decide as we speak.

b) Underline the best form of the verb in these sentences.

1 I have to go to the station to meet my friend. Her train *arrives/'s arriving* at 6.45.
2 A: Do you want anything to eat?
   B: Yes, *I'm going to have/I'll have* an apple, thanks.
3 I *meet/'m meeting* my friends for coffee next Saturday afternoon. Would you like to come?
4 We*'re not going to catch/don't catch* the train tomorrow because my father's lending us the car.
5 Our course *is finishing/finishes* tomorrow, so we're planning a party.
6 A: I've got terrible toothache!
   B: Oh, dear, have you? *I'm going to phone/I'll phone* the dentist for you.
7 I'm not sure what I*'m going to do/do* when I finish my course. But I*'m not getting/don't get* a job immediately.

2 Function: different kinds of messages

Look at Instructions 1–9 and match them to the sentences a)–i) below.

> In Writing Part 2, the instructions tell you to write different kinds of messages.

1 accept an invitation ....
2 apologise for something you didn't do ....
3 arrange to meet someone somewhere ....
4 ask someone to do something for you ....

5 say you can't do something with someone and explain why ....
6 invite someone to do something with you ....
7 thank someone and refuse an invitation ....
8 suggest that someone should do something ....
9 tell someone how to do something ....

a) Unfortunately I can't go swimming with you because I have to revise for an exam.
b) I can see you at half past ten outside the library.
c) You need to go the ticket office and show them your student card in order to get a discount.
d) I'm really sorry I forgot to post your card.
e) Would you like to come to a concert with us next month?
f) I think you'd better phone the college and ask for more information.
g) I'd love to come to New York with you.
h) I'm sorry I won't be able to come to your party, but thank you for inviting me.
i) Could you possibly collect my jacket from the dry cleaners?

3 Exam Task

a) Now write your answer to this question.

> An English friend of yours called Hannah is visiting your town on Saturday. Write an e-mail to Hannah. In your e-mail, you should
> - invite Hannah to meet you
> - arrange where you will meet
> - ask what time she is arriving.
> Write **35–45 words** on your answer sheet.

b) When you have finished, check your work carefully.

- Have you included all the information?
- Have you written no more than 45 words?
- Is your grammar correct?
- Is your spelling correct?

Writing Part 3

In Part 3 there are two writing tasks: an informal letter and a story. You answer ONE task only.

▶ Strategy

1 Read the instructions to Part 3 opposite.

1 How many questions do you answer?
2 How many words do you write?
3 Where do you write your answer?
4 Where do you put the question number?

▶ Strategy: letter

1 Read the instructions to the Exam Task opposite.

1 Who are you going to write to?
2 What does your penfriend ask you to write about?
3 Where must you write your answer?

2 Planning your answer

a) Write down three ideas for your letter.

Example:

shopping
clubbing
football

b) Write down five useful words and phrases to use in your letter.

Example:

city centre
café
in the evening
I don't enjoy
on Sundays

c) Decide how your answer will begin and end. Match the sentence halves.

1 Thank you very much   ....
2 I hope   ....
3 It was great   ....
4 Write back soon   ....
5 I'm looking forward to ....
6 I've just read   ....

a) hearing about your hobbies.
b) and tell me what you like doing.
c) your interesting letter.
d) to get your letter.
e) for your letter.
f) you'll write back soon.

d) Which three sentences can you use at the beginning of a letter? Which three sentences can you use at the end of the letter?

3 Writing your letter

Read Answers A and B to Question 7 opposite.

1 Which letter has unnecessary information?
2 Which letter is the right length?
3 Which letter has a good beginning?
4 Which letter copies whole sentences from the question?
5 Which letter answers all parts of the question?
6 Which is the best answer?
7 Can you find three grammar mistakes in Letter B?

4 Checking and correcting your work

Work with a partner and compare the mistakes you found. Correct the mistakes together.

> •• *Exam tip!* ••••••••••••••••••••••••
> Check that you give all the information you are asked for.

Speaking Part 1, Exam Task (page 45)

Student B, ask your partner these questions.

1 What's your name?
2 Where do you go to school?
3 What time do you start lessons?
4 How long have you studied English?
5 Do you enjoy studying English? Why?/Why not?
6 What road is your school in?
7 Can you spell the name of the road for me, please?

Part 3

Write an answer to **one** of the questions (**7** or **8**) in this part.
Write your answer in about **100 words** on your answer sheet.
Put the question number in the box at the top of your answer sheet.

Question 7

- This is part of a letter you receive from an English penfriend.

  In your next letter, please tell me about what you like doing in your free time. Do you stay at home or do you like going out?

- Now write a letter, telling your penfriend what you like doing.

- Write your **letter** on your answer sheet.

A

Dear Max
  I hope you'll write back soon. I've been at school today and it was boring. I don't like Thursdays because we do sport in the afternoon and I have to play volleyball. I'm not very tall, so I never get the ball. I prefer swimming, but we don't do that. Sometimes I go swimming when I'm on holiday. I want to learn to dive next year. I like going out if the weather is good and sitting in the park with my friends. We can buy very good ice cream at the café.
  In your next letter, please tell me about what you like doing in your free time. Do you stay at home or do you like going out?
      Best wishes
      Flora

B

Dear Judith
Thank you very much for your letter. It was great hearing about your hobbies. You want to know what I like doing in my free time. Well, I love going out with friends. I don't enjoy stay at home. On Saturdays, we often go to the city centre and look around the shops, then we go to the park and have an ice cream. There's café in the park which is really good. On the evening we sometimes go clubbing.
  On Sundays I play football if I'm not too tired.
  Please write back soon.

    Love
    Pietro

Writing Part 3

 Strategy: story

1 Read the instructions to the Exam Task below.

1 How must you begin your story?
2 Where must you write your answer?

2 Planning your answer

Before starting your story, it is important to make a plan. Your story must be simple enough to finish in about 100 words.

a) Write down some ideas for the story. Think about these questions.

1 Who answered the telephone?
2 Who was the call from?
3 Why did she/he call so early in the morning?
4 What did she/he say?
5 What happened next?

b) How will your story end? Think about this question.

How did she/he feel?

c) Write down five useful words and phrases that you can use in your story.

Example:

> sleepy
> earlier than (we) expected
> explain
> as quickly as possible
> get ready

3 Writing your story

Read Answers A and B to Question 8 on page 33.

1 Which story is better? Why?
2 Why is the other story not so good?
3 Can you find five grammar mistakes in that answer?

4 Checking and correcting your work

Work with a partner and compare the mistakes you found. Correct the mistakes together.

> •• **Exam tip!** ••••••••••••••••••••••••
> It is better to tell a simple story in correct English. Don't try to write a complicated story that needs words you don't know.

Part 3

Question 8

- Your English teacher has asked you to write a story.

- Your story must begin with this sentence:

    At six o'clock in the morning, the telephone rang.

- Write your **story** on your answer sheet.

A

At six o'clock in the morning, the telephone rang. I was very sleepy because I'd been out to dinner the night before. 'Who's that?' I said.

'It's Azita. I'm at the railway station.'

It was my sister. She was home a day early from a job interview in London.

'OK, I'll get ready as quickly as possible and come to fetch you.' I told her.

While I was driving to the station, I realised that I hadn't asked her about the job. But when I saw her, she looked so happy that I knew the answer. I said 'Congratulations!'

B

At six o'clock in the morning, the telephone rang. It was my brother Sami. 'Who's that?' I said.

He was at the airport.

'OK, I'll fetch you' I told. I was very tired because I'd been in a party the night before. I got ready as quickly as possible. While I have driven to the airport, I realised that I had forgot to ask him about his interview. He went to Paris for a university interview and had returned early.

But he looked so happy when I saw him that I knew the answer. 'Congratulations!' I said.

Language practice: Writing Part 3

Grammar: narrative tenses

a) Read Sentences 1–8 and find examples of verbs to match the descriptions in the box.

1   At six o'clock in the morning, the telephone rang. I ran down the stairs.

2   While I was running down the stairs, I fell over the cat.

3   When I reached the bottom of the stairs, the phone had stopped ringing.

4   But the noise had woken my baby brother, and he was crying.

5   I was talking to him when the phone started ringing again!

6   I walked down the stairs carefully.

7   When I answered the phone, it was my friend Tom.

8   I had completely forgotten that we had agreed to go fishing.

We use:

A   past simple for a completed action in the past.

B   past continuous for a continuous action in the past.

C   past continuous for an interrupted action in the past.

D   past perfect for an action completed before another action in the past.

---

b) Put the verbs in brackets in the correct forms: past simple, past continuous or past perfect.

1   While I .... (walk) to the city centre, I .... (see) an advertisement for a concert on Saturday.

2   A lot of other people .... (already/see) the advertisement before me.

3   They .... (stand) outside the theatre when I .... (arrive) there.

4   We .... (wait) for a long time.

5   At last a man .... (come) out of the theatre and .... (put) up a notice.

6   They .... (sell) all the tickets for Saturday!

7   We .... (wait) so long that we .... (feel) angry.

8   Why .... (not/tell) us earlier?

Writing Part 3: Exam Practice

 Strategy: choosing your question

1 Read both the Exam Tasks below.

- Write down two ideas for your letter.
- Write down five useful words or phrases that you can use in your letter.
- Write down two ideas for your story.
- Write down five useful words or phrases that you can use in your story.
- Look at your notes. Which question is easier for you?

2 Make a plan on your exam paper.

3 Write your answer.

4 Check and correct your work.

Question 7

- Does your letter have a good beginning and ending?
- Have you answered all parts of the question?
- Have you used your own words (not copied sentences from the question)?
- Is your letter the right length?
- Have you added unnecessary information?

Question 8

- Is the story clear?
- Is the story the right length?
- Can you find any mistakes? Underline any grammar mistakes and correct them.

> **Exam tip!**
> Practise writing about 100 words. You don't need to write exactly 100, but it is useful to know what 100 words looks like in your writing.

Part 3

Write an answer to **one** of the questions (**7** or **8**) in this part.
Write your answer in about **100 words** on your answer sheet.
Put the question number in the box at the top of your answer sheet.

Question 7

- This is part of a letter you receive from an English penfriend.

> I went to a great concert last week with some friends. Do you ever go to concerts and do you collect CDs? Tell me about the musicians you like.

- Now write a letter, answering your penfriend's questions.

- Write your **letter** on your answer sheet.

Question 8

- Your English teacher has asked you to write a story.

- Your story must begin with this sentence:

  I checked that my ticket was in my bag and locked the front door.

- Write your **story** on your answer sheet.

Listening Part 1

▶ Strategy

1 **Listen to the introduction to the test.**

1 How many parts does the Listening test have?
2 How many times will you hear each part?
3 Where do you write your answers?
4 What will you do at the end of the test?
5 How long will you have?

2 **Read and listen to the instructions for Part 1 below.**

1 How many questions are there?
2 How many pictures are there for each question?
3 What do you have to do?

3 **Look at the example and listen to the recording.**

1 What is the question?
2 What is the answer?
3 How do you know?

4 Look at Question 1. Think about what you are going to hear.

1 What information must you listen for?
2 Look at the three pictures. What different ways are there of saying the times in pictures A, B and C?
3 Listen to the recording for Question 1. Which of the times did you hear?
4 Listen again and mark your answer.
5 Why is A wrong?
6 Why is C wrong?
7 Why is B the correct answer? What does Paula say?

5 Do Questions 2–7 in the same way.

•• **Exam tip!** ••••••••••••••••••••••
: Use the pictures to help you. You can guess a
: lot about what you are going to hear by looking
: at them.
•••••••••••••••••••••••••••••••••••••

Part 1

Questions 1–7

There are seven questions in this part.
For each question, there are three pictures and a short recording.
Choose the correct picture and put a tick (✓) in the box below it.

Example: What will the boy take back to the shop?

A ✓   B ☐   C ☐

[Turn over

1 What time will Paula pick Julie up?

A ☐   B ☐   C ☐

2 What will they get first?

A ☐   B ☐   C ☐

3 Where did the woman leave her keys?

A ☐   B ☐   C ☐

4 What does the man decide to eat?

A ☐   B ☐   C ☐

5 What time is the woman's new appointment?

A ☐   B ☐   C ☐

6 What was cancelled?

A ☐   B ☐   C ☐

7 What did Jason enjoy doing on Saturday?

A ☐   B ☐   C ☐

1 Vocabulary: word sets

> In Listening Part 1, there is a range of questions about different topics, so you need to revise the vocabulary you know.

a) **Work with a partner. Put the words in the box into groups. Decide what heading to give each group of words. How many other words can you add to each group?**

neck	cheque	horse	football	credit cards
ankle	stomach	duck	tennis	volleyball
chicken	purse	wallet	thumb	swimming
shoulder	sheep	coin	cycling	turkey

b) **Compare your lists with the rest of the class to see who has the most words in each group.**

2 Grammar: saying when things happen

a) **Complete the sentences with a linking word from the box.**

while	during	after	before	as soon as
~~until~~	since			

0 The film doesn't start .....until..... 8.15.

1 I want to get a film for my camera in this shop .... we're here.

2 We'll get the fruit last, ... we've bought your trainers.

3 We'll buy your trainers first, ... we get the fruit.

4 It's hours .... we had lunch.

5 It rained heavily .... the afternoon.

6 We only just arrived in time. The coach left .... we arrived.

b) **Complete the second sentence so that it means the same as the first, using no more than three words.**

1 Our train arrives at midnight.

Our train doesn't arrive .... midnight.

2 The last train left hours ago.

It's hours .... the last train left.

3 When I arrive at the station, I'll phone my sister immediately.

I'll phone my sister .... I arrive at the station.

4 We found a seat and then we went to the buffet car.

We went to the buffet car .... finding a seat.

5 We couldn't get on the train until we'd shown our tickets.

We had to show our tickets .... we got on the train.

3 Speaking: habits and routines

▶▶ Extra Language for the Speaking Test, Section 5, page 160

a) **Work in groups. Find out what time everyone:**

- gets up
- has breakfast
- has lunch
- arrives home
- goes to bed.

Example:

What time do you get up?

At quarter past seven.

At about 7.30.

Not until eight o'clock!

b) **Now tell the class.**

- Who gets up/goes to bed the latest/the earliest?
- Who has breakfast at the same time?
- Who has lunch before/after one o'clock?
- Who arrives home first/last?

▶ Strategy

1 🎧 **Read and listen to the instructions to the Exam Task below.**

1   How many questions are there?
2   Who will you hear?
3   What will she talk about?
4   Who is Robert?
5   Who is Ben?
6   What do you have to do?
7   How many times will you hear the recording?

2   Read the questions and make guesses about what you will hear.

Which of the following points do you think the woman will talk about? Put a tick next to them.

1   how long the journey took ☐
2   how they prepared for the journey ☐
3   problems on the journey ☐
4   where they stopped ☐
5   Robert's father ☐
6   meeting other families ☐
7   what she is doing now ☐

3 🎧 **Listen to the recording the first time.**

a) **Look at Question 8. Listen to what Vanessa says about last year and tick the correct answer.**

CLUE: What word that you hear means the same as *travel by boat*?

b) **Look at Question 9. Listen to what Vanessa was worried about. Tick the correct answer.**

CLUE: What word does Vanessa use which means the same as *worried*?

c) **Now do Questions 10–13 in the same way.**

4 🎧 **Listen to the recording again.**

Check the answers you have marked and try to do any you missed the first time. If you still don't know, guess! Do not leave any questions unanswered.

> •• *Exam tip!* ••••••••••••••••••••••
> The questions always follow the same order as what you hear on the recording. Use the questions to help you understand the recording.

Part 2

Questions 8–13

You will hear a woman, Vanessa, talking about a journey she made with her husband, Robert, and her baby, Ben.
For each question, put a tick (✓) in the correct box.

---

8   What did Vanessa and Robert decide to do last year?

   A   get married ☐
   B   travel to England by boat ☐
   C   look for new jobs ☐

9   Vanessa was worried that

   A   they wouldn't be prepared. ☐
   B   the conditions would be bad. ☐
   C   the baby would get ill. ☐

10 How did Vanessa feel when they reached Singapore?

    A She wondered if she should fly home. ☐

    B She was worried about the boat. ☐

    C She enjoyed the break from travelling. ☐

11 Why was Vanessa's father-in-law particularly helpful?

    A He was a good cook. ☐

    B He looked after the baby. ☐

    C He helped to sail the boat. ☐

12 Because of spending so much time on the boat, the baby

    A learnt to walk late. ☐

    B doesn't play by himself. ☐

    C only likes certain food. ☐

13 What is Vanessa's advice for people sailing with children?

    A Don't take more than one child. ☐

    B Go for a short time. ☐

    C Don't let children get bored. ☐

Language practice: Listening Part 2

1 Vocabulary: -ing and -ed adjectives

a) Look at these examples.

- *We gave up our jobs because we were getting **bored**.*
- *We spent six **boring** weeks in Singapore.*

Which adjective describes how they felt?

b) For each sentence, choose the correct word for each space.

amazed/amazing

1 My brother cooked an .... meal last night.

2 My neighbour was .... to find her brother at the door because she thought he was in Australia.

surprised/surprising

3 I was .... to win the competition.

4 It's ...., that Anthony got the job, since he has no experience of working in a hotel.

interested/interesting

5 The Modern Art museum is much more .... than the National Museum.

6 I was so .... in what I was reading that I forgot to have lunch.

tired/tiring

7 I'm really .... today because I went to bed too late last night.

8 It can be very .... to speak a foreign language for a long time.

excited/exciting

9 For an adventure film, it wasn't very ....

10 When I was little, I was always very .... the night before we went on holiday.

c) Work with a partner. Ask and answer these questions.

1 Do you enjoy going to museums or do you think they are boring?

2 What do you do if you get bored at the weekend?

3 What free-time activities do you think are most interesting?

2 Grammar: verbs followed by *to* + infinitive

a) Look at these examples from the Exam Task. What do you notice about the form of the second verb in bold?

- ... we **decided to sail** back to England.
- How long did it **take** you **to get ready** for the trip?
- I hadn't **expected to hit** bad weather so soon.

b) Complete these sentences with a suitable verb from the box.

| ~~pass~~ travel buy paint study play |
| reply tell swim meet come |

0 My brother expects ....*to pass*........ his driving test because he's had lots of lessons.

1 I learnt .... in the sea when I was ten.

2 Would you like .... to a party on Saturday?

3 My mother hopes .... round the world when she retires.

4 I've decided .... chemistry at university.

5 I had planned .... my bedroom at the weekend, but I didn't have time.

6 Sara promised .... to my e-mail immediately, but I still haven't had an answer.

7 If she offers .... her violin to you, find an excuse to leave!

8 We had intended .... him the truth, but we weren't brave enough.

9 I wanted .... that new CD, but I'd spent all my money.

10 I've arranged .... my friend after class tomorrow.

c) Work with a partner. Ask and answer these questions.

1 Have you arranged to do anything this weekend?

2 What do you hope to do when you leave school/college?

3 What do you plan to do during the holidays?

3 Speaking: journeys

a) Complete these sentences about some journeys you make regularly.

1 I get to .... (work/school/etc.) by .... It takes about ....

2 When I go on holiday, I travel by ....

3 My favourite way of travelling is by .... because ....

b) Tell a partner about an interesting journey. It can be a real journey you've made, or you can invent one. Use these questions and the language in the box below to help you.

- Who did you go with?
- Where did you go? (to an island? to the mountains? to a foreign city?)
- How did you get there? (by train? by plane? by car? by boat?)
- What was good and bad about your journey?

| Useful language |
| I went by myself/with ... |
| I/We went to ... because I wanted ... |
| We travelled by ... |
| The most interesting thing was ... |
| ... was very exciting. |
| I was very surprised by ... |
| ... was a little boring. |

c) After listening to you, your partner must decide if the journey was real or invented.

Listening Part 3

TEST 1, LISTENING PART 3   41

▶ Strategy

1 🎧 **Read and listen to the instructions to the Exam Task below.**

1 How many questions are there?

2 What sort of word is *Willingham*? How do you know?

3 Who will you hear? What will they talk about?

4 What do you have to do?

2 Look at the Exam Task and guess what kinds of words are missing.

1 Look at Questions 14, 15, 17 and 18. What kind of word can go in each space? How do you know?

2 Look at Question 16. What kind of information do you need here? How do you know?

3 Look at Question 19. What kind of word can go here? How do you know?

3 🎧 **Listen to the recording the first time.**

Try to answer as many questions as you can. If you miss a gap, don't worry. You can fill it in the second time you listen.

4 🎧 **Listen to the recording again.**

Check the answers you wrote the first time. Fill in any answers you missed.

5 Check your answers.

* How many words did you write in each space?
* Is the meaning correct?
* Is the grammar correct?
* Is the spelling correct?

••• *Exam tip!* ••••••••••••••••••••••••
A small spelling mistake in a difficult word is OK, for example *castel* for *castle*. But simple words, for example *green*, must be correct.
•••••••••••••••••••••••••••••••••••

Part 3

Questions 14–19

You will hear someone talking on the radio about the Willingham Museum.
For each question, fill in the missing information in the numbered space.

Willingham Museum

In the museum, visit:
* a 19th-century **(14)** ....
* a 1950s dining room
* a new exhibition about **(15)** .... which will open on **(16)** ....

The museum is:
* in a building which was a **(17)** ....
* near the **(18)** .... outside the town

To get there:
* follow the **(19)** .... signs from the town centre.

1 Grammar: prepositions

In Part 3, prepositions can often help you to decide what sort of word can go in a gap, so it's important to practise understanding and using them correctly.

a) **Look at Gap 16 from the Exam Task on page 41.**

16 *open* + *on* is followed by a day or date.

b) **Underline the correct preposition in each pair.**

A Visit to Historic Willingham

Cars are not allowed (0) <u>into</u>/to the centre of Willingham, so it is very pleasant to walk (1) *above/around* the town. If you come by car, you have to leave it in the car park just (2) *next/outside* the centre. A free bus service takes you (3) *from/in* there (4) *to/at* the main square.

There are lots of interesting things to see (5) *in/at* Willingham. If you want to go shopping, be sure to visit the new shopping mall (6) *in/into* the centre. When you have finished your shopping, why not see a film (7) *in/by* the new multiplex cinema? It is easy to find the cinema because there is a big sign in front (8) *of/from* it. You can buy tickets by phone or from the box office. It is open every weekday (9) *by/until* 10 p.m. and closes later (10) *on/in* Saturdays and Sundays.

2 Vocabulary: compound nouns

a) **Look at this example from the notes on the Willingham Museum.**

*If you visit Willingham Museum, you can see a 1950s **dining room**.*

What do you notice about the spelling of *dining*?

b) **Add *-ing* to the verbs in the box and fill in the gaps to form a compound noun. Be careful about spelling!**

sleep   drive   wash   swim   fry   wait
walk   write

1 My sister passed her .... test last week.
2 The hotel has a pool, so take your .... costume.
3 Do you have a .... bag for when we go camping?
4 I usually wash my clothes in the .... machine.
5 Please take a seat in the .... room. The doctor will see you soon.
6 We can cook the sausages in this .... pan.
7 I wrote to my aunt on my new .... paper.
8 My father is using a .... stick because he has a bad knee.

3 Vocabulary: places to visit

In the exam, you often have to read, write or speak about places to visit. It's useful to know the names of things you find in them.

Complete the text with a word or phrase from the box.

antique furniture   café   guided tour
old books   sculptures   cloakroom   paintings
fast-food kiosks   jewellery   funfair   rides
gift shop   pottery   exhibition   souvenirs

Wellington Hall offers you the chance to visit a beautiful house and garden. In the 18th-century house, you can see rooms filled with (0) ..*antique*.. ..*furniture*.... and a wonderful collection of (1) .... on the walls. There are three gardens which contain some interesting (2) .... You can have lunch in the old kitchen which is now a (3) .... The old dining room is used as an art gallery, and there is a new (4) .... there every month. If you want to know more about the history of the house, take a (5) .... They leave every half an hour from the library. While you're there, have a look at the (6) .... – some of them have been there for several hundred years. A wide range of (7) .... can be bought in the (8) .... next to the main entrance.

4 Speaking: places to visit

Work with a partner. Tell them about a museum, art gallery, theme park or other interesting place you have visited. Use these questions to help you.

- Where is it?
- What is it called?
- What can you see and do there?
- Did you have a good time?
- What was the best thing about it?

Listening Part 4

► **Strategy**

1 🎧 **Read and listen to the instructions to the Exam Task below.**

1 How many sentences are there?
2 How many people will you hear?
3 What is the boy's name?
4 What is the girl's name?
5 Where are they?
6 What do you have to do?

2 **Read the six sentences. Underline the names in each sentence.**

•• **Exam tip!** •
The instructions tell you the names of the people and who they are. Make sure you know which speaker is which, as this is important for answering the questions.
• •

3 **Make guesses about what you will hear.**

a) Underline six nouns which tell you what William and Sophie's conversation will be about.

b) **Compare your list of words with another student.**

4 🎧 **Listen to the recording and answer the questions.**

Mark the answers you are sure of. If you miss one, don't worry. You can listen for the answer when you hear the recording again.

5 🎧 **Listen again and check your answers.**

Try to fill in any answers you missed the first time. If you're still not sure, guess! Don't leave any questions unanswered.

Part 4

Questions 20–25

Look at the six sentences for this part.
You will hear a conversation between a boy, William, and a girl, Sophie, in a music shop.
Decide if each sentence is correct or incorrect.
If it is correct, put a tick (✓) in the box under **A** for **YES**.
If it is not correct, put a tick (✓) in the box under **B** for **NO**.

		A YES	B NO
20	Sophie's mother works in the town where they live.	☐	☐
21	Sophie enjoys shopping in Birmingham.	☐	☐
22	William feels confident about finding his way around Birmingham.	☐	☐
23	Sophie thinks the band 521 has improved.	☐	☐
24	William persuades Sophie to buy a different CD from him.	☐	☐
25	Sophie is disappointed to have her birthday present early.	☐	☐

1 Vocabulary: words with similar meanings

In Part 4, you hear people talking about their feelings, giving opinions, and agreeing or disagreeing with each other. They use different words for the same meaning.

a) Look at this example from the Exam Task on page 43.

Sophie says: *Their music has got a lot better recently.*

Question 23 says: *Sophie thinks the band 521 has improved.*

Does *has improved* mean the same as *has got a lot better recently*?

b) Complete the second sentence so it means the same as the first, using a word or phrase from the box. Remember to put the verb in the correct form.

feel think persuade ~~enjoy~~ be disappointed suggest prefer be keen recommend

0 'I really like shopping for clothes.'
   She .....*enjoys*..... shopping for clothes very much.

1 'I'm sure I can climb to the top of the mountain.'
   He .... confident about climbing to the top of the mountain.

2 '*The Riders'* new CD is better than their old one.'
   He .... *The Riders'* new CD to their old one.

3 'Why don't we go away for the weekend?'
   She .... going away for the weekend.

4 'In my opinion, this book is really boring.'
   He .... the book is really boring.

5 'I really want to visit the market while I'm here.'
   She .... to visit the market while she's here.

6 'If I were you, I'd try the fish soup.'
   He .... the fish soup.

7 'I hoped to go sailing this weekend, but the weather is bad.'
   She .... that she can't go sailing.

8 'I'm going to a really good club tonight. Why don't you come?'
   He tried to .... her to come to a club with him.

2 Grammar: *if* sentences (unreal situations)

a) Look at the following sentences from William and Sophie's conversation.

William: *If we **had** a map, it **wouldn't be** a problem for me.*

Sophie: *If we **were** together, it **would be** OK.*

b) Match the sentence halves.

1 If I earned more money, ...
2 If my brother wasn't so shy, ...
3 If they lived in the country, ...
4 If I had a bicycle, ...
5 If we knew his address, ...
6 If the city was nearer, ...

a) he'd join my band.
b) they'd miss the shops.
c) we'd go there more often.
d) I'd go to work by taxi.
e) I'd get more exercise.
f) we'd visit him.

c) Complete these sentences with your own ideas.

1 If I had lots of money, ...
   ....

2 If I was a film star, ...
   ....

3 If I could live anywhere in the world, ...
   ....

4 If I met a famous pop star, ...
   ....

5 If my friends gave a party for me, ...
   ....

6 If my hair was green, ...
   ....

3 Speaking: shopping

Work with a partner. Answer the following questions.

1 What sort of shops do you often go to?
2 When do you usually go shopping?
3 Do you like going shopping?
4 Who helps you choose your clothes?
5 Do you decide quickly what to buy?
6 Do you like buying presents?

Speaking Part 1

▶ Strategy

The test begins with a general conversation between the examiner and the candidates. Be ready to:

- answer questions about personal details, e.g. where you live
- answer questions about your daily life, likes/dislikes, habits, etc.
- spell out words (e.g. names, addresses)

1 Sample interview

▶▶ Extra Language for the Speaking Test, Section 5, page 160

You are going to hear two candidates doing Part 1 of the test.

a) Read these questions, then listen once. Which questions does the examiner ask? Tick the ones you hear.

1 What's your name? ☐
2 What's your family name? ☐
3 How do you spell that? ☐
4 Where do you come from? ☐
5 How long have you lived there? ☐
6 What do you study? ☐
7 What do you do there? ☐
8 What do you enjoy doing in your free time? ☐
9 What did you do last weekend? ☐
10 Do you think English will be useful for you in the future? ☐

b) Listen again and answer these questions.

1 What does the examiner ask for first?
2 Who does the examiner introduce?
3 What word are the students asked to spell?
4 What does Anna say when she doesn't understand?
5 Anna says: 'I work in an office.' Then she adds: 'I'm a secretary'. This is extra information. What extra information does Carlo give the examiner?

> •• **Exam tip!** •
> Practise spelling words in English until you can say the letters of the alphabet easily.
> •

2 Spelling

a) Look at the letters of the alphabet below.

1 What are the names of the letters?
2 What do you say when a letter is repeated, for example the *m* in *grammar*?

I E X K Q U O V W H R A Z S C G J Y

b) Work with a partner.

Student A: Look at the bottom of page 47.

Student B: Write down what your partner says in your notebook. When you have finished, show your words to Student A. Are they spelt correctly?

c) Change roles.

Student B: Look at the bottom of page 48.

Student A: Write down what your partner says in your notebook. When you have finished, show your words to Student B. Are they spelt correctly?

d) Now take turns to spell the names of the places where you live and study. Write the names in your notebooks and then check them.

3 Exam Task

▶▶ Extra Language for the Speaking Test, Sections 4 and 5, page 160

a) Work with a different partner.

Student A: You are the examiner. Ask your partner the questions at the bottom of page 22. For Question 7, write down what your partner says so that you can check it later.

Student B: Answer the questions your partner asks you.

When you have finished, check the answer to Question 7. Is it spelt correctly?

b) Change roles.

Student B: You are the examiner. Ask your partner the questions at the bottom of page 30. For Question 7, write down what your partner says so that you can check it later.

Student A: Answer the questions your partner asks you.

When you have finished, check the answer to Question 7. Is it spelt correctly?

Speaking Part 2

▶ Strategy

In Part 2, the examiner describes a situation, and you and your partner talk about it for two or three minutes. The examiner gives you some pictures to help you. Be ready to:

- make suggestions
- explain your opinion
- agree or disagree.

1 Sample interview

You are going to hear two candidates doing Part 2 of the test.

a) **Look at page 162. There are some pictures of places to visit. Listen to the first part of the recording. What does the examiner tell the candidates to do?**

b) **Listen to the candidates. Where do they decide to go? Tick the places they choose.**

2 Functions: making plans

a) **While doing the task, the candidates used some of these expressions. Tick the ones you heard.**

1 What do you want to do?   ...a....
2 Right, we'll do that.   ....
3 Shall we go to ... ?   ....
4 Where would you prefer to go first?   ....
5 That sounds good. Let's do that.   ....
6 Can we try something else?   ....
7 Where would you like to go?   ....
8 What shall we do ... ?   ....
9 Let's go to ...   .
10 How about going to ... ?   ....
11 Right, we'll do that.   ....
12 That's a great idea.   ....
13 Sure, I'd like to do that.   ....
14 I'm not so sure about that.   ....
15 All right, let's do that!   ....

b) **Match the expressions 1–15 above with the descriptions a)–e) below.**

a) finding out what your partner wants to do
b) making a suggestion
c) agreeing with a suggestion
d) disagreeing
e) agreeing that a decision has been made

c) **Read the following conversation between Jeanne and Martin who are planning their day. Fill each space with a suitable word.**

Jeanne: Let's plan our day.
Martin: OK. Where shall we (0) ......go...... first?
Jeanne: How (1) .... going to look round the market?
Martin: What can we (2) .... there?
Jeanne: We might buy a few souvenirs.
Martin: I'm not so (3) .... about that. If we buy anything, we'll have to carry it all day.
Jeanne: That's true. So where (4) .... you like to go first?
Martin: What (5) .... the castle?
Jeanne: Well, what can we (6) .... there?
Martin: They have lots of old paintings there.
Jeanne: OK. And what (7) .... we do after that?
Martin: (8) .... go somewhere for lunch.
Jeanne: That's a great (9) .... Where shall we go?
Martin: Shall we go for a burger?
Jeanne: Sure. I'd (10) .... to do that. And what shall we do after lunch?
Martin: Well, then we could go to the funfair.
Jeanne: All right. (11) .... do it!
Martin: OK. I'm ready.

d) **Listen and check your answers.**

e) **Work with a partner. Practise reading the conversation aloud.**

3 Exam Task

▶▶ Extra Language for the Speaking Test, Sections 6–10, pages 160–161

> **Work with a partner. Turn to page 162 and look at the pictures. Decide together which three places you are going to go to and which you will go to first.**

> Which places would you prefer to go to?

> How about ... first? I like ...

> OK, that sounds good. Let's do that.

> What shall we do after that?

•• **Exam tip!** ••••••••••••••••••••••••
Listen carefully to what your partner says, so that you can give a suitable answer.
••

Strategy

In Part 3, the examiner gives you a photograph. You talk about it by yourself for about a minute. Then your partner talks about another photo on the same topic.

Be ready to say:

- what you can see in different parts of the photo
- what is happening/what people are doing
- what people look like and what they are wearing
- how people are feeling and why.

1 Describing where things are in a picture

Work with a partner.

a) Look at the pictures (A–C). What does each picture show?

Picture A shows a boy studying in his bedroom.
Picture B is probably a room in ....
Picture C ....

b) Label the numbered parts of the pictures. If you don't remember the names of all the things, look in your dictionary.

c) Take turns to say where things are in each picture. Use the phrases in the box to help you.

> on one side (of)   on the left (of)
> on the right (of)   on top of   next to
> in the/one corner   in the other corner
> between   in front of   by (the window)
> in the middle (of)

> In Picture A, there's a bed in the middle of the room. In one corner, there's a wardrobe …

B

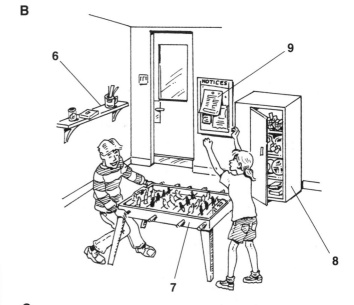

C

d) Write four sentences describing where the furniture is in the room where you are now.

A

> Speaking Part 1, Exercise 2 (page 45)
>
> **Student A:** Spell the names of the following countries for your partner.
>
> 1 Germany   2 Australia   3 Egypt
> 4 Greece   5 Venezuela

2 Describing people

a) Work with a partner. Look at the pictures on page 47 for a few moments.

Now cover page 47. Can you remember what the people are doing in each picture? Correct the mistakes in these descriptions.

1 In Picture A, a boy is sitting on the bed. I think he's about 15 years old. There's a book open in front of him, but he isn't studying. He's watching TV. He's wearing a dark jumper. There's a computer on the table.

2 In Picture B, a boy and a girl are playing table football. The boy is on the right and he's wearing a striped T-shirt and jeans. The girl's wearing a T-shirt and a pair of jeans. There's a picture on the wall.

b) Now look back at page 47 and check your answers.

c) Write a similar description of Picture C.

3 Describing how people are feeling

a) Look at the words in the box. Which could you use to describe the people in Pictures A, B and C? Which don't fit any of the pictures?

busy	calm	excited	tired	happy
cheerful	worried	depressed		anxious
amused	cross	unhappy		thoughtful
miserable	lonely	impatient		grateful
disappointed	astonished		nervous	

b) Now make sentences about each of the people. Say how you think they are feeling and give a reason for your opinion. Use the language in the box to help you.

Example: The boy in Picture A looks bored and miserable. I think he's probably studying for a test, but he'd rather go out and be with his friends.

> **Useful language**
> He/She seems/looks …
> They look as if …
> He/She/They might/could be …

4 🎧 Sample interview

You are going to hear a candidate doing Part 3 of the test.

a) Look at Photographs 1A and 1B on pages 168 and 171. Listen to the first part of the recording. What does the examiner ask Carlo to do with the photographs?

b) Listen to Carlo and Anna talking about their photographs. Mark the points in the list below which they talk about.

	Carlo	Anna
what kind of room it is		
what people he/she can see		
what the people are wearing		
where the people are in the room		
what things he/she can see		
his/her opinion about the things		
what the people are doing		
how the people are feeling		

5 Exam Task

▶▶ Extra Language for the Speaking Test, Sections 11–16, page 161

> Work with a partner. Do the Exam Task below.
>
> **Candidate A:** Look at Photograph 1A on page 168.
> **Candidate B:** Look at Photograph 1B on page 171.
>
> Think about your photograph for a few seconds. Describe it to your partner for about one minute. Use the points in Exercise 4b to help you.

•• *Exam tip!* ••••••••••••••••••••••••
: Talk about the place as well as the people and give
: an opinion.
••

Speaking Part 1, Exercise 2 (page 45)

Student B: Spell the names of the following cities for your partner.

1 Venice   2 Athens   3 Barcelona
4 Buenos Aires   5 Vienna

Speaking Part 4

▶ Strategy

In Part 4, the examiner asks you to talk to your partner about a topic for about three minutes. The topic is the same as the pictures in Part 3.

- DO give your opinions and explain what you prefer.
- DO ask your partner questions and respond to what he/she says.
- DO NOT talk to the examiner, only to your partner.

1 Sample interview

You are going to hear two candidates doing Part 4 of the test.

a) **Listen to the first part. What does the examiner ask the candidates to do?**

b) **Anna and Carlo ask each other's opinions.**

How does Anna ask Carlo's opinion?

How does Carlo ask Anna's opinion?

c) **Which of these expressions do Anna and Carlo use to agree with each other?**

1 Yes. ☐
2 Me too. ☐
3 That's OK sometimes. ☐
4 That's correct. ☐
5 No. ☐
6 I agree. ☐
7 That's my opinion too. ☐
8 You're right. ☐

2 Thinking about study habits

Write down the answers to these questions. You will use your answers in the Exam Task in Exercise 4.

1 Where do you usually study?
2 Do you listen to music while you study?
3 Do you study alone?
4 Do you watch TV while you study?
5 Do you use a computer to write your work?
6 Do you use the internet?

3 Vocabulary: television programmes

a) **What kind of TV programmes do you watch? Write how many times a week you watch the different kinds of programmes below. You will use your answers in the Exam Task in Exercise 4.**

Programme	Number of times I watch per week
the news	
political documentaries	
nature programmes	
comedy series	
quiz shows	
concerts/music programmes	
competitions	
sports programmes	
films	
TV dramas	
soap operas	

b) **Work with a partner. Compare the kind of TV programmes you like. Are your partner's answers in Exercise 3a similar to your own?**

> I like watching sports programmes, especially football. What about you?

> Yes, me too! / So do I.

4 Exam Task

▶▶ Extra Language for the Speaking Test, Sections 17 and 18, page 161

Work with a partner. Look at the Exam Task below, then look back at your answers to Exercises 2 and 3. Take turns to shut your book while your partner asks you these questions.

Ask and answer these questions:

1 Which of the photographs on pages 168 and 171 looks more like the way you study?
2 When and where do you study?
3 Do you ever watch television at the same time?
4 What kinds of TV programmes do you prefer?
5 Do you spend more time studying or watching TV?

•• *Exam tip!* ••••••••••••••••••••••
Don't worry if you can't think of much to say at first.
The examiner will help you by asking you questions.
•••••••••••••••••••••••••••••••••••••

TEST 2

Reading Part 1

 Strategy

1 Read the instructions to the Exam Task on the opposite page.

1 How many questions do you have to answer?

2 What do you have to decide?

3 Where do you mark your answers?

2 Look at the example.

1 What kind of text is this?

   a) a message on a board   b) a sign
   c) an e-mail

2 Where might you see it?

3 A is the correct answer. Let's decide why.

   Look at A. Underline the words which mean *phoning the cinema*.

   Underline the words which mean *contact Nell*.

4 Why is B wrong? When should John ring Nell?

5 Why is C wrong? How should John find out when the film starts?

3 Look at Question 1.

1 What kind of text is this?

   a) an e-mail message   b) a notice
   c) a phone message

2 Where might you see this sign? What words help you to decide? Underline them.

3 Can 'saver' tickets be used on the 10.15 train?

4 Can you use 'saver' tickets on later trains? How do you know?

5 Can you use 'saver' tickets on earlier trains?

6 Look at **A**, **B** and **C**.

   Which one means the same as the message? Mark it.

   What words in the message tell you? Underline them.

7 Look at the other sentences. Decide why they are wrong.

4 Look at Questions 2–5.

For each question:

• decide what kind of text it is

• choose the correct answer

• mark the answer on your answer sheet.

·· Exam tip! ··

Some of the words in the incorrect sentences are often the same as in the text. Don't choose too quickly. Make sure you understand the meaning of the whole sentence before you decide.

··

Speaking Part 1, Exam Task (page 89)

Student A, ask your partner these questions.

1 What's your name?

2 What school do you go to?

3 Which class are you in?

4 Can you spell the name of your maths teacher, please?

5 What time do you finish school each day?

6 What's your favourite subject? Why?

7 How long do you spend on homework?

Part 1

Questions 1–5

Look at the text in each question.
What does it say?
Mark the correct letter **A**, **B** or **C** on your answer sheet.

Example:

0

> John
>
> Can you call the cinema from home and check film time before leaving? Let me know what time we should get there.
>
> Nell

John should

A contact Nell after phoning the cinema.

B ring Nell after arriving at the cinema.

C go to the cinema to check when the film starts.

Answer:

1

> SAVER TICKETS CAN
> BE USED ON THE
> 10.15 TRAIN AND
> ANY TRAIN AFTER THAT

A The first train you can travel on with a 'saver' ticket is the 10.15.

B 'Saver' tickets cost extra if you travel after 10.15.

C The 10.15 is the only train you can travel on with a 'saver' ticket.

2

> TELL RECEPTIONIST
> YOUR NAME ON ARRIVAL,
> THEN GO TO DENTIST'S
> WAITING ROOM

A Do not leave the waiting room until the receptionist calls your name.

B Do not go to the waiting room before telling the receptionist you are here.

C The receptionist will tell the dentist that you have arrived.

3

> *Dear all*
> *We're staying by the sea for a few days at present instead of going straight to the mountains. It's very relaxing after driving for two days to get here.*
> *Michael*

A Michael has spent two days driving to the mountains.

B Michael visited the mountains before going to the coast.

C Michael is having a break from travelling at the moment.

[Turn over

4

THIS OFFICE CAN ONLY TAKE
BOOKINGS AT LEAST
TWENTY-FOUR HOURS
IN ADVANCE OF DEPARTURE

A This office doesn't take bookings for the same day as you travel.

B If you book tickets here, you'll receive them a day later.

C You can book tickets at this office twenty-four hours a day.

5

Students wanting to go on the trip should go to the office within the next two days with the correct money. We no longer accept credit cards or give change.

Students should

A pay the exact amount for the trip in cash.

B make sure they have a credit card for the trip.

C take enough change with them on the trip.

Language practice: Reading Part 1

1 Grammar: time words and phrases

In Part 1, time words and phrases, for example *after that*, *at present*, *later* and *until* can be very important when you are choosing your answer.

a) Find and <u>underline</u> examples of time expressions in the Exam Task on pages 51–52.

b) Rewrite the sentences below in your notebook using the expressions from the box instead of the words <u>underlined</u>.

later   ~~at present~~   every fifteen minutes
in advance   within a fortnight   no longer
until   in time   at the moment

0 The restaurant is not open <u>now</u>.
   The restaurant is not open at present.

1 I'm on holiday <u>from now to</u> Tuesday.

2 That film is <u>not</u> showing <u>any more</u>.

3 The museum is closed for lunch, but it will be open <u>afterwards</u>.

4 There's a tram from here to the city centre <u>four times an hour</u>.

5 I promise I'll reply to your request <u>in less than two weeks</u>.

6 Harry's not here <u>now</u>, can I take a message?

7 We need to know how many people are coming to the performance <u>before it starts</u>.

8 You must be here <u>early enough</u> to catch the ferry.

2 Vocabulary: words you see in signs

a) The words in the box below often appear on the signs and notices in Part 1. Choose the correct word or phrase for each gap in the notices below.

assistant   available   arrival   cancelled
credit card   discount   emergency   ~~entrance~~
forbidden   ~~luggage~~   responsible   permitted
on time   out of order   reception   security
staff   urgent

0

THIS .... *entrance* .... IS FOR PASSENGERS
WITHOUT .... *luggage* .... ONLY.

1

THIS LIFT IS ....
PLEASE ASK AN .... FOR
HELP IF YOU CANNOT USE THE STAIRS.

2

For very .... enquiries,
please ring the bell on the .... desk.

3

Ten per cent .... on group bookings.
Pay by ....

4

> *All the trains are running* .... *today,*
> *except the 10.05 which is* .... *.*

5

> At weekends the doctor is only
> .... in an ....

6

> On .... , visiting students must wait here
> to be met by the teacher who is .... for sports.

7

> **SMOKING IS** .... **DURING**
> **LECTURES, BUT IS** ....
> **DURING THE COFFEE BREAK.**

8

> For .... Reasons, Only ....
> Are Allowed Beyond This Gate.

b) Where might you see the signs (1–8) above?

3 Grammar: *before/ after + -ing*

Signs and messages often talk about things happening *before* or *after* each other. They sometimes use the words *before* or *after + -ing*.

a) Find and underline examples of *before* or *after + -ing* in the Exam Task on pages 51–52.

b) Make sentences in your notebook using *before* or *after + -ing*.

0 Always read the instructions/use the equipment (before)
   Always read the instructions before using the equipment.

1 You must take a shower/use the swimming pool (before)

2 Please clear the table/eat a meal (after)

3 You'll have to ask permission/use this telephone (before)

4 Don't forget to pick up your rubbish/finish your picnic (after)

5 Employees must wash their hands/prepare a meal (before)

6 Remember to lock the door/put out the rubbish (after)

7 Passengers must buy a ticket/get on the train (before)

8 Switch off your mobile/enter the theatre (before)

4 Vocabulary: money words

The texts in Part 1 are often about buying things. You need to know words for talking about money, for example:
Saver tickets **cost extra** *if you travel after 10.15.*
We no longer accept **credit cards** *or give* **change***.*

Complete the text with a word or phrase from the box.

> ~~buy~~   change   cheaper   correct money
> cost extra   credit card   discount
> expensive   pay   sell

When you go to London on the train you can
(0) ......buy........ your ticket at the local station using
a (1) .... Sometimes you can get a
(2) .... ticket, because there is a
(3) .... on the fare at certain times
of the day. Make sure you have plenty of
(4) .... with you, because when
you arrive in London, you can use it to
(5) .... for your underground ticket from a
machine. If you don't have the (6) .... ,
you may have to queue at the ticket office. You
can also go to London by coach. This is less
(7) .... than the train, although it takes
longer. The driver can (8) .... you a ticket,
and it doesn't (9) .... to travel at busy times
of the day.

5 Speaking: *Are you a spender or a saver?*

a) Work with a partner. Discuss some of the questions below. Look again at the language in Exercise 4 before you start.

1 Do you get pocket money?
2 Do you earn money? How?
3 Do you often run out of money?
4 Do you ever borrow or lend money?
5 Do you have a bank account?
6 Do you have a credit card?
7 Can you save money, if you have to?
8 Are you a spender or a saver?

b) Tell the rest of the class whether your partner is a spender or a saver, and say why.

▶ **Strategy**

1 Read the instructions to the Exam Task opposite.

1 How many questions are there?
2 What do all the people want?
3 What are the reviews about?
4 How many reviews are there?
5 What do you have to decide?
6 Where do you mark your answers?

2 Look at the pictures.

Each question describes a different person or group of people. What kind of people do the pictures show?

3 Look at Questions 6–10.

a) **All the people are looking for something different. Look at the underlined parts of Question 6. What is important for Ryan?**

1 Does Ryan like modern films?
2 What is his favourite kind of film?
3 What kind of actors does he like?
4 What kinds of film doesn't he like?

b) **Now underline the important parts of Questions 7–10.**

4 Look at Texts A–H to find the important information.

a) **Look at Question 6 again.**

1 Which films are comedies?
2 Which of these films is best for Ryan?

b) **Check your answer.**
- Is the film funny?
- Is it old-fashioned?
- Are the actors famous?
- Is it a musical or a thriller?

c) **Mark the letter (A, B, C, etc.) by Question 6 on your answer sheet.**

d) **Look at the important points you underlined for Questions 7–10. Use them to decide which films are the most suitable for the other people. Mark your answers on your answer sheet.**

> •• *Exam tip!* •••••••••••••••••••••••
> Remember there are eight texts and only five
> people, so three texts are not needed.

Part 2

Questions 6–10

The people below all want to watch a film on TV. On the opposite page, there are reviews of eight films.

Decide which film would be the most suitable for the following people.

For questions **6–10**, mark the correct letter **(A–H)** on your answer sheet.

---

6  Ryan likes watching old-fashioned films on TV. He prefers comedies, particularly those with famous actors. He is not keen on musicals or thrillers.

7  Tom's hobby is reading and he enjoys watching films on TV whose stories are taken from literature. His favourite books are those by famous authors of the past. He reads books about the cinema, too, and likes watching famous actors.

8  Elena likes to relax by watching the latest romantic films on TV, especially if they make her laugh. She particularly likes those which have some music in them.

9 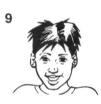 Belinda enjoys watching thrillers. She prefers adventures which actually happened to people in real life, as she is interested in the lives of other people.

10  Carol loves listening to pop music and reading magazines about it. She doesn't mind what sort of film she sees, if it's a new one about pop stars or their music.

Darius Alexander reviews this week's films on TV

A   *See you in Sicily* ....

This is about a journey across Europe in the 1960s. A group of young people travel across Europe in an old van, but nothing really exciting happens to them and it isn't actually very funny. It's a weak comedy film with singing. I had never heard of the actors before, although some of them could certainly sing.

B   *The moon and stars* ....

This follows the usual love story – boy meets girl, they fall in love and sing some songs about it. It's an enjoyable film, although there's nothing special about the singing, and it has its amusing parts. It comes to the TV screen very quickly, as it was only made a year ago.

C   *Mad for music* ....

This film came out last month, and all the young people are queuing to see it. There will be a whole generation of fans watching because the music of this group, Sure Fire, is everyone's favourite at the moment.

D   *The house by the lake* ....

Although the main roles are all acted by well-known stars of film or TV, I got bored by the dialogue which seems so slow compared to modern films. However, people who like Henrietta Browne's writing will enjoy it because it is beautifully filmed, and the story keeps perfectly to the novel written two hundred years ago.

E   *Seaside story* ....

This funny film was made in the past, but is still as good as it was 25 years ago when I first saw it. The main actors, who were already famous when it was made, made several more films together later on. The story takes place in a very unusual hotel at the seaside where the guests have lots of problems.

F   *Shooting for freedom* ....

Photographer Valerie Maine planned to work in a dangerous part of the world for six weeks. This adventure film tells how she escaped from the people who held her prisoner for over a year. It is difficult to believe that this actually happened to someone who is still alive.

G   *Escape to Jupiter* ....

This film about adventures in space isn't supposed to be funny, but I'm afraid I wanted to laugh sometimes. Although this is one of several very similar films made recently, it's one of the better ones, as it certainly holds your attention.

H   *Another part of town* ....

This film manages to show some serious problems of a family in modern Britain without depressing the audience. If you haven't read Michael Stone's book of the same name yet, you'll be pleased to watch this excellent film. And you'll still enjoy the film if you have already read it. There is some excellent acting from some completely unknown actors.

1 Vocabulary: expressions with similar meanings

> In Part 2, it's important to understand when different words or phrases have similar meanings.

The phrases on the left are from Questions 6–10 on page 54; those on the right are from the texts on page 55. Match the ones with similar meanings.

1 old-fashioned film   a) funny film
2 musical   b) well-known stars
3 thriller   c) film with singing
4 romantic film   d) love story
5 comedy film   e) this actually happened
6 in real life   f) adventure film
7 famous actors   g) film made in the past

2 Grammar: present perfect

a) Match the questions in A with the answers in B.

0 Have you spoken to Mary recently? ....h....

1 Have you finished that book yet? ....
2 Have you already seen this film? ....
3 Have you booked your plane ticket? ....
4 Have you just changed your clothes? ....
5 Have you seen Ian? ....
6 Have you had some lunch? ....
7 Have you studied Spanish for a long time? ....

a No, let's watch it.
b Yes, I've already had some sandwiches, thank you.
c No, I'm only half way through.
d No, I still haven't decided when I need to leave.
e No, I began last year.
f Yes, I'm going out in a minute.
g No, he's been away recently.
h ~~Yes, I phoned her two days ago.~~

b) Which time words are used with the present perfect? Underline them.

c) Complete each sentence with a word or phrase from the box.

| ago | already | during | for | in | just | last month |
| later | ~~since~~ | still | yet | | | |

0 We've been on holiday ......since....... the end of June.

1 I ordered that CD a month .... , but it .... hasn't arrived.
2 We get lots of tourists here .... the winter, but not so many .... the summer.
3 You've finished your homework .... , but I've .... started mine!
4 I don't want to stop work .... , so I'll make myself a snack ....
5 I saw that band in a concert .... , but they didn't play .... long.

3 Grammar: time expressions

Complete the second sentence so that it means the same as the first, using no more than three words.

0 It's been eight months since we swam in this pool. We .....haven't swum...... in this pool for eight months.

1 He joined that pop group last year.
He .... in that pop group since last year.
2 She wrote that e-mail a week ago.
It's a week .... that e-mail.
3 They've worked there for a month.
They .... work there last month.
4 He was in the garden until a moment ago.
He .... come into the house from the garden.
5 She's already told that joke twice before.
This .... the third time she's told that joke.

4 Vocabulary: word sets

a) **Put the words in the box into the correct columns in the table.**

actor	article	camera	CD	cinema
contents	concert	crossword	director	
drummer	game	guitarist	headline	
keyboard	make-up	mouse	movie	
musician	photograph	program	rock	
screen	software	story	website	

Film	Music	Magazine	Computer
actor			

b) **Compare your lists with a partner. Are there any words which can go in more than one column? Do they have the same meaning in both columns?**

c) **Match each description with a word from the box in Exercise 4a.**

0   He or she plays the drums. ...*drummer*......

1   This is at the top of a magazine article.

2   You can look at millions of these on your computer.

3   This word means *film*.

4   This tells you which page to look at in a magazine.

5   He or she tells the actors what to do.

5 Speaking: films

a) **Think of a film you have enjoyed. Make notes about it.**

- What kind of film is it?
- What happens in it?
- Why did you like it?

b) **Work with a partner. Tell your partner about your film, but don't tell him/her the title. Your partner should try to guess the name of the film you are describing. Do you both like the same kinds of film?**

> This film is about …
>
> The best part of the film is when …
>
> It's one of my favourite films because …

6 Writing: an e-mail or letter about a film

a) **Fill each space in this e-mail with one word.**

Hi Steve

I went to the cinema with Jack last night. We saw the film 'Moving Out'. It's (1) .... a young man, Rashid, who goes to live in London. I'm not very (2) .... on films about everyday life, so I didn't really want to go because I (3) .... watching films like thrillers and space adventures.

But now 'Moving Out' is one of my (4) .... films because it's really (5) .... I laughed all the time. And it's about ordinary young people, just (6) .... you and me. The (7) .... part of the film is (8) .... Rashid's mum comes to visit him. He's (9) .... got home from a party, and the flat's very untidy. The (10) .... aren't well-known, but they're really good. Go and see it soon!

See you

Sami

b) **Write an e-mail or letter to a friend about a film, play or video you have seen recently. Use Sami's e-mail to help you plan what to write.**

Reading Part 3

 Strategy

1 Read the instructions to the Exam Task opposite.

1 How many sentences are there?

2 What are the sentences about?

3 What do you have to read?

4 What do you have to decide?

5 When do you mark A on your answer sheet?

6 When do you mark B on your answer sheet?

2 Read Sentences 11–20 to get a good idea what the text is about.

Match the sentences to the following topics.

a) buying food ......16......

b) learning a new sport ....

c) who should read this ....

d) the opening times of an office ....

e) something which gives information about accommodation ....

f) singing or playing for an audience ....

g) improving your skill in a leisure activity ....

h) something many people want to do ....

i) something which helps you to spend less money ....

j) who you can ask about something ....

3 Read the text to find the information you need.

For each sentence (11–20), <u>underline</u> the part of the text where you think the answer is. The first two are done for you.

4 Look at the sentences again.

• Compare them with your underlined text.

• Decide whether the sentence is correct or incorrect.

• Mark your answer on your answer sheet.

> **•• Exam tip!** ••••••••••••••••••
> The questions are in the same order as the information you need in the text.

Part 3

Questions 11–20

Look at the sentences below about advice for new students at a university.
Read the text on the opposite page to decide if each sentence is correct or incorrect.
If it is correct, mark **A** on your answer sheet.
If it is not correct, mark **B** on your answer sheet.

___

11 This information is to help students who have arrived after the start of the university term.

12 The Welfare Office is usually closed in the morning.

13 A list of flats available for rent can be seen in the Welfare Office.

14 You can save money on books if you have a student card.

15 You should ask older students for advice about where to buy books.

16 Having all your meals in the canteen is the cheapest way to eat.

17 Lots of students want to join the cookery class.

18 You can take up golf at a local club.

19 You can join a part-time course at the Music School if you already play reasonably well.

20 At musical open evenings, you can perform even if you have no experience.

19th September

WELCOME!

As a new student, you've arrived two days before term starts to look around and get settled in before your course begins and the place fills up. Here is some information to make all that a bit easier (we hope!).

The Student Welfare Office is normally open from 4 p.m. till 8 p.m. Monday to Friday. Today and tomorrow it will be open all day, from about 9 a.m. This is the place to come if you have any problems, for example about money or accommodation (we have a list of rental agencies and also advertise any rooms which become available in the university hostels at the end of term). We also give out the university identity cards which you need to join the library and which allow you to get discounts at a number of local shops (including bookshops) and places of entertainment, such as clubs and cinemas.

On Monday and Tuesday of next week, second-year students will be running a book sale in the canteen from 10–3. Many of the books on your first-year reading list will be available, and we suggest you should look here first before spending too much on new books.

The university canteen (open from 7.30 a.m. till 7.30 p.m.) sells hot meals fairly cheaply, as well as snacks and drinks, but it'll save you money to cook at least some of your own meals. There is a basic cookery course starting next week (run by students for students, so it's really practical). If you don't know how to boil an egg, this is for you. It's always full, so get your name on the list in the Welfare Office NOW!

The sports centre is open from today. Look on the noticeboards there for information about athletics, swimming, team games and so on. It is also possible to join some local city clubs, such as golf or squash, at a discount (show them your card) if you can play at a reasonable level. Addresses in the sports-centre office.

The Music School welcomes all members of the university, whatever their main subject of study, for part-time courses. Why not take the opportunity to start learning the guitar, violin or piano while you're here? Many advanced students offer really cheap lessons. There are also open evenings when anyone can take the chance to perform in front of an audience. Look out for notices advertising times and dates.

1 Vocabulary: student life

The words and phrases in the box are used in the sentences and in the text on page 59. Match them with the explanations below.

> advanced   canteen   club   full-time course
> hostel   noticeboard   part-time course
> reading list   rent   sports centre   student card
> ~~university term~~   welfare office

0 part of the students' year = ..university term....

1 money paid to your landlord ....

2 a place where students can go for general help and advice ....

3 something you can use to prove that you are a student ....

4 a place to eat ....

5 a group who join together for a leisure activity ....

6 studying for a few hours every week ....

7 studying all day, from Monday to Friday ....

8 a place for students to live cheaply ....

9 the books that students must read for their course ....

10 where you can play volleyball, do gymnastics, etc. ....

11 where people put posters and other information ....

12 a word to describe students who know a lot about their subject ....

2 Speaking: your school/college

a) **What do you think makes a good school? Look at the list below and number it in order of importance.**

☐ friendly atmosphere   ☐ uniform
☐ lots of computers   ☐ good exam results
☐ hard-working students   ☐ strict teachers
☐ good sports facilities   ☐ clear rules
☐ modern classrooms

b) **Compare your list with a partner. Tell each other why you put things in that order.**

c) **Imagine that you have to give a talk about the school or college where you study to some visitors. Spend two minutes thinking about what you would say. Use the expressions in the box to help you.**

> **Useful language**
> The school has ...
> The best classes ...
> Most of the students enjoy ...
> Nobody likes ...
> The students are usually ...
> We have lots of ...
> There aren't any ...

d) **When you are ready, work with a partner. Talk about your school for one minute. Then listen to what your partner has to say. Did you talk about the same things? Do you agree with each other's opinions?**

3 Grammar: adverbs of frequency (*how often?*)

a) **Look at the words in the box. We use these words to show how often something happens.**

> always   often   frequently   regularly   sometimes
> usually   normally   rarely   seldom   never

*Example: The Student Welfare Office is **normally** open from 4 p.m. till 8 p.m. (text page 59)*

Complete this diagram with the words in the box.

always
|
100%————————50%————————0%
   |
usually

b) **Complete these sentences truthfully, using words from the box in Exercise 3a.**

1 I .... do my homework in the morning.

2 My classmates .... have problems with grammar.

3 Our teacher .... speaks English in the classroom.

4 My classmates and I .... meet after class.

5 We .... listen to music by English bands.

6 My family .... helps me with words I don't understand.

7 I .... watch English films on TV.

8 We .... eat English food in my house.

9 My friends .... take a holiday in August.

10 I .... use an English dictionary to check words I don't know.

c) **Compare your sentences with other students.**

4 Speaking: everyday activities

In PET Reading and Listening, you may read or hear about someone's everyday life. In PET Writing and Speaking, you often need to write or speak about your own everyday life.

Work with a partner. Talk about how often you do the following activities. Use words from Exercise 3.

go jogging   drive a car   play football use a computer   visit art galleries go to the cinema   do the washing-up go to bed after midnight   get up after midday

Example:

Student A: How often do you go jogging?

Student B: I never go jogging. / I usually go jogging on Saturday mornings.

5 Grammar: relative clauses

Understanding how short sentences can be joined to make longer ones is useful both for understanding Reading texts in the exam and writing your answers in the Writing paper.

a) **Look at these sentences. They are made from two shorter ones.**

1 *We also give out the university identity cards **which** you need to join the library.*

= We also give out the university identity cards. + You need ~~the cards~~ to join the library.

2 *Students will be running a book sale in the canteen **where** many of the books on your reading list will be available.*

= Students will be running a book sale in the canteen. + Many of the books on your reading list will be available ~~there~~.

3 *There are also open evenings **when** anyone can take the chance to perform.*

= There are also open evenings. + Anyone can take the chance to perform ~~on those evenings~~.

b) **Complete these sentences with the correct pronoun. Use *who* (for people), *which* (for things), *where* (for places) or *when* (for times).**

0 This photo shows the hotel *where* we stayed.

1 That's the CD .... got to number 1.

2 That's the school .... I used to go.

3 My music teacher was the person .... helped me most.

4 These jeans are the ones .... need mending.

5 Do you remember the day .... we went to London and got lost?

c) **Make longer sentences by joining these pairs. Use a pronoun to replace the words <u>underlined</u> in the second sentence.**

0 Mary's giving me a lift in the new car. She bought <u>the car</u> last week. (which) *Mary's giving me a lift in the new car which she bought last week.*

1 A group of students share the flat. Keith's father owns <u>the flat</u>. (which)

2 We often have a party at weekends. We don't have classes <u>at weekends</u>. (when)

3 Most students live in hostels. Parties aren't allowed <u>in hostels</u>. (where)

4 This is my penfriend. <u>He</u>'s coming to stay next month. (who)

5 I usually study in the college library. Most of my friends study <u>in the college library</u> too. (where)

6 It's a pity we have exams in the summer. The weather is very hot <u>in the summer</u>. (when)

d) **Complete the second sentence so that it means the same as the first, using no more than three words.**

1 A famous rock star used to live in that house. That's the house .... a famous rock star used to live.

2 I usually buy clothes from my cousin's shop. My cousin owns the shop .... buy my clothes.

3 This note was left on my desk. This is the note .... left on my desk.

4 If a person steals things, he's a thief. A thief is .... steals things.

5 Some mornings I don't have school and I go swimming instead. I go swimming on .... I don't have school.

Reading Part 4

 Strategy

1 Read the instructions to the Exam Task opposite.

1 What do you have to read?
2 What do you have to do?
3 Where do you mark your answers?

2 Read the text quickly to get a good idea of what it is about.

1 What sort of place is the text about?
2 Why does the writer enjoy going there?
3 What happened there in 1975?

3 Read Questions 21–25.

<u>Underline</u> the best word or phrase to complete each sentence.

1 Question 21 asks about *when/why/where* the writer wrote the text. (This is always a general question.)
2 Question 22 asks about *a person/a place/an event*. (This is always a question about detail or opinion.)
3 Question 23 asks about *opinions towards/information about/plans for* Lake Vinney. (This is always a question about detail or opinion.)
4 Question 24 asks about the writer's *plans/opinions/discovery*. (This is always a question about detail or opinion.)
5 Question 25 asks about a way of *persuading people to visit/warning people of a danger/telling people about changes*. (This is always a general question.)

4 Read the text and answer Questions 21–25.

- Read the text again more carefully.
- Choose the correct answer for each question.
- Mark your answers on your answer sheet.

• • Exam tip! •
If you are not sure of the answer to one question, do the others and come back to it at the end. It may be easier then.

Part 4

Questions 21–25

Read the text and questions below.
For each question, mark the correct letter
A, **B**, **C** or **D** on your answer sheet.

Lake Vinney

My favourite place for watersports is Lake Vinney, but it has only existed since 1975 when the valley was filled with water to provide electricity. Under the water is the village, Vinnthorpe. Last week I talked to Pat Smithers, who runs a shop on the edge of the lake and looks after the huge car park. She gets up early to travel to her shop to sell newspapers and food and doesn't finish work till late because of the car park. She said drowning the village was the best thing that ever happened, as it brought a lot of business to the area, and the number of visitors from all over the country continues to increase, especially as there is a new road which means it is easier to get to. When I asked people enjoying the watersports, they said they never thought about the drowned houses and streets. When I spoke to some people sitting in the café overlooking the lake, I was surprised to find they still get angry about what happened. They used to live in Vinnthorpe and were moved to other places in the area, among them thirty children who are now middle-aged, but they still miss the village. They say that nobody asked them what they wanted – they were told one day that everything was decided. They were separated from their friends and had to get buses to new schools instead of walking there together. It is a shame that these people lost their homes, and I hope something similar never happens again in the future. I would miss the watersports if they weren't there, however, and I must say that I hadn't ever thought about what was under the water until last week.

21 What is the writer trying to do?

    A describe what people think about the drowned village

    B persuade people to take up watersports on Lake Vinney

    C discuss what might happen to Lake Vinney in the future

    D explain why people like living by Lake Vinney

22 What do we learn about Pat Smithers?

    A She lives beside the lake.

    B She used to live in Vinnthorpe.

    C She often visits the area on holiday.

    D She earns her living near Lake Vinney.

23 What do we find out about Lake Vinney?

    A It attracts tourists from abroad.

    B There are lots of houses on the banks.

    C More people are visiting it every year.

    D Mainly local people do watersports there.

24 What does the writer think about Vinnthorpe?

    A He agrees with Pat Smithers.

    B He feels sorry for the people who lived there.

    C He thinks it should now be forgotten.

    D He has always felt guilty about water-skiing there.

25 Which of these is an advert for Lake Vinney?

A

> Come to Lake Vinney and water-ski or sail. No ugly car parks, shops or cafés around the lake to spoil the views.

B

> Come to Vinnthorpe and stay in a hotel in the village. Enjoy the walks around the lake in complete peace and quiet.

C

> Lake Vinney is perfect for all kinds of watersports. Wonderful café by the side of the lake and plenty of car-parking space.

D

> Enjoy water-skiing on Lake Vinney, but leave time to visit the old village beside the lake – nothing has changed there for 30 years.

Language practice: Reading Part 4

1 Function: expressing attitudes

In this part of the exam, at least one question is about people's attitudes and opinions. In the text on page 62, several people express attitudes.

a) Match the people (a–d) with the attitudes (1–8).

Who...

1 said drowning the village was the best
   thing that ever happened? ....
2 never think about the drowned houses? ....
3 was surprised? ....
4 still feel angry about what happened? ....
5 still miss the village? ....
6 thinks it's a shame? ....
7 hope something similar never
   happens again? ....
8 would miss the watersports? ....

a) the shop owner
b) the writer of the text
c) people who used to live in Vinnthorpe
d) people doing watersports

b) Complete these sentences with your own ideas.

1 I think it's a shame that some people ....
2 I feel angry when ....
3 I sometimes miss ....
4 I really hope ....

2 Grammar: reported speech

a) In the text on page 62, the writer reports what people said:

... *they said **they** never **thought** about the drowned houses* ...

The people actually said:

We never **think** about the drowned houses.

What differences do you notice?

b) Now compare these and <u>underline</u> the differences.

1 He said he would visit them the next day.

I'll visit you tomorrow.

2 She said she could help us with our luggage.

I can help you with your luggage.

3 They told us they weren't going to leave that
   evening.

We aren't going to leave this evening.

4 We told them we had already locked the door.

We've already locked the door.

5 I said I hadn't been there the day before.

I wasn't here yesterday.

c) Complete the second sentence so it means the same as the first, using no more than three words.

0 John said he didn't want any coffee.
   John said, 'I ....*don't want*.......... any coffee.'

1 They said the book was in the post.
   'The book .... in the post,'
   they said.
2 She explained she usually worked there in the
   evenings.
   She explained, 'I .... in the
   evening.'
3 She told us she was going home.
   She told us, '.................................... home.'
4 You said you expected to arrive before lunch.
   You said, '.................................... to arrive
   before lunch.'
5 We said we would help with the housework at
   the weekend.
   'We .... with the housework
   at the weekend,' we said.
6 He informed us we had to pay extra.
   'You .... extra,' he informed
   us.
7 I told them I would phone the next day.
   'I .... ,' I told them.
8 You told me you could speak Spanish.
   'I .... Spanish,' you told me.
9 He said my sister had already phoned the hospital.
   He said, '.................................... already phoned
   the hospital.'

3 Grammar: patterns after reporting verbs

Complete the second sentence so that it means the same as the first, using no more than three words.

0   My friend suggested going to the cinema.
    My friend said, 'Why ......*don't we*...... go to the cinema?'

1   My father advised me to walk so I got some exercise.
    My father said, 'You ....
    walk so you get some exercise.'

2   Sarah invited Giacomo to her party.
    Sarah said, 'Would .... to come to my party?'

3   The sign reminded us to drive on the left in England.
    The sign said, 'Don't .... to drive on the left in England.'

4   The man refused to give his wallet to the thief.
    The man shouted, 'No, I ....
    give you my wallet.'

5   Matilda apologised for starting the fire.
    Matilda said, '.............................. I started the fire.'

4 Vocabulary: get

> **Get** is a very common word in English and has lots of different meanings. You will meet and need to use it in many parts of the exam.

Get is used in four different ways in the text:

a)   *It is easier to get to.*
b)   *They had to get buses to new schools.*
c)   *She gets up early.*
d)   *They still get angry.*

a) Match the sentences a–d to their meanings 1–4.

1   *get* + adjective = *become*
2   *get to* + place = *travel to*
3   *get* + transport = *catch*
4   *get up* = *leave the bed*

b) Write a number 1–4 next to each of these sentences to show which meaning get has.

a)   Are you getting the bus?   ....
b)   I'd get wet if it rained.   ....
c)   I have to get up early for college.   ....
d)   How do you get to work?   ....

c) Complete the sentences below with an expression from the box.

> got to the sports club   get a lift   get any e-mails
> get to know   get out of bed   getting off
> ~~gets very tired~~   get married   get home
> get to school   get it back

0   Angelo has two jobs, so he ....*gets very tired*.... .

1   How do you .... ? By bus or on foot?

2   I realised I had forgotten my tennis racket when I ....

3   I lent that CD to Jenny – I must remember to ....

4   My computer isn't working and I can't ....

5   In the winter I find it really difficult to ....

6   She slipped as she was .... the bus and hurt her ankle.

7   I missed the last bus, so I had to ....

8   My sister and her boyfriend have decided to ....

9   Maria didn't .... until midnight. Her parents were really angry.

10   Peter is an interesting person, and I'd like to .... him better.

5 Speaking: past habits (*used to*)

> In the text on page 62, we read about people who used to live in Vinnthorpe, but don't live there any more.
> We say *used to* when we talk about something we did in the past that we don't do now.

Work with a partner. Talk about things you used to do that you don't do now. For example, think about:

- what you used to eat and drink
- what you used to wear
- what activities you used to like/dislike doing
- what you used to do in the evenings/at weekends.

I used to drink milk with my breakfast. Now I prefer coffee.

I never used to like playing football, but now I love it.

I used to take my little brother to the park on Saturdays. Now he goes with his friends.

▶ Strategy

1 Read the instructions to the Exam Task on the opposite page.

1 What do you have to read?

2 What do you have to choose?

3 Where do you put your answers?

2 Look at the title of the text and make guesses about the text.

Can you guess which of the following people the text might be about?

- a man who lives in an airport
- a man who works in an airport
- a man who likes visiting airports
- a man who designs airports

3 Read the text quickly and check your guess.

Don't worry about the numbered spaces for now. Did you guess correctly?

4 Look at the example (0) and read the first sentence of the text carefully.

1 What is the answer to the example?

2 Why are the other answers not possible?

5 Look at Questions 26–35 and choose the answers for the ones you are certain about.

For each question:

- read the whole of the sentence which contains the space
- write the word you choose in the space – it may help you to understand the text.

•• **Exam tip!** ••••••••••••••••••••••

Choose the answers for the spaces you are certain about first. Then go back and guess the other answers.

•••••••••••••••••••••••••••••••

6 Go back and guess the other answers.

7 Check your work.

When you have finished, read the text again all the way through. Do your answers make sense?

8 Mark your answers on your answer sheet.

Check that you have put them in the right place.

Speaking Part 1, Exam Task (page 89)

Student B, ask your partner these questions.

1 What's your name?

2 What's the name of your school?

3 What part of the town is that in?

4 How long have you been at that school?

5 Can you spell the name of your school for me, please?

6 Which subject is easiest for you?

7 Which subjects do you dislike? Why?

Part 5

Questions 26–35

Read the text below and choose the correct word for each space.
For each question, mark the correct letter **A**, **B**, **C** or **D** on your answer sheet.

Example:

0   **A** left   **B** went   **C** removed   **D** departed

Answer:
0	A	B	C	D
	■	☐	☐	☐

The airport man

Yesterday Ahmed **(0)** .... his home for the first time in eleven years. But his home is a very unusual one – he has **(26)** .... the last eleven years living in an international airport. Ahmed had no family in his own country, so eleven years ago he set off to search **(27)** .... his sister who lived in Scotland. He hadn't heard from her for **(28)** .... , but he had an old address. He never **(29)** .... Scotland, however, because while he was **(30)** .... for a connecting flight, all his documents **(31)** .... stolen and he had to ask for new ones. **(32)** .... he had nowhere to go, he stayed in the airport. After a **(33)** .... weeks, he was still there. He became **(34)** .... as 'Sir George' and all the airport staff liked him. Eleven years **(35)** .... his documents arrived and he was free to go. But he no longer wanted to!

26	**A** taken	**B** passed	**C** spent	**D** used
27	**A** to	**B** for	**C** from	**D** at
28	**A** years	**B** times	**C** long	**D** ever
29	**A** got	**B** arrived	**C** travelled	**D** reached
30	**A** waiting	**B** thinking	**C** booking	**D** sitting
31	**A** had	**B** were	**C** are	**D** have
32	**A** Although	**B** Even	**C** As	**D** If
33	**A** several	**B** many	**C** lot	**D** few
34	**A** called	**B** known	**C** told	**D** said
35	**A** following	**B** since	**C** later	**D** next

1 Grammar: preposition or no preposition after a verb

> In Part 5, you often need to know which preposition (if any) follows a certain verb.

Look at the following sentences. Each verb is followed by a space. Decide whether you need to put a preposition in each space. If you do need a preposition, decide which one.

0 My uncle lived ..in... Africa when he was young.

1 The boys got .... home very late on Saturday.

2 The shop assistant brought .... the customer several different pairs of shoes.

3 I'm looking .... a birthday present for my uncle.

4 The plane didn't reach .... Sydney until the next day.

5 Nobody can enter .... the building without an identity card.

6 We're staying .... friends until our new flat is ready.

7 I took my coat .... the hook and put it in my case.

8 Please can you pass .... me an apple?

9 What time does the ferry arrive .... the island?

10 A thief stole .... my wallet when I was in the cinema.

2 Grammar: words that describe *how much* or *how many*

> In Question 33 on page 67, you should have chosen *few* to fill the space *after a ...... weeks*. *Several* and *many* do not fit the space because they do not follow *a*. *Lot* will only fit in this space if it is followed by *of*.

a) Underline the correct word or words in each sentence.

0 Have you got *many/much* homework tonight?

1 Please hurry. We've only got *a few/a little* minutes before the film starts.

2 I need *an/some* information about evening classes.

3 Can I make *a/some* suggestion?

4 We've got *a/some* bread, but there's only *a few/a little* cheese.

5 There isn't *a/any* room for your coat in your suitcase, so you'll have to carry it.

6 I enjoyed the party, but Bob didn't have *many/much* fun because his girlfriend was ill.

b) Add *of* where necessary in these sentences.

0 You only need shorts and a couple ..of.. T-shirts to wear on the beach.

1 I phoned the tourist office and got lots ...... information about hotels.

2 I saw several ...... my friends at the party.

3 We didn't wash up until every ...... guest had left.

4 Both ...... David and Gabrielle are taller than me.

5 The singer gave each ...... his fans a signed photograph.

6 All ...... children need a loving home.

3 Vocabulary: *like/as*

> It's important to remember when we use *like* and when we use *as*.

Complete each sentence with either *like* or *as*.

0 Alecia Moore is better known .as. Pink.

1 Has anyone ever told you that you look ...... Britney Spears?

2 I worked ...... a waiter to pay my college fees.

3 Julia's father is very rich. Their house is ...... a palace.

4 Are you sure this is butter? It smells ...... cheese to me!

5 John's teachers remembered him ...... a clever student when he was young.

6 Although Saskia is fifteen, she still behaves ...... a ten-year-old sometimes.

7 Milo's English was so good he got a job ...... an interpreter.

8 Even if we run ...... the wind, we'll still be late for class.

9 On the plane, I used my jacket ...... a pillow and soon fell asleep.

10 The opera house closed last year, but reopened ...... a cinema last week.

4 Vocabulary: at the airport

a) Choose three people and three places from the following list. Write a sentence explaining what each one is. Use the language in the box below to help you.

- baggage hall
- check-in desk
- customs officer
- departure lounge
- duty-free shop
- flight attendant
- information desk
- passenger
- pilot
- snack bar

> **Useful language**
> This is someone who …
> This is the person who …
> This is the place where …

This is someone who flies planes.

pilot

b) Work with a partner. Read aloud what you have written. Your partner will guess which person or place you are describing.

c) Now imagine that you are at the airport and that you are going to fly somewhere. With your partner, think of the order in which you might go to the places in the list.

> When you arrive at the airport, you go to the check-in desk, then you …

5 Vocabulary: words that go together

> Learning verbs and nouns in matching pairs will help you remember vocabulary.

a) Match each verb in List A with the correct noun phrase from List B.

A	B
cash	a seat
cross	the flight
fasten	the border
miss	your suitcase
pack	your seat belt
reach	your destination
reserve	some traveller's cheques

b) Now choose one of the expressions from Exercise 4a to complete these sentences, putting the verb in the correct form.

0 I ..... missed the flight ..... because there was a terrible traffic jam on the way to the airport.

1 The train stopped for half an hour when we .... between Italy and Switzerland.

2 You'd better .... so that you've got plenty of money when we go shopping.

3 I always .... on the train because I like to sit by the window.

4 'Did you .... yourself?' asked the man at the check-in desk.

5 You should .... while the plane is taking off.

6 When you .... , make sure you take all your luggage with you.

6 Speaking: travelling

a) Work with a partner. Say which way you would prefer to travel and explain why.

> **Useful language**
> I'd rather …   dangerous
> exciting   expensive
> (un)comfortable

b) Now ask and answer these questions.

1 Have you ever flown on a plane or helicopter? When? Where did you go? Why?

2 Have you ever missed a plane? What happened?

3 What are the advantages and disadvantages of flying compared to other kinds of transport?

Writing Part 1

 Strategy

1 Read the instructions to the Exam Task below.

1 How many sentences are there?
2 What are the sentences about?
3 What do you have to do?
4 How many words can you use?
5 Where do you write your answers?
6 How much do you write there?
7 Where can you do your rough work?

2 Compare the two sentences in the example.

1 Read the first sentence. What information does it give you about the cinema?
2 Now read the second sentence. Does it give you the same information as the first sentence?

3 Answer Question 1.

1 Read the first sentence. What information does it give you about the cinema?
2 Now read the beginning and end of the second sentence. How does it begin? How does it end?
3 How can you complete it? Write your answer.

4 Check your answer.

- Does your sentence give the same information as the first sentence?
- Is the grammar correct?
- How many words have you used?

5 Answer the other questions in the same way.

Write the answers to Questions 2–5 on your answer sheet.

Remember you can write your answers on the exam paper first if you wish and then copy them.

•• *Exam tip!* ••••••••••••••••••••••••
   Don't write more than three words.
••••••••••••••••••••••••••••••••••••

Part 1

Questions 1–5

Here are some sentences about a cinema. For each question, complete the second sentence so that it means the same as the first. **Use no more than three words.**
Write only the missing words on your answer sheet.
You may use this page for any rough work.

Example:

0 The cinema is near the shopping mall.

The cinema is .... from the shopping mall.

Answer:	0	not far

---

1 The cinema opened two years ago.

The cinema .... here for two years.

2 It has twelve screens.

There .... twelve screens.

3 The tickets cost less during the week.

The tickets are .... at weekends.

4 My sister told me she had seen a great new film there last week.

My sister said, 'I .... a great new film there this week.'

5 My boyfriend advised me to book tickets.

The boyfriend said I .... book tickets.

1 Grammar: matching patterns

> In Part 1, the same grammar patterns are often tested. It is a good idea to study these patterns so that you can recognise them.

a) Read the twelve sentences below. Find the six pairs which have the same meanings.

1 The waiter said I should try the fish soup. ....7....
2 It's too cold to sit outside. ....
3 The restaurant is not far from the river. ....
4 The meals cost a lot in the evening. ....
5 It's not warm enough to sit outside. ....
6 My girlfriend told me she had really enjoyed her meal. ....
7 The waiter advised me to try the fish soup. ...1....
8 You won't get a table unless you book early. ....
9 My girlfriend said, 'I really enjoyed my meal.' ....
10 The restaurant is near the river. ....
11 The meals are more expensive in the evening. ....
12 If you don't book early, you won't get a table. ....

b) Match each pair of sentences above with one of these patterns.

0 modal verbs ...1.... and ..7....

a) similar meanings .... and ....
b) *too / enough* .... and ....
c) reported speech ➜ direct speech .... and ....
d) opposites .... and ....
e) *if not ➜ unless* .... and ....

c) Complete the second sentence so that it means the same as the first, using no more than three words.

1 My suitcase was on top of my sister's on the shelf.
My sister's suitcase was .... on the shelf.
2 We said we were looking for our books.
We said, 'We .... our books.'
3 If I were you, I'd buy that CD.
Why .... buy that CD?

4 Your jeans are clean enough to wear.
Your jeans aren't .... wear.
5 This shop is closed on Saturday afternoons.
This shop isn't .... on Saturday afternoons.
6 We'll go to the tennis club if it doesn't rain.
We'll go to the tennis club .... it rains.
7 Which band do you like best?
Which is your .... band?
8 He said he ate in the canteen every day.
He said, 'I .... in the canteen every day.'
9 This house is close to the sports ground.
This house isn't .... the sports ground.
10 She explained she hadn't got any money.
She said, 'I .... money.'

2 Correcting mistakes

Read these pairs of sentences. There is a mistake in the second sentence. Can you correct it?

0 He's called Robert.
            is
His name ~~called~~ Robert.

1 My flat isn't as big as yours.
My flat is smaller as yours.

2 My brother is a member of the tennis club.
My brother is belong to the tennis club.

3 My sister suggested I should go swimming with her.
'Why not you come swimming with me?' suggested my sister.

4 You can't get a table unless you book.
You can get a table if you don't book.

5 I like modern shops better than old ones.
I prefer modern shops from old ones.

Writing Part 2

 Strategy

1 Read the instructions to the Exam Task opposite.

1 What are you going to write?
2 Who are you writing to?
3 How many things do you have to write about?
4 How many words do you have to write?
5 Where do you write your answer?

2 Planning your answer

Before you begin to write, look at the words in the instructions. Mark the words that tell you what information you should include. Think about what extra information you need to add.

1 What has Eva borrowed?
2 When?
3 How will you start your note?
4 What do you have to ask her to do?
5 Why do you need it back?

3 Writing your answer

Read the notes A, B and C opposite.

1 Which is the best answer? Why?
2 What is wrong with the other two answers?

4 Checking and correcting your work

a) Read this e-mail. It has eight grammar mistakes. Find and <u>underline</u> the mistakes.

> Dear Adriana
> Do you remember to camp in Wales last year? Would you like coming to Ireland with me in next month? My exam's finish after two weeks and my cousins have invited me going with them. We can use my brothers' tent because he needn't it.

b) Work with a partner and compare the mistakes you found. Correct the mistakes together.

Part 2

Question 6

A friend, Eva, borrowed your rucksack two weeks ago and hasn't returned it.

Write a note to Eva. In your note, you should

- remind her that she has your rucksack
- ask her to return it
- explain why you need it.

Write **35–45 words** on your answer sheet.

A

> Hi Eva
>
> I hope you're well. Did you enjoy your camping holiday with your friends? I hope the weather was good. Was my rucksack useful? Please can you return it before next weekend? Thank you very much.
>
> Sergio

B

> Hi Eva
>
> Do you remember that you borrowed my rucksack two weeks ago? Could you give it back to me soon, please? I need it before next weekend because I'm going camping with some friends.
> Thanks,
>
> Andreas

C

> Hi Eva
>
> Do you remember that you lent me a rucksack two weeks ago? If you don't need it yourself, can I borrow it again next weekend, please?
> I need it because I'm going camping with some friends.
> Thanks,
>
> Estelle

1 Grammar: possessives

a) Look at these sentences and answer the questions below.

- *We visited several of the **students' houses**.*
- *She lost all her **sister's money**.*
- *I found the **children's socks**.*

1 Why is the apostrophe (') in a different place in *students'* and *sister's*?

2 Is *children* a singular word or plural word?

3 What is unusual about *children's*?

b) Rewrite the sentences below in your notebook, adding apostrophes in the correct places.

0 When he got angry, you could hear my fathers voice in the next street.
   *When he got angry, you could hear my **father's** voice in the next street.*

1 I have two brothers and two sisters – my brothers school is near our house, but my sisters school is three kilometres away.

2 I looked through all the womens clothes in the shop, but there was nothing suitable.

3 I tried not to laugh when I saw Janes new hairstyle.

4 Her friends parents all agreed that the party should finish at eleven.

5 I don't like borrowing other peoples clothes.

2 Grammar: verbs followed by *-ing* or infinitive

Complete these sentences using one of the verbs in the box in the correct form.

apply	arrive	buy	drive	know	learn
leave	~~meet~~	phone	talk	tidy	~~travel~~

0 Would you like ...*to meet*..... me after work tomorrow?

00 I've often imagined ....*travelling*.. around the world, but I never have.

1 I hope .... a new language next year.

2 They didn't want .... at the party too early.

3 Will you promise .... me as soon as you get home?

4 Jake caught the bus because he disliked .... in the city centre.

5 She asked her sister .... her a pair of tights.

6 Please don't forget .... the kitchen before you go out.

7 When we came into the room, everyone stopped .... and looked at us.

8 Would you consider .... for a new job?

9 He pretends .... a lot about art, but he doesn't really.

10 My uncle always regretted .... school at fifteen.

3 Exam Task

a) Write your answer to this question.

> An English friend, Saskia, is spending the day at your home next Sunday. You want to tell her what to expect.
>
> Write a note to Saskia. In your note, you should
> - tell her who she will meet
> - say what kind of meal she will have
> - ask how she would like to spend the day.
>
> Write **35–45 words** on your answer sheet.

b) When you have finished, check your work carefully.

- Have you included all the information?
- Have you written no more than 45 words?
- Is your grammar correct?
- Is your spelling correct?

> **Exam tip!**
> Make sure you answer all three parts of the exam question.

In Part 3 there are two writing tasks: an informal letter and a story. You answer ONE task only.

 Strategy: letter

1 Read the instructions to the Exam Task below.

1 Who are you going to write to?
2 What does your friend ask you to write about?
3 Where must you write your answer?

2 Planning your answer

a) Write down three ideas for your letter.

Example:

> city centre
> two bedrooms
> quiet street

b) Write down five useful words and phrases that you can use in your letter.

Example:

> a block of flats
> a balcony
> plenty of space
> to move in
> to paint

c) Decide how your answer will begin and end. (Look back at Test 1 page 30 if you are not sure.)

3 Writing your letter

Read Answers A and B to Question 7 opposite.

1 Which is the best answer? Why?
2 Why is the other answer not so good?
3 Can you find eight grammar mistakes in that answer?

4 Checking and correcting your work

Work with a partner and compare the mistakes you found. Correct the mistakes together.

Part 3

Question 7

• This is part of a letter you receive from an English-speaking friend.

> In your last letter, you gave me your new address. Please write and tell me what your new home is like. Is it in a similar place? What do you like best about it?

• Now write a letter, telling your friend about your new home.

• Write your **letter** on your answer sheet.

A

Dear Alex

Thanks for your letter. You want to know what is the new flat like. Well, I love it! It's into a block of flats near of the city centre, but it's in a quiet street. It's not so small than our old one, so I don't had to share a room with my brother. I've got plenty of space for my computer. I painted my room before we move in. But the better thing about this flat is the balcony. It's really big and we are having breakfast there every morning.
I hope you'll come and see it soon.
All the best

Marco

B

Dear Tom

Thanks for your letter. You want to know about our new flat. Well, it's great! It's in the city centre, but the street is quiet. It's on the ground floor of a small block of flats. It's much bigger than our old one, so I have my own bedroom. My bedroom is painted blue and white and there's plenty of space for eveything I need. My favourite part of this flat is the balcony. It's big and sunny, so we can eat there at weekends.
I hope you'll visit us here soon.
All the best   Roberto

Language practice: Writing Part 3

1 Vocabulary: describing houses and flats

In the exam, you often have to describe your home, or someone else's.

Use the words in the boxes to label the picture. You can use a dictionary to help you.

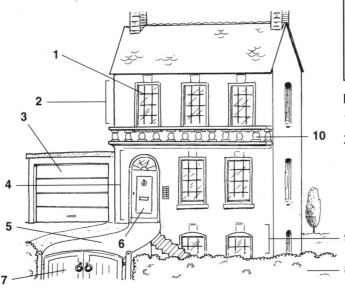

| basement   first floor   ground floor   front door |
| path   window   gate   hedge   garage   balcony |

2 Vocabulary: things in your room

a) **Alex has a computer in his room. What do you have in yours? Mark the things on the list below which you have in your room, then compare your list with a partner.**

air conditioning armchair basin blind
carpet CD player chest of drawers computer
cupboard curtain desk fridge mirror
radiator radio rug shower television
wardrobe

b) **Talk about these questions.**

1 What other things do you have in your rooms?

2 What other things would you like to have in your rooms?

▶ **Strategy:** story

1 Read the instructions to the Exam Task below.

1 What title must your story have?
2 Where must you write your answer?

2 Planning your answer

Before starting your story, it is important to make a plan. Your story must be simple enough to finish in about 100 words.

a) Write down some ideas for the story. Use these ideas to help you.

• Begin with someone feeling sad.
• Describe a good surprise.

b) How will your story end? Think about this question.

How did he/she feel?

c) Write down five useful words and phrases that you can use in your story.

Example:

> birthday
> be disappointed
> discover
> guess
> a plan

3 Writing your story

Read Answers A and B to Question 8 on page 77.

1 Which is the best answer? Why?
2 Why is the other answer not so good?
3 Can you find five grammar mistakes in that answer?

4 Checking and correcting your work

Work with a partner and compare the mistakes you found. Correct the mistakes together.

•• *Exam tip!* ••••••••••••••••••••
Remember to keep your story simple. You only have 100 words.
••••••••••••••••••••••••••••••••••

Part 3

Question 8

• Your English teacher has asked you to write a story.

• Your story must have this title:

   The surprise

• Write your **story** on your answer sheet.

A

The surprise

I knew a boy called Timmy. He used to stealing things from shops. He had lots money. Nobody liked him. He told his friends he stole things. They weren't interested in.

One day he was talking to some other boys in a café. A young man came in. He sat at the same table. He said Timmy, 'I don't believe you really steal things.' Timmy showed him a CD. He'd stolen the CD that morning. 'Do you believe me now?' he asked.

'Yes,' said the young man. 'I'm arresting you. I'm policeman.'

Timmy was very surprised. He didn't know what to say.

B

The surprise

I usually spend Friday evenings with my friend, Mina. Last Friday was my birthday. At school, some of my classmates said 'Happy birthday' when I came into the classroom, but I was a little bit disappointed, because Mina didn't suggest meeting that evening.

I thought, 'Perhaps her family has visitors.' When I got home, my father made me sit in the car, then he covered my face with a scarf and drove somewhere.

I discovered we were at Mina's house. And there was Mina with all our friends, ready for a party. I was really surprised because I hadn't guessed their plan.

Language practice: Writing Part 3

1 Improving your story: using linking words

Look at Answer A again. It has too many short sentences, so it isn't very interesting to read. Use a word from the box to fill each space in the text below and make the story more interesting.

> although and but so that who
> when which

I knew a boy called Timmy (1) .... used to steal things from shops. (2) .... he had lots of money, nobody liked him. He told his friends that he stole things, (3) .... they weren't interested. One day, he was talking to some other boys in a café (4) .... a young man came in (5) .... sat at the same table. He said to Timmy, 'I don't believe you really steal things.' Timmy showed him a CD (6) .... he'd stolen that morning. 'Do you believe me now?' he asked.

'Yes,' said the young man, 'I'm arresting you. I'm a policeman.'

Timmy was (7) .... surprised (8) .... he didn't know what to say.

2 Improving your story: adding information

a) **Here is part of a different story. Read the story and then look at the phrases in the box below. Decide which one fits best in each space.**

(1) .... , I decided to go on a bus tour one afternoon. The tour goes through a part of London (2) .... (3) .... , I saw a strange castle beside the road. I asked the man (4) .... 'What is that castle?'

He looked at me (5) .... and said, 'There hasn't been a castle here for a hundred years.'

> a) While the bus was waiting at some traffic lights
> b) which has lots of famous old buildings in it
> c) Although the weather was wet
> d) very strangely
> e) who was sitting next to me

b) **Add your own ideas to make some interesting sentences.**

1 The young man lived in a small flat which ...
2 The film director met his wife while ...
3 The girl shouted ...... and everyone heard her.
4 Although the party began late, ...
5 There's a new student in our class who ...

Writing Part 3: Exam Practice

▶ Strategy: choosing your question

1 Read both the Exam Tasks below.
- Write down two ideas for your letter.
- Write down five useful words or phrases that you can use in your letter.
- Write down two ideas for your story.
- Write down five useful words or phrases that you can use in your story.
- Look at your notes. Which question is easier for you?

2 Make a plan on your exam paper.

3 Write your answer.

4 Check and correct your work.

(Look back at Test 1, page 34.)

Part 3

Write an answer to **one** of the questions (**7** or **8**) in this part.
Write your answer in about **100 words** on your answer sheet.
Put the question number in the box at the top of your answer sheet.

Question 7

- This is part of a letter you receive from an English penfriend.

> *You told me in your last letter that you sometimes stay with your cousins in the summer. What kind of place do they live in? Can you tell me about it?*

- Now write a letter, answering your penfriend's questions.

- Write your **letter** on your answer sheet.

Question 8

- Your English teacher has asked you to write a story.

- Your story must have this title:

    A new member of the family

- Write your **story** on your answer sheet.

Listening Part 1

▶ **Strategy**

1 **Listen to the introduction to the test.**

1 How many parts does the Listening test have?
2 How many times will you hear each part?
3 Where do you write your answers?
4 What will you do at the end of the test?
5 How long will you have?

2 **Read and listen to the instructions for Part 1 below.**

1 How many questions are there?
2 How many pictures are there for each question?
3 What do you have to do?

3 **Look at the example and listen to the recording.**

1 What is the question?
2 What is the answer?
3 How do you know?

4 **Look at Question 1. Think about what you are going to hear.**

1 What information must you listen for?
2 Look at the three pictures. What are the names of the places in Pictures **A**, **B** and **C**?
3 Listen to the recording for Question 1. Which of the places did you hear?
4 Listen again and mark your answer.
5 Why is **A** wrong?
6 Why is **B** wrong?
7 Why is **C** the correct answer? What does the woman say?

5 **Do Questions 2–7 in the same way.**

•• **Exam tip!** ••••••••••••••••••••••••••
: Remember you will hear each recording twice
: so you have a second chance to choose the
: answers.
••

Part 1

Questions 1–7

There are seven questions in this part.
For each question, there are three pictures and a short recording.
Choose the correct picture and put a tick (✓) in the box below it.

Example: What will the boy take back to the shop?

A ✓

B ☐

C ☐

[Turn over

1 Where will they meet?

A ☐ B ☐ C ☐

2 What is the woman looking for?

A ☐ B ☐ C ☐

3 Which photograph are they looking at?

A ☐ B ☐ C ☐

4 Where is the boy's flat?

BUS STOP BUS STOP BUS STOP

A ☐ B ☐ C ☐

5 Who is coming to stay with the girl?

A ☐ B ☐ C ☐

6 What was the weather like on Tom's holiday?

A ☐ B ☐ C ☐

7 Where is the desk now?

A ☐ B ☐ C ☐

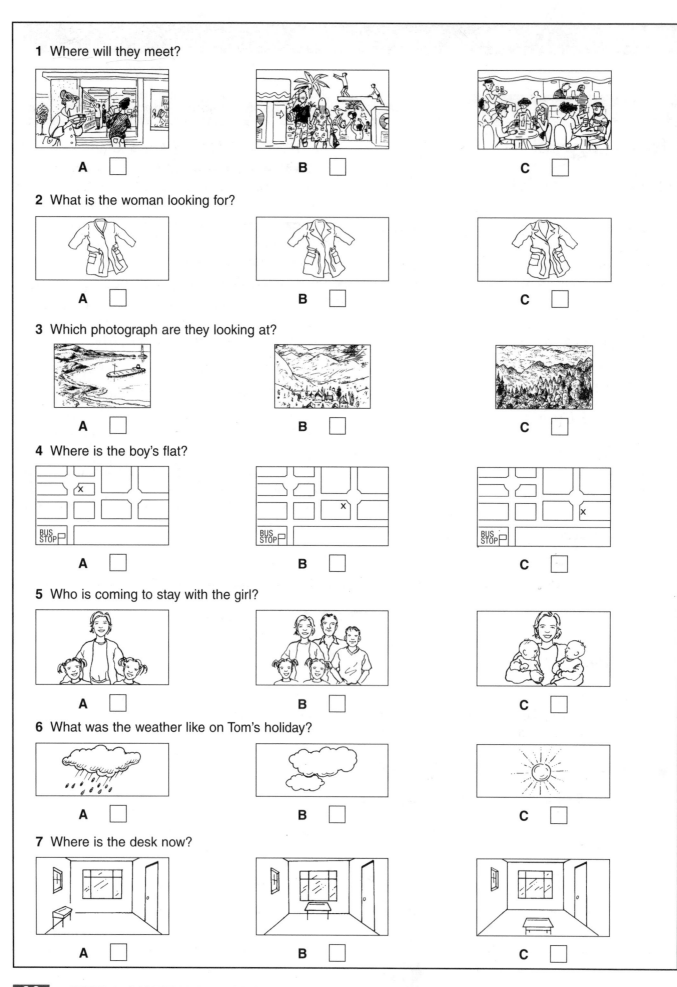

1 Vocabulary: weather

> In Part 1, there is often a question about the weather. In Question 6 on page 80, the boy talked about bright sunshine, the rain and cloudy weather.

Match the following sentences to the pictures. Some sentences can be used with more than one picture.

- It's sunny.
- It's icy.
- It's freezing.
- It's windy.
- It's frosty.
- It's damp.
- It's foggy.
- It's snowing.
- It's wet.
- It's cloudy.
- It's raining.
- It's misty.

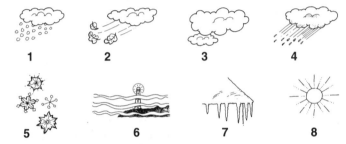

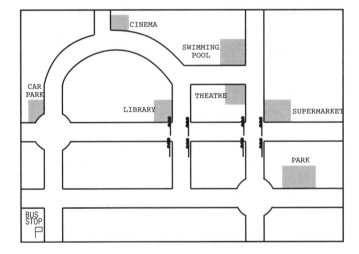

2 Functions: giving and understanding directions

a) Look at the map. Read these directions and fill in the gaps.

1 Get off the bus and go straight on at the crossroads. Turn right at the roundabout, then take the first turning on the left. The .... is on the left.

2 Get off the bus and turn right at the crossroads. Turn left at the roundabout. Go straight on at the traffic lights. The .... is on the next corner on the left.

b) Work in pairs. Choose a place on the map. Don't tell your partner what it is. Tell your partner how to get there from the bus stop.

c) Give your partner directions from your school to somewhere in your town or city. Don't say the name of the place. Does he/she arrive in the correct place?

3 Vocabulary: clothes

a) Here are some words that you may meet in the exam. Decide which words in the box belong with the different clothes. (Some of them can go in all the columns!)

belt V-neck silk knee-length pockets collar short sleeves buttons zip round neck leather high heels sleeveless wool cotton

skirt	coat	jacket	dress	shirt	boots
belt	belt	belt	belt		

b) Complete this conversation between a man and a lost-property officer using some of the words above.

Officer: Good morning. Can I help you?

Man: Yes, please. I've lost a jacket. I think I left it on the train.

Officer: OK. Can you describe it?

Man: Yes. It's brown with a (1) .... up the front. It's got two (2) .... and it's made of (3) ....

Officer: Does it have a (4) .... ?

Man: No, it doesn't.

c) Write about someone in the class. Describe the clothes they are wearing. Then read your description to the class. How quickly do they guess who you are describing?

▶ **Strategy**

1 🎧 **Read and listen to the instructions to the Exam Task below.**

1 How many questions are there?
2 Who will you hear?
3 Who is she talking to?
4 What is she talking about?
5 What do you have to do?
6 How many times will you hear the recording?

2 Read the questions. They give you some information about what you will hear.

Which of the following points do you find out from the questions? Put a tick next to them.

1 They will come back to the hotel in the early evening. ☐
2 They will visit a town. ☐
3 They will have coffee in a hotel. ☐
4 Something about the trip has changed. ☐
5 Brampton is a village. ☐
6 They will stop in the countryside for a drink. ☐
7 They will visit a wildlife park. ☐

3 🎧 **Listen to the recording the first time.**

a) **Look at Question 8. Listen to what the tour guide says about the change of plan and tick the correct answer.**

Be careful – she mentions a town, a university and a wildlife park, but there is only one change to the plans.

b) **Look at Question 9. Listen to where they will stop for a coffee. Tick the correct answer.**

c) **Now do Questions 10–13 in the same way.**

4 🎧 **Listen to the recording again.**

Check the answers you have marked and try to do any you missed the first time. If you still don't know, guess! Do not leave any questions unanswered.

•• **Exam tip!** ••••••••••••••••••••••••
You must choose the answer which really gives the information asked for in the question, so read the question very carefully.
••••••••••••••••••••••••••••••••••••••

Part 2

Questions 8–13

You will hear a tour guide talking to a group of tourists about a coach trip.
For each question, put a tick (✓) in the correct box.

---

8 What is the change of plan?

    A They will visit two towns. ☐

    B They will look round a university. ☐

    C They will visit a wildlife park. ☐

9 Where will they stop for coffee?

    A near a waterfall ☐

    B by a lake ☐

    C on a mountain ☐

10 The town of Brampton became well known because of its

A shops ☐

B university ☐

C museum ☐

11 What animals will they see in the wildlife park?

A lions ☐

B monkeys ☐

C tigers ☐

12 What time will they arrive back at the hotel?

A 5.30 ☐

B 6.45 ☐

C 7.15 ☐

13 The tour guide asks if anyone

A needs more information. ☐

B would like to go on another trip. ☐

C wants to ask any questions. ☐

Language practice: Listening Part 2

1 Grammar: possessives

In the Listening on pages 82–83, the tour guide talks about *some friends of mine*. This is another way of saying *my friends* or *some of my friends*.
She also says *a colleague of mine*.
This is another way of saying *my colleague* or *one of my colleagues*.
We can say *a friend of my mother's* or *(one of) my mother's friends*.

Complete the second sentence so that it means the same as the first, using no more than three words.

0 Andrew's friend is studying to become an actor.
   A ....*friend of Andrew's*.... is studying to become an actor.

1 One of my neighbours is having a party.
   A .... is having a party.

2 My brother's friend has just sailed across the Atlantic Ocean.
   A friend .... has just sailed across the Atlantic Ocean.

3 My sister keeps wearing my shoes.
   My sister keeps wearing some shoes ....
   ....

4 One of her students has won a competition.
   A .... has won a competition.

5 One of their cousins lives in China.
   A .... lives in China.

6 Sally's friends are hoping to rent a flat together.
   Some friends .... are hoping to rent a flat together.

2 Grammar: reported questions

a) Look at Question 13 from the Exam Task.

The tour guide asks if anyone ...

A needs more information.

B would like to go on another trip.

C wants to ask any questions.

> Compare these direct and reported questions. How do we form reported questions?
> '*Do you need more information?*'
> → She asks **if** they need more information.
> '*What information do you need?*'
> → She asks **what** information they need.

b) Report what these people are asking.

0 'Is that book David's?' The teacher asks .if that. book is David's ....

1 'When does the match start?' She asks ....
....

2 'What's the time?' The man asks ....
....

3 'Is it far to the cinema?' She wants to know ....
....

4 'Are you busy tonight, Paola?' Peter asks ....
....

5 Where's the nearest bus stop?' They want to know
....

6 'Are they coming to the cinema?' We ask ....
....

c) Complete the second sentence so that it means the same as the first, using not more than three words.

0 He asked what the time was.
'What ....is.............. the time?' he asked.

1 She wanted to know where I lived.
'Where .... ?' she wanted to know.

2 They asked if they could sit near the window.
They said, '................................. near the window?'

3 I wondered when the rain would stop.
'When .... the rain stop?' I wondered.

4 He inquired whether there were any seats available.
He said, '................................. any seats available?'

5 Monica wanted to know how Clare knew about her problems.
'How .... about my problems?' asked Monica.

6 John asked Rosemary why she hadn't phoned him in the morning.
'Why .... me in the morning?' said John to Rosemary.

3 Vocabulary: the environment

Choose the correct word for each space.

0 The sun .... over the hills and then it was dark.
(A set) B rose   C finished   D started

1 We spent the afternoon walking through the .... near the village.
A hedge   B green   C tree   D forest

2 The children ran across the sandy .... to the sea.
A cliff   B coast   C beach   D rock

3 The sky was completely blue, except for one dark ....
A cloud   B moon   C star   D sun

4 The race began at the café, went round the .... and back to the café.
A ocean   B lake   C river   D stream

5 The boys camped in the .... , away from the cold wind.
A waterfall   B island   C valley   D mountain

6 This region is divided into five smaller ....
A continents   B districts   C lands   D countries

4 Speaking: the environment

Talk to your partner. Answer these questions.

1 Do you live near the countryside?

2 Do you like going into the countryside?

3 Which parts of your country are famous for their natural beauty?

4 Do you ever visit them?

5 Do you prefer spending a day in the countryside or the city?

> **Useful language**
> I live in/quite near/a long way from the countryside.
> The north/south/east/west of my country is famous for ...

Listening Part 3

▶ Strategy

1 🎧 **Read and listen to the instructions to the Exam Task below.**

1 How many questions are there?

2 Who will you hear? What will they talk about?

3 What do you have to do?

2 Look at the Exam Task and guess what kinds of words are missing.

1 Look at Questions **14** and **16**. What kind of word can go in these spaces. How do you know?

2 Look at Question **15**. What kind of information do you need here? How do you know?

3 Look at Question **17**. What kind of information can go here? How do you know?

4 Look at Question **18**. What kind of word do you need here? How do you know?

5 Look at Question **19**. What sort of information can go here? How do you know?

3 🎧 **Listen to the recording the first time.**

Try to answer as many questions as you can. If you miss a gap, don't worry. You can fill it in the second time you listen.

4 🎧 **Listen to the recording again.**

Check the answers you wrote the first time. Fill in any answers you missed.

5 Check your answers.

• How many words did you write in each space?

• Is the meaning correct?

• Is the grammar correct?

• Is the spelling correct?

•• **Exam tip!** •••••••••••••••••••••
You usually need to write one or two words, and
never more than three.

Part 3

Questions 14–19

You will hear a woman talking on the radio about a competition.
For each question, fill in the missing information in the numbered space.

This month's competition

Prize: a computer + a **(14)** .... printer

Write a story

• length: fewer than **(15)** .... words

• subject: a short **(16)** .... story which

  takes place in **(17)** ....

Write your name, address, telephone number and

(18) .... at the end.

Story must arrive on or before **(19)** ....

Language practice: Listening Part 3

1 Writing dates and numbers

In Part 3, it is important to be able to write dates and numbers correctly.

a) **Look at the Exam Task on page 85. Where must you write a date or number?**

b) **Write the following dates correctly in your notebook.**

0 teusday 9th juli 2015
   Tuesday 9th July 2015......

1 febuary 21th 2002
2 wensday 2 marsh 2005
3 septembre 4st 2009
4 thrusday aprille 19th 2020

c) **Now say and write these numbers.**

0 $3\frac{1}{2}$ ...three and a half.........

1 $7\frac{1}{4}$ 2 $\frac{1}{3}$ 3 1st   4 2nd   5 3rd   6 4th
7 75%   8 0.35   9 1,580   10 200,000

d) **Listen to your teacher read some dates and numbers and write them down. Be careful with your spelling and punctuation.**

2 Grammar: expressions of purpose

We can use *in order to* + verb or *so that* + subject + verb to explain the purpose of an action.

a) **Match Questions 1–6 to the correct answer a)–f).**

1 Why did you buy a computer? ....
2 Why are you wearing that old shirt? ....
3 Why are you phoning the station? ....
4 Why are you whispering? ....
5 Why have you come to see me? ....
6 Why do you want to have guitar lessons? ....

a) in order to apologise
b) in order to book seats on the train to Paris
c) in order to use the internet
d) so that I can join my boyfriend's band
e) so that no one can hear me
f) so that my clothes don't get dirty

3 Vocabulary: computer words

Find eight words connected with computers in the wordsearch box and use some of them to complete the sentences below.

K	T	W	F	E	S	U	O	M	G
B	E	N	M	A	O	X	C	V	F
V	N	Y	K	U	F	I	O	Q	R
G	R	J	B	U	T	N	R	W	E
M	E	I	E	O	W	E	E	R	K
W	T	M	T	J	A	E	F	T	A
E	N	C	A	F	R	R	C	H	E
R	I	V	Y	I	E	C	D	N	P
N	A	J	T	D	L	S	Z	B	S
L	R	E	T	N	I	R	P	I	P

1 You can get information on almost any subject on the ....
2 You need .... in order to run a computer program.
3 You need a .... if you want to listen to music.
4 You can use arrows on the keyboard to move around the screen, or you can use a ....
5 Instead of writing a letter to someone, you can send an .... from your computer.

4 Speaking: communicating with other people

Talk to your partner. Answer these questions.

1 How often do you send an e-mail?
2 Do you just send e-mails to your friends or to other people, too?
3 Do you prefer to send an e-mail or talk on the phone?
4 How many text messages do you send every week?
5 How often do you write a letter?

Listening Part 4

▶ **Strategy**

1 🎧 **Read and listen to the instructions to the Exam Task below.**

1 How many sentences are there?

2 How many people will you hear?

3 What is the man's name?

4 What is the woman's name?

5 How do they know each other?

6 What do you have to do?

2 Read the six sentences. <u>Underline</u> the names in each sentence.

3 Make guesses about what you will hear.

a) <u>Underline</u> six words or phrases which tell you what Marcus and Cora's conversation will be about.

b) Compare your list of words with another student.

4 🎧 **Listen to the recording and answer the questions.**

Mark the answers you are sure of. If you miss one, don't worry. You can listen for the answer when you hear the recording again.

•• *Exam tip!* ••••••••••••••••••••••••••
: When a question is about agreeing or
: disagreeing, you need to listen carefully to
: what both speakers say on that subject.
••

5 🎧 **Listen again and check your answers.**

Try to fill in any answers you missed the first time. If you still don't know, guess! Do not leave any questions unanswered.

•• *Exam tip!* ••••••••••••••••••••••••••
: Remember, at the end of the exam you are
: given six minutes to transfer all your listening
: answers to the answer sheet. Make sure you
: copy carefully.
••

Part 4

Questions 20–25

Look at the six sentences for this part.
You will hear a conversation between a man, Marcus, and a woman, Cora, who work in the same office.
Decide if each sentence is correct or incorrect.
If it is correct, put a tick (✓) in the box under **A** for **YES**.
If it is not correct, put a tick (✓) in the box under **B** for **NO**.

	A YES	B NO
20 Marcus is often late for work.	☐	☐
21 Cora disagrees with Marcus about the cause of traffic jams.	☐	☐
22 Marcus agrees that cycling to work would be good for him.	☐	☐
23 Marcus believes employers should provide buses.	☐	☐
24 Marcus agrees to try coming to work by bus tomorrow.	☐	☐
25 Cora suggests that Marcus is lazy.	☐	☐

1 Functions: agreeing and disagreeing

> In Part 4, you often need to understand when people are agreeing and disagreeing with each other.

a) **Look at the phrases below. Write A next to the ones which we use to agree, and D next to the ones which we use to disagree.**

1 I don't think so. .....D.....
2 That's not right. ....
3 I quite agree. ....
4 Exactly. ....
5 I just don't accept that. ....
6 I don't agree. ....
7 That's where you're wrong. ....
8 That's right. ....

b) **Work with a partner. Take turns at reading out a statement. Say whether you agree or disagree with it.**

1 Football players earn too much money.
2 Graffiti is art and should be encouraged.
3 The government should give children pocket money.
4 There are too many television channels.
5 Adverts should not be aimed at children.

2 Vocabulary: traffic problems

> In the exam, you often meet or need to use words about traffic problems.

a) **Complete the following sentences with a word or phrase from the box.**

```
motorway   petrol   car park   pollution
speed limit   tunnel   pedestrians   pavement
traffic jam   traffic lights
```

0 Some cities have stopped cars from going into the centre because of the .....pollution.........

1 Someone took my space in the ....
today, so I had to leave my car in the street.

2 The fire engine didn't stop at the .... ,
even though they were red. Luckily there were no
.... trying to cross the road.

3 If you're driving on an empty .... ,
it's easy to forget the .... is 90kph.

4 I never drive through the city centre because there's always a .... by the market square.

5 We stopped at the garage to buy some
....

6 It's very dangerous to walk along that road because there's no ....

7 The journey is much quicker now because there's a .... under the river.

b) **Work with a partner. Decide if you agree or disagree with these suggestions for reducing traffic in cities. Tick the ones you think are the best.**

1 Cars should be forbidden from the city centre. ☐

2 Each family should only be allowed to have one car. ☐

3 The government should make public transport free in cities. ☐

4 Young people should not be allowed to own a car until they are 21. ☐

5 Everyone should pay a fee before they drive into a town or city. ☐

c) **Can you add any more ideas?**

> Another idea is to ...
> The government could ...
> It would help if we ...

3 Speaking: where you live

a) **Think about the town where you live. Think about:**
- traffic
- transport
- activities for young people
- things to do and see (e.g. libraries, museums)
- parks and green spaces.

b) **In your notebook, write down the two things you like best about your town and the two things you like least.**

c) **Work with a partner. Discuss the things you wrote. What do you agree or disagree about?**

Speaking Part 1

 Strategy

The test begins with a general conversation between the examiner and the candidates. Be ready to:

- answer questions about personal details, e.g. where you live
- answer questions about your daily life, likes/dislikes, habits, etc.
- spell out words (e.g. names, addresses).

1 Giving personal information

a) Here are some questions the examiner might ask in Part 1. Read the questions, then match them to the answers below.

1 What's your name and surname? ....
2 Where do you live? ....
3 What school do you go to? ....
4 How long have you been there? ....
5 Can you spell the first word of your school's name for me, please? ....
6 How far is the school from your home? ....
7 How do you get to school? ....
8 What is your favourite subject? ....

a) Usually by bike, but sometimes I catch the bus if I have too many books.
b) Diana Mann.
c) Science.
d) Longbridge Road School. It's near the hospital.
e) About two and a half kilometres.
f) Five months.
g) L-O-N-G-B-R-I-D-G-E.
h) 16, Milford Hill Flats.

b) Look carefully at the answers.

1 Are they all complete sentences?
2 Which of them give extra information?

c) Work with a partner. Ask each other the questions in Exercise 1a above. Try to give some extra information for some of the questions. When you have finished, write the answers you gave in your notebook.

2 Vocabulary and pronunciation: school subjects

a) Tick which school subjects you study.

chemistry   biology   physics   environmental science   geography   history   philosophy   music   computing   religion   modern languages   literature

b) 🎧 Some of the subjects above look almost the same in many languages, but they are pronounced differently. Listen and underline the syllable with the main word stress. Then practise saying them.

Example: <u>che</u>mistry   bi<u>o</u>logy

> It's important to put the correct stress on words. This will make it easier for other people to understand you.

c) Have you ever studied any other subjects?

1 What are they called in English?
2 Write the names down in your notebook.
3 Make sure you know how to pronounce them.

3 Exam Task

▶▶ Extra Language for the Speaking Test, Sections 4 and 5, page 161

---

a) Work with a partner.

Student A: You are the examiner. Ask your partner the questions at the bottom of page 50. For Question 7, write down what your partner says so that you can check it later.

Student B: Answer your partner's questions.

When you have finished, check the answer to Question 4. Is it spelt correctly?

b) Change roles.

Student B: You are the examiner. Ask your partner the questions at the bottom of page 66. For Question 7, write down what your partner says so that you can check it later.

Student A: Answer your partner's questions.

When you have finished, check the answer to Question 5. Is it spelt correctly?

•• *Exam tip!* ••••••••••••••••••••••••

Short answers are usually better than complete sentences, but don't answer questions with just *Yes* or *No* – always try to give an extra piece of information.

••••••••••••••••••••••••••••••••••••

Speaking Part 2

▶ Strategy

In Part 2, the examiner describes a situation, and you and your partner talk about it for two or three minutes. The examiner gives you some pictures to help you. Be ready to:

- ask your partner's opinion
- say what you think is best
- give a reason for your opinion.

Make sure you listen to your partner and ask his/her opinion. Give reasons for your ideas.

1 Vocabulary: presents (1)

You are going to buy a present for some neighbours who are going to live in another city. Look at the picture of your neighbours on page 163 and some of the things you might buy. Do you know what they all are in English?

2 Functions: choosing a present

a) **Match these expressions (1–7) with the descriptions a)–c) below.**

1 What kind of thing would be best? ....
2 But they might already have one. ....
3 Do you think a CD is a good idea? ....
4 I don't think we should choose a cookery book because they don't like cooking. ....
5 Don't you think a book would be better? ....
6 I think she'd prefer some earrings because she likes jewellery. ....
7 Do you think they would like some chocolates? ....

a) asking your partner's opinion
b) say what you think is best
c) give a reason for your opinion

b) **Read the following conversation between Kika and Owen who are deciding what to buy for a friend. Fill each space with a suitable word.**

Kika: We should buy Janetta a present when she leaves school.

Owen: Yes. What (1) .... of thing would be best?

Kika: I'm not (2) .... Do you think she'd like a box of chocolates?

Owen: She might, but do you think that's a good (3) .... ? I know she worries about her weight. I think she'd prefer a book (4) .... she likes reading.

Kika: But she (5) .... already have the book we choose.

Owen: That's true. I don't think we should choose a video, because she doesn't like (6) .... to the cinema.

Kika: Yes, I know. She's quite unusual. But she enjoys art. What (7) .... a painting?

Owen: Don't you think a photo would be (8) .... ? We can't afford a really good painting.

Kika: Yes, you're right. Let's choose one today.

Owen: OK.

c) **Work with a partner. Practise reading the conversation aloud.**

3 Vocabulary: presents (2)

Work with a partner. Look again at the presents in Exercises 1 and 2.

Tell your partner which of these things you would like:

a) for your birthday

b) if you moved into a new house.

Explain why.

4 Exam Task

▶▶ Extra Language for the Speaking Test, Sections 6–10, pages 160–161

> Work with a partner. Turn to page 163 and look at the picture. Do the task in Exercise 1. Decide together what you are going to buy.

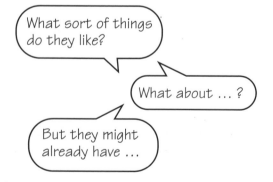

•• **Exam tip!** •••••••••••••••••••••••••
You don't have to agree with everything your partner says, but it's good if you can agree at the end.

Speaking Part 3

▶ Strategy

In Part 3, the examiner gives you a photograph. You talk about it by yourself for about a minute. Then your partner talks about another photo on the same topic.

Be ready to say:

- what you can see in different parts of the photo
- what is happening/what people are doing
- what people look like and what they are wearing
- how people are feeling and why.

1 Talking about things you don't know the name of

Work with a partner. Take turns to choose one of the things in the list below, but don't tell your partner. Use the expressions below to explain it and see if your partner can understand which thing you mean.

a) a zebra   f) a burger
b) a museum   g) a CD player
c) a mobile phone   h) a keyboard
d) a wardrobe   i) a restaurant
e) a pineapple   j) a tiger

> *It's a sort of …*
> *It's a place where …*
> *It's a thing which you use to …*

Examples:
Student A: It's a place where you can see lots of old things.
Student B: A museum?
Student A: Right.

Student B: It's a sort of a horse.
Student A: A zebra?
Student B: Yes.

•• Exam tip! ••••••••••••••••••••
Don't worry if you don't know a word – try to say it in another way, e.g. if you don't know the word **rucksack**, you can say **a sort of bag**.

2 Describing photos

a) Look at Photos A and B and read the description below. Which photo is described?

A

B

In the photo I can see several young people. I think they're students. They look quite happy and relaxed. Some of them are talking. They're outside a café and they're sitting around tables. There are some other tables in the background and all the tables have, I don't know what you call them, but they keep the sun away from you. There are some flowers and a fountain. It looks quite warm, but not too hot.

b) Now work with a partner. Describe the other photo together.

3 Exam Task

▶▶ Extra Language for the Speaking Test, Sections 11–16, page 161

Work with a partner. Do the Exam Task below.
Candidate A: Look at Photograph 2A on page 168.
Candidate B: Look at Photograph 2B on page 171.

Think about your photograph for a few seconds. Describe it to your partner for about one minute. Tell your partner about these things:

- the kind of place it is
- what you can see in different parts of the picture
- what kind of people you can see
- what they are doing
- whether they look happy or not
- why you think they are there.

Speaking Part 4

▶ Strategy

In Part 4, the examiner asks you to talk to your partner about a topic for about three minutes. The topic is the same as the pictures in Part 3.

- DO give your opinions.
- DO talk about your own or other people's experiences.
- DO ask your partner questions and respond to what he/she says.
- DO NOT talk to the examiner, only to your partner.

1 Talking about your own or other people's experiences

Match these questions and answers.

1 Have you ever played in a concert? ....
2 Do you often forget your homework? ....
3 Do you know anyone who has recorded a CD? ....
4 Do any of your friends own sports cars? ....
5 Have any of your friends ever appeared in a film? ....

a) Yes, my cousin has. He plays in a band.
b) No, none of them has enough money.
c) No, I can't sing or play an instrument.
d) No, but one of them was in a show at the theatre.
e) Yes, all of my friends do that sometimes.

2 Talking about some of the people in a group

a) Look at the picture. Complete the sentences below using the phrases in the box. You need some of the words more than once.

All of Both of One of None of Two of

1 .... them are carrying books.
2 .... them are wearing T-shirts.
3 .... the boys are wearing jeans.
4 .... them has a mobile phone.
5 .... them has a rucksack.
6 .... them could be students.

b) Complete these sentences truthfully.

1 Most of my friends …
2 Some of my classmates …
3 One of my neighbours …
4 None of my family …
5 All of my teachers …

3 Telling someone about yourself and people you know

Work with a partner. Ask each other Questions 1–5 in Exercise 1. Answer three questions truthfully and two questions untruthfully. Guess which questions your partner answered truthfully. Find out if your guesses were right.

4 Exam Task

▶▶ Extra Language for the Speaking Test, Sections 17 and 18, page 161

> **Work with a partner. Look at the Exam Task below.**
>
> **Ask and answer these questions:**
>
> 1 Which of photographs on pages 168 and 171 looks like a place you'd like to visit?
> 2 Do you use the internet?
> 3 Do any of your friends ever use internet cafés?
> 4 What do they use them for?
> 5 Do any of your friends or family play computer games?
> 6 Have you ever visited an internet chatroom?
> 7 Do you think it's useful for students to have computers? Why/why not?

•• **Exam tip!** ••••••••••••••••••••
If you haven't done something yourself, try to think of other people who have and talk about them.
•••••••••••••••••••••••••••••••••••

TESTS 3-6

Tests 3, 4, 5 and 6 give you the opportunity to practise what you have learned in Tests 1 and 2.

Test 3 contains *Exam tips* to help you with each task.

You can use these tests for timed practice, so you get used to doing the tasks under exam conditions.

When you have finished, you will be ready to take the exam with confidence.

Good luck!

PAPER 1   Reading and Writing Test   (1 hour 30 minutes)

Reading

Part 1

Questions 1–5

Look at the text in each question.
What does it say?
Mark the correct letter **A**, **B** or **C** on your answer sheet.

Exam tip!
Think about the meaning of the whole text before you choose your answer. The answer with the same words as the text may not be correct – check the other answers too.

Example:

0

> IT IS FORBIDDEN TO
> MOVE COMPUTERS FROM
> THIS ROOM WITHOUT
> PERMISSION FROM
> THE HEADTEACHER

A You mustn't take the computers out of this room without asking the headteacher.

B You should check with the headteacher before using the computers in this room.

C You must ask the headteacher for permission to move the computers into this room.

Answer:

1

> Dad,
> Andy wants you to phone him. I said you'd be back very late but he didn't mind. I've gone out. Back about midnight.
>
> x Penny

A Penny wanted to go out with Andy.

B Penny's father will arrive home late.

C Andy didn't agree with Penny's suggestion.

2

Job applications to be left at reception not with security guard

A Give your application form to the receptionist.

B There is a job available as a security guard.

C Reception can pass a message to the security guard.

3

Please go to Customer Services on ground floor if you wish to exchange goods

A You can try on clothes on the ground floor.

B You can change your money at Customer Services.

C You change things you don't want at Customer Services.

4

To	Everyone
From	Nina

I'm having my computer repaired, so I won't be able to receive e-mails for five days.

Phone me 237702

Nina

A Nina is mending her computer herself, so she can send e-mails.

B Nina's friends can't get in touch with her by e-mail for five days.

C Nina is doing a short course to learn how to repair her computer.

5

WAIT OUTSIDE STATION FOR AIRPORT BUS – EVERY 15 MINUTES

A It takes 15 minutes from the station to the airport.

B The bus waits to collect passengers from the station.

C The airport bus stops regularly at the station.

Part 2

Questions 6–10

The people below all want to do an English course.
On the opposite page there are descriptions of eight courses.
Decide which course would be most suitable for the following people.
For questions **6–10**, mark the correct letter **(A–H)** on your answer sheet.

•• **Exam tip!** •••••••••••
Underline the important parts
of each question. You can only
choose each text (A–H) once.

---

6  Paolo is good at speaking and understanding English, but he needs to do a full-time course to improve his writing and spelling before he starts a business course next year. He can come to England for one month in December or January.

7  This Spanish family would like to spend two or three weeks attending a part-time language course. The girls are nineteen and eighteen and know quite a lot of English. The parents know very little English.

8  Nikos is fourteen and his sister Anastasia is sixteen. Their parents would like them to spend a month on a language course where they can learn new hobbies and be looked after by their teachers.

9  Mehdi has just finished university and wants to spend some time touring round the world. He would like to do a course for a week or two before he starts his trip as he has never studied English.

10  Dorit is leaving school in June and will start a course to become a tour guide about four months later. Her English is good, but she must get a language qualification before she starts college.

Kinghall English Courses – something for everyone!

A

Activity language learning

For teenagers up to age sixteen with any level of English. Fully qualified staff and instructors make learning fun and safe. Spend two weeks or a month in small classes, improving your English while you paint, make music, play tennis, volleyball, etc. and take part in many other activities.

B

Family summer school

Classes at all levels for adults (over sixteen) and ten- to fifteen-year-olds in the same building. Meet for meals and evening leisure activities. Accommodation in modern flats near the school. A full-day study timetable for one, two or three weeks.

C

Get around in English

This course is aimed at beginners who want to feel comfortable using English to buy tickets, book hotel rooms and make new friends. Although you will spend most of the course simply taking part in conversations, you will work hard and you will be surprised how much progress you make in just two weeks.

D

Examination course 1

For students over sixteen, three-month courses preparing for a certificate recognised by international companies and employers around the world. Full-time courses for students who are prepared to work seriously hard.

E

Examination course 2

For students over sixteen, these courses last six months, and are part-time in the first three months, with a choice of afternoon leisure activities, changing to full-time for the second three months, with increased homework as the examination approaches.

F

Special skills courses

These one-, two- or three-month courses take place from January to March and are aimed at students who wish to improve particular language skills. Listening, writing, reading and speaking are all offered, together or separately. Students are not advised to take more than two skills in one month.

G

English for tourism

A six-month course for students with some knowledge of the language. The course covers areas such as ticket sales, making reservations and telephone work. Several trips to important English tourist centres are included. A very useful course for people planning to make a career in the travel business.

H

Adults' language breaks

These courses offer serious study during the morning, followed by the opportunity to join short trips to places of interest in the afternoon if you wish. Minimum three weeks, up to six weeks. Minimum age eighteen, all levels from beginners to advanced.

Part 3

Questions 11–20

Look at the sentences below about a group of islands.
Read the text on the opposite page to decide if each sentence is correct or incorrect.
If it is correct, mark **A** on your answer sheet.
If it is not correct, mark **B** on your answer sheet.

Exam tip!
Read the sentences
first to find out what
the text is about.

11 St Margaret Island is smaller than St Michael Island.

12 There was no one living on the islands in the 1980s.

13 There are several restaurants on the islands.

14 Flowers are for sale in the island shop.

15 The church is at the top of the highest hill.

16 There is one beach on St Michael Island where it is safe to swim.

17 It is possible to take a boat trip on a Saturday.

18 There is a fee for landing on the islands.

19 The journey to the islands lasts half an hour.

20 There is an exhibition centre on the islands.

Ferndig Islands

Three miles across the water from the town of Blascott lies the group of islands known as the Ferndigs. The main island is St Michael. Separated by a narrow channel of water is St Michael's little sister, St Margaret. People first lived on these islands 1,500 years ago. By the 1950s the population had gone down to below twenty, and in 1960 the last person left the islands. But in 1991 two families moved back, and since then more people have followed. Tourists now visit regularly to enjoy the beautiful scenery.

Visit the one shop on the islands which sells butter, cheese and bread produced by the families who live there. The produce is also taken by boat to restaurants in Blascott, where it can be enjoyed by visitors to the area. Perhaps more interestingly, a range of perfumes is made from the wild flowers and herbs which grow on the island and can be bought in the shop. They are produced mainly for export and are very special. So a visit to the shop is a must!

St Michael Island is easily explored on foot but, in the interests of safety, visitors are requested to keep to the main footpaths. From where the boat lands, walk along the cliff until you reach a steep path signposted to the church. When you get there, it is worth spending a moment in this lovely old building. Carry on along the same path which continues to climb to the highest point on the island. There is a wonderful view from here along the coastline. If it is warm, you may like to finish your day relaxing on the beach. Priory Beach on the eastern side of the island is safe for swimming. Sandtop Bay on the western side is the other sandy beach, but swimming is not advised here.

It is possible to hire a boat to cross to the islands, or you can take one of the boat trips which depart from Blascott harbour in summer, Monday to Friday. The islands are always open to visitors apart from on Sundays. Buy a ticket for a boat trip from the kiosk in Blascott harbour. The charge for landing on the islands is included in the ticket but, if you take your own boat, remember to take some money. The crossing takes thirty minutes, and boats run every fifteen minutes.

Before you set off on a trip, visit the exhibition centre which tells the history of the islands and gives information about birds and wildlife you may see when you get there.

Part 4

Read the text and questions below.
For each question, mark the correct letter **A**, **B**, **C** or **D** on your answer sheet.

> **•• Exam tip! ••••••••**
> The text will be about
> opinions and attitudes
> as well as information.

James

My name is James, I'm fourteen, and I moved to this town with my family three months ago. My parents lived here when they were young, but my brother and I didn't know anyone here except a few aunts and uncles we'd met when we'd spent a couple of weeks with my grandparents, during school holidays. When I started school, one of my cousins, Sophie, who was in my class, was very friendly for the first week and I was happy to have a friend in a strange place. Then, for no reason, she stopped talking to me and I felt very hurt and lonely for several weeks.

In the end I made some more friends and since I got to know them, I've been fine. Now Sophie is having a disco party for her birthday next week and she has invited me. I don't want to go. My brother says he heard someone say she only asked me because her parents said she had to. But my mum and dad say it would be rude not to accept. Some of my new friends are invited, too. How can I show Sophie that she can't behave so badly towards me without causing a family quarrel?

21   What is the writer trying to do in the text?

   A explain a problem

   B describe a family

   C offer advice

   D refuse an invitation

22   Who did James know in the town six months ago?

   A no one

   B a few relatives

   C only his grandparents

   D Sophie's friends

23 At the beginning of term, Sophie's behaviour made the writer feel

    A embarrassed.

    B unhappy.

    C grateful.

    D surprised.

24 The writer wants Sophie to realise

    A that he still hasn't forgiven her.

    B that her friends think she behaved rudely.

    C that his parents dislike her.

    D that she has fewer friends than he has.

25 Which of these is an answer to the text?

    A Ask your friends to come with you and we can all have a good time together.

    B Why not go to the party and ask Sophie why she stopped being friendly? At least everyone will know what's happening.

    C Please phone my parents and explain the situation to them, so that they'll stop worrying.

    D What about cooking a meal with Sophie and inviting all your relatives? That will be a good way to stop them quarrelling.

Part 5

Questions 26–35

Read the text below and choose the correct word for each space.
For each question, mark the correct letter **A**, **B**, **C** or **D** on your answer sheet.

•• *Exam tip!* ••••••••
Write the words in the spaces.
When you have finished, read
through the text and check
they sound right.

Example:

0   **A** of   **B** from   **C** by   **D** to

Answer:
0	A	B	C	D
	■	☐	☐	☐

Weather

Weather influences the lives (**0**) .... everyone. The climate of any country depends on its position on Earth, its (**26**) .... from the sea and how high it is. In countries which have sea all (**27**) .... them, like Britain and New Zealand, winters are mild and summers are cool. There is not a huge change from one season to (**28**) ....

Countries near the Equator have hot weather all year with some (**29**) .... rain, except in deserts where it rains (**30**) .... little. Above the desert there are no clouds in the sky, so the (**31**) .... of the sun can easily warm the ground during the day, but it gets very cold at night.

People are always (**32**) .... in unusual weather, and pictures of tornadoes, for example, are shown on television. Strong winds and rain can (**33**) .... a lot of damage to buildings, and in spite of modern (**34**) .... of weather forecasting they can (**35**) .... surprise us.

26	**A** distance	**B** space	**C** depth	**D** length
27	**A** through	**B** beside	**C** around	**D** near
28	**A** next	**B** another	**C** later	**D** other
29	**A** thick	**B** large	**C** heavy	**D** great
30	**A** not	**B** quite	**C** more	**D** very
31	**A** heat	**B** fire	**C** light	**D** temperature
32	**A** attracted	**B** interested	**C** keen	**D** excited
33	**A** make	**B** happen	**C** have	**D** cause
34	**A** jobs	**B** tools	**C** methods	**D** plans
35	**A** yet	**B** still	**C** already	**D** ever

Writing

Part 1

Questions 1–5

Here are some sentences about having a haircut.
For each question, complete the second sentence so that it means the same as the first.
Use no more than three words.
Write only the missing words on your answer sheet.
You may use this page for any rough work.

Example:

0   I need a haircut.

   My hair .... **cutting.**

Answer:

0	needs

---

1   The hairdresser last cut my hair six months ago.

   I last .... **my hair cut six months ago.**

2   When I phoned, she asked what time I wanted to go.

   When I phoned, she asked, 'What time .... **to come?'**

3   My brother cuts his hair himself.

   My brother cuts .... **hair.**

4   He says the hairdresser is too expensive for him.

   He says he .... **to go to the hairdresser.**

5   Unfortunately, he doesn't do it very well.

   Unfortunately, he's not very .... **doing it.**

Part 2

Question 6

An English-speaking friend called Jimmy has sent you a T-shirt as a present.

Write a card to Jimmy. In your card, you should

- thank him for the T-shirt
- ask him where he got it
- say when you plan to wear it.

Write **35–45 words** on your answer sheet.

Exam tip!

Remember to answer all three parts of the question.

Part 3

Write an answer to **one** of the questions (**7** or **8**) in this part.
Write your answer in about **100 words** on your answer sheet.
Put the question number in the box at the top of your answer sheet.

Exam tip!

When you finish writing, read through your letter or story carefully to check for any mistakes.

Question 7

- This is part of a letter you receive from your English penfriend.

> I guess you'll get this when you've just come back from your holiday. I'd like to hear about it. Where did you go? What did you do there? What sort of place did you stay in?

- Now write a letter to this penfriend.

- Write your **letter** on your answer sheet.

Question 8

- Your English teacher has asked you to write a story.

- Your story must have this title:

  My lucky day

- Write your **story** on your answer sheet.

Part 1

Questions 1–7

There are seven questions in this part.
For each question, there are three pictures and a short recording.
Choose the correct picture and put a tick (✓) in the box below it.

Example: What will the boy take back to the shop?

A   B ☐   C ☐

---

1   Which is the woman's house?

A ☐   B ☐   C ☐

2   Where is the traffic jam?

      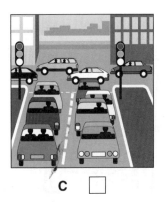

A ☐   B ☐   C ☐

[Turn over

3 Which wedding present has the man bought?

A ☐

B ☐

C ☐

4 How did the man get home?

A ☐

B ☐

C ☐

5 What did Simon hurt?

A ☐

B ☐

C ☐

6 Which is the man's mother?

A ☐

B ☐

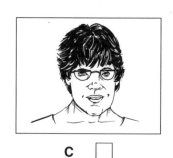

C ☐

7 Which poster are they looking at?

A ☐

B ☐

C ☐

Part 2

Questions 8–13

You will hear a successful fashion designer talking about his career.
For each question, put a tick (✓) in the correct box.

· · Exam tip! · · · · · · · · · · · ·

The questions are in the same order as the information you hear, so if you can't answer a question at first, leave it and do the others.

---

8 How well did the speaker do at school?

    A He was an average student. ☐

    B His parents helped him. ☐

    C He had problems passing exams. ☐

9 What did he do when he left school?

    A He got a job to earn a lot of money. ☐

    B He did a business course. ☐

    C He went to art college. ☐

10 What did he learn from his part-time job?

    A how to sew ☐

    B how clothes are made ☐

    C how to run a large business ☐

11 When did he go to London?

    A at the age of seventeen ☐

    B as soon as he had enough money ☐

    C when he won a prize ☐

12 How long did he stay in Milan?

    A three months ☐

    B nine months ☐

    C three years ☐

13 Why did he have difficulties in New York?

    A He wanted to be nearer his home. ☐

    B He could not start a company there. ☐

    C The work was more stressful than he had expected. ☐

Part 3

You will hear a tour guide talking to some tourists about a visit to a shopping centre.

For each question, fill in the missing information in the numbered space.

> **Exam tip!**
>
> Use the words around the spaces to help you decide what kind of answer is needed.

Visit to shopping centre

Bank is on the **(14)** ....

Get a **(15)** .... from the newsagent.

Restaurant is opposite the **(16)** ....
in the main square.

Snack bar next to the **(17)** ....

closes at **(18)** ....

Meet outside shop called **(19)** ....

Part 4

Questions 20–25

Look at the six sentences for this part.
You will hear a conversation between a girl, Alice, and a boy, Sam,
about a play their school is doing called *Romeo and Juliet.*
Decide if each sentence is correct or incorrect.
If it is correct, put a tick (✓) in the box under **A** for **YES**. If it is not correct,
put a tick (✓) in the box under **B** for **NO**.

•• *Exam tip!* •••••••••••
Look carefully at the verbs in
the statements (e.g. *decided,
agrees, persuades*) because
they are all very important
in helping you choose the
answer.

		A YES	B NO
20	They are going to have the practice outdoors today.	☐	☐
21	Sam has decided he no longer wants to be Romeo.	☐	☐
22	Alice agrees with Miss Hayes about Sam's voice.	☐	☐
23	Sam agrees that Alice should speak to Miss Hayes about the problem.	☐	☐
24	Alice persuades Sam to take a smaller part in the play.	☐	☐
25	Someone is needed to produce the scenery.	☐	☐

Part 1

General conversation: saying who you are, giving personal information, spelling

•• Exam tip! •••••••••••••••••••••••••••••
Remember to try to add some extra information when you answer.
••

Take turns to be the examiner. Ask your partner questions to find out some information about each other.

Ask each other at least four of these questions:

- What's your name?
- How long have you been studying English?
- Where do you study?
- How many students are there in your class?
- How many hours a week do you have English?
- Can you spell your teacher's surname for me, please?

Part 2

Simulated situation: exchanging opinions, saying what you think is necessary

•• Exam tip! •••••••••••••••••••••••••••
Speak to your partner, not the examiner, and listen to what he / she says.
•••••••••••••••••••••••••••••••••••••••

The examiner gives you both a picture. You do a task together.

You are going to travel by coach together for a whole day. Look at page 164. There are pictures of some things you might take for the journey. Decide together what you will take. Think about what you need.

Ask and answer questions like these:

- What do we need?
- What would amuse us?
- What would be interesting to do?
- Would that be too big / noisy?
- Do you think we'll really use that?

Part 3

Responding to photographs: describing situations and settings

•• Exam tip! •••••••••••••••••••••••••••••
Don't worry if you don't know the name of something – describe it instead.
••

You take turns to tell each other about a photograph.

Candidate A: look at Photograph 3A on page 169.
Candidate B: look at Photograph 3B on page 172.

Think about your photograph for a few seconds. Describe it to your partner for about one minute.

Tell your partner about these things:

- what kind of place it is
- what sport the people are playing
- why they are doing it
- whether they are enjoying it
- what you can see in the background.

Part 4

General conversation about the photographs: talking about likes, dislikes and preferences

•• Exam tip! •••••••••••••••••••••••••••
If you agree or disagree, don't just say 'Yes' or 'No' – explain why.
•••••••••••••••••••••••••••••••••••••••

The examiner asks you to talk to your partner. You give your opinion about something and explain what you prefer.

Tell each other about sports you enjoy doing or watching (now or in the past).

Use these ideas:

- Say if you like football or volleyball.
- Say what other sports you like.
- Say if you enjoy sports competitions and why.
- Say if you prefer watching sport or doing it and why.

TEST 4

Reading

Part 1

Questions 1–5

Look at the text in each question.
What does it say?
Mark the correct letter **A**, **B** or **C** on your answer sheet.

Example:

0

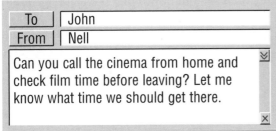

John should

A   contact Nell after phoning the cinema.

B   ring Nell after arriving at the cinema.

C   go to the cinema to check when the film starts.

Answer:

1

Polly — I phoned the bike shop about getting yours mended. If they're closed, leave your bike outside (locked, of course) and put your keys in their letter box.

A   Polly can leave her bicycle for repair even when the shop is closed.

B   Polly should leave her keys so that the repair shop can lock her bicycle.

C   Polly's bicycle will be left outside when it is repaired.

2

Choose a pair of gloves
FREE
when you buy a coat today

A   You can get a discount on a coat if you buy some gloves today.

B   You are given some gloves if you buy a coat today.

C   We have gloves to match the coats we sell.

[Turn over

3

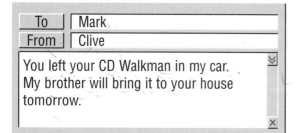

ANY LOST PROPERTY
LEFT HERE AFTER
TWO WEEKS IS SOLD

A We give lost property away if it is not collected after two weeks.

B We will look after your property for two weeks if you pay a fee.

C We keep things people have lost for a maximum of two weeks.

4

To | Mark
From | Clive

You left your CD Walkman in my car. My brother will bring it to your house tomorrow.

A Clive borrowed Mark's Walkman.

B Clive's brother will return the Walkman to Mark.

C Mark wants to use Clive's Walkman on a journey.

5

PHOTOCOPYING

Serve yourself
Count number of copies
Pay assistant at till on way out

A Do your photocopying and pay for it when you leave.

B Put your money in the photocopier before you start to use it.

C Tell an assistant how many photocopies you need.

Part 2

Questions 6–10

The people below all want to buy a book.
On the opposite page there are descriptions of eight books.
Decide which book would be most suitable for the following people.
For questions **6–10**, mark the correct letter **(A–H)** on your answer sheet.

6  Jan is sixteen and she loves shopping for clothes and reading stories about people and things in the news. She wants to read some entertaining light fiction.

7 Paul is nineteen and is very keen on sport. He doesn't enjoy fiction much, but does like reading about the lives of sporting heroes of the past.

8  Susan is eighteen and enjoys good writing. She would like something which offers information as well as entertainment. She's interested in history and plans to travel round Europe this summer.

9  Michael is twenty-three, a computer expert, whose interests include travel and sport. He has to go abroad for work and wants a novel to read on his journey with plenty of action and excitement.

10 Sonia is twenty-four and works for an international airline. She enjoys love stories of the past, especially if they contain descriptions of beautiful houses, clothes and parties.

Recommended New Books

A **The Beauty** by Sophie Harper

The lovely Emmaline Barton was an American girl who came to Europe in the nineteenth century and won the hearts of young men in every great city. This entertaining novel shows us the wonderful silk dresses, the beautiful rooms and Emmaline's sparkling eyes in a well-imagined world of palaces and gardens.

B **European Hotels and Guesthouses** by Andrew Peters

A very clear and helpful book which lists accommodation in most main European cities, with brief descriptions and a good price guide. Its small size makes it easy for the traveller to pack, and the organisation of the information makes it quick and easy to use.

C **Getting There** by Will Jenkins

This is the first part of the autobiography of the international gymnastics star. He writes his own story well, hiding none of the difficulties that he had to face, and he brings to life the heartaches, as well as the joys, of young sportsmen and women who really want to find success.

D **Trains and Boats and Planes** by Rachel Bryant

Sometimes funny, sometimes exciting, occasionally sad, this beautifully written little book describes the adventures of a group of American students who spent a year working and studying in Europe. There are lively descriptions of some of the great cities and their inhabitants, past and present.

E **What People Wore** by Annabel Stoneman

An extremely interesting history of clothes, written by a history teacher. It will be a very useful book for anyone who needs to design clothes for the theatre or who is interested in the everyday lives of people in the past. There are not many pictures, but lots of detailed notes.

F **Future Pop** by Terry Orpen

The pop music industry has changed enormously in the past few years. With electronics and computers in the studio and at concerts, what is the future for the human musician? This book is by one of the top performers of computer pop music, and he discusses the way it will probably develop in the future.

G **Goal Posts** by Simon Brown

A very well-written and fast-moving adventure story, set in an imagined world of international football stars. The matches are well described, as well as the problems of the players as they fight for their careers, on and off the pitch. A great read for sports fans.

H **The Fashion House** by Julia Davis

This amusing novel is just right for reading on holiday. It reveals the lives and loves of the designers, models and customers of a famous fashion house. It's written by a former model and gives away many of the modern fashion world's secrets.

Part 3

Look at the sentences below about a holiday in Tasmania, an island off the south coast of Australia.
Read the text on the opposite page to decide if each sentence is correct or incorrect.
If it is correct, mark **A** on your answer sheet.
If it is not correct, mark **B** on your answer sheet.

11   There are few traffic jams in Tasmania.

12   There are several buses every day on most routes.

13   It is essential to reserve accommodation in advance.

14   There is a limit on the number of hotel tickets you can buy.

15   Ruby Hotels are the cheapest.

16   Taz Hotel tickets can only be used in Taz Hotels.

17   The most attractive scenery you see on the second day is by Russell Falls.

18   The third day is spent in the car.

19   There are good views of Cradle Mountain from the edges of Dove Lake.

20   The trip finishes where it started.

See Tasmania!

Rich in old-world charm and with magnificent National Parks, Tasmania is well covered by a good road network. Light traffic and wonderful views make driving these roads a pleasure. Though the bus system is reliable, on many routes services may only run once daily. So hire a car and see this beautiful and interesting island at your own speed.

There is a variety of places to stay, and although booking is strongly advised, particularly at peakholiday times, it should not be too difficult to arrange things as you go, if you prefer. We sell you a set of Taz Hotel Pass vouchers and Tasmania is yours. The Taz Hotel Pass offers the visitor a simple and convenient way to stay anywhere in Australia. Each hotel ticket is paid for in advance and is for one night's accommodation. There is no maximum or minimum number of hotel tickets you can buy, and we will give you your money back on unused tickets, less a small administrative charge. Taz Hotels are divided into simple colour categories, with Ruby being the most basic and Diamond representing the highest quality. We recommend that you buy a mixture of tickets, as we cannot give you your money back if you use a higher-value ticket when staying at a lower-value hotel. If you travel to an area where Taz have no hotels, then we will find other reasonably priced accommodation for you in exchange for your Taz tickets.

Here is the planned route for our holiday in Tasmania:

Day 1: Arrive Hobart airport, pick up your car and spend some time in the capital, perhaps driving up to the Old Signal Station on Mount Nelson.

Day 2: Drive through the Derwent Valley, stopping at Russell Falls. Later the scenery becomes even more amazing as you pass Lake St Clair National Park. Spend the night in the fishing town of Strahan.

Day 3: We take you on a half-day cruise from Strahan on the famous Gordon River. Then set off for a leisurely drive to Cradle Mountain National Park.

Day 4: Enjoy the wild beauty of the Park. Go fishing or horse-riding. Or walk around beautiful Dove Lake, from where there are wonderful views of the mountain itself.

Day 5: Explore the fascinating country towns as you drive north and along the coast to Launceston, Tasmania's second-largest city.

Day 6: A pleasant drive through peaceful countryside to Hobart. On route, you pass the charming towns of Ross and Oatlands. Return to the airport in time for your flight.

Part 4

Read the text and questions below.
For each question, mark the correct letter **A**, **B**, **C** or **D** on your answer sheet.

The businessman

There is a story going round at the moment about a well-known journalist who went to interview Jack Parrish at a smart New York restaurant. The journalist was late, but fortunately, when he arrived, he found the great man was not yet there. On the way to his table, the journalist noticed a colleague from his paper and stopped to chat to her. After fifteen minutes, a waiter approached him. 'There's some young man at the door who says he's supposed to be having lunch with you. I think he's trying to be funny, because he says his name is Jack Parrish!'

But of course it was. The twenty-four-year-old is becoming famous for the fact that he doesn't look like the owner of one of the world's most successful computer companies. His manner is polite, his voice is quiet and his clothes are clearly not expensive. Two years ago, when he started his own company, no one had heard of him. Friends say that he hasn't changed at all. He hasn't even moved out of his parents' house. So what does he do with his money? It's all used for business. But some people in the computer world are getting nervous – and they are right. It won't be long before someone in another company picks up the phone to hear that quiet voice saying that he's the new boss.

21 Someone could find out from this text

   A   how Jack Parrish runs his business.

   B   what Jack Parrish said in an interview.

   C   how to get a job in Jack Parrish's company.

   D   what the writer thinks Jack Parrish will do next.

22 How did the journalist pass the time while he was waiting?

   A   He phoned his office.

   B   He talked to another journalist.

   C   He talked to a man at the next table.

   D   He interviewed a woman in the restaurant.

23 The waiter thought the young man at the door of the restaurant

    A   was a journalist.

    B   was behaving rudely.

    C   was not as old as he said he was.

    D   was pretending to be someone else.

24 What is the writer's attitude to Jack Parrish?

    A   He is more important than he appears.

    B   He is a good example for young people.

    C   He should be more careful how he runs his business.

    D   He would be an interesting person to work for.

25 Which of these headlines does the writer expect to see soon?

    A

> ## Too much success too fast – was that the end of Parrish's luck?

    B

> ### Jack Parrish doesn't worry about money – he gives it away to old friends

    C

> ### And the new owner of our top computer company is Jack Parrish!

    D

> ## SPEND, SPEND, SPEND – how Jack furnishes his new million-dollar home

Part 5

Questions 26–35

Read the text below and choose the correct word for each space.
For each question, mark the correct letter **A**, **B**, **C** or **D** on your answer sheet.

Example:

0	**A** won	**B** took	**C** beat	**D** held

Answer:

0	A	B	C	D
	■	☐	☐	☐

Olympic hopes

Yesterday Eleanor Preston **(0)** .... an international swimming competition for girls **(26)** .... under sixteen. She swam faster **(27)** .... girls from ten other countries. This **(28)** .... even better when you learn that Eleanor is only thirteen. She had to have special **(29)** .... to enter, because normally competitors are fourteen or older.

Eleanor has been **(30)** .... on swimming for a long time – **(31)** .... she was three in fact. I wondered whether she found it hard to **(32)** .... several hours a day training. She **(33)** .... me that sometimes she has problems finding time for homework, but that's all. 'My parents have given up so **(34)** .... time driving me to local competitions, I think it's been harder for them, actually.' Her aim is to swim at the Olympics.

After yesterday's performance, I think she may **(35)** .... there.

26	**A** age	**B** aged	**C** ages	**D** ageing
27	**A** that	**B** from	**C** than	**D** of
28	**A** suggests	**B** means	**C** sounds	**D** shows
29	**A** permission	**B** attention	**C** opportunity	**D** accommodation
30	**A** happy	**B** good	**C** pleased	**D** keen
31	**A** until	**B** since	**C** when	**D** ever
32	**A** take	**B** use	**C** spend	**D** pass
33	**A** told	**B** explained	**C** said	**D** agreed
34	**A** often	**B** much	**C** long	**D** many
35	**A** reach	**B** find	**C** get	**D** make

Writing

Part 1

Questions 1–5

Here are some sentences about a house.
For each question, complete the second sentence so that it means the same as the first.
Use no more than three words.
Write only the missing words on your answer sheet.
You may use this page for any rough work.

Example:

0   I live in this house.

This is the house .... **I live.**

Answer: | **0** | *where* |

---

1   My family has lived in this house for two months.

My family .... **to this house two months ago.**

2   It was formerly my grandparents' home.

My grandparents used .... **here.**

3   They said they didn't need so much space.

They said, '.. **need so much space.'**

4   They were bought a new flat by my parents.

My parents .... **a new flat.**

5   It isn't necessary for me to share a room in this house.

I .... **to share a room in this house.**

Part 2

Question 6

An English-speaking friend called Leo has invited you to go to a football match with him on Saturday.

Write an e-mail to Leo. In your e-mail, you should

- thank him for asking you
- say how you feel about going
- invite him to a meal afterwards.

Write **35–45 words** on your answer sheet.

Part 3

Write an answer to **one** of the questions (**7** or **8**) in this part.
Write your answer in about **100 words** on your answer sheet.
Put the question number in the box at the top of your answer sheet.

Question 7

- You are going to stay with an English family. This is part of a letter you receive from them.

> Can you tell us about your work or school, your hobbies and interests and say what you hope to do while you are in England?

- Now write a letter to this family.

- Write your **letter** on your answer sheet.

Question 8

- Your English teacher has asked you to write a story.

- Your story must have this title:

    A new friend

- Write your **story** on your answer sheet.

Part 1

Questions 1–7

There are seven questions in this part.
For each question, there are three pictures and a short recording.
Choose the correct picture and put a tick (✓) in the box below it.

Example: What will the boy take back to the shop?

A ✓   B ☐   C ☐

---

1   Which job does the woman do now?

A ☐   B ☐   C ☐

2   Where will they meet?

A ☐   B ☐   C ☐

[Turn over

3 Where is the car park?

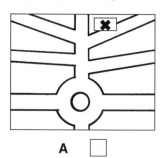 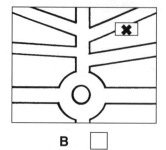 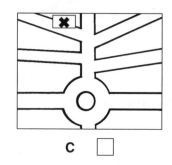

A ☐   B ☐   C ☐

4 Which date is Brian's birthday?

A ☐   B ☐   C ☐

5 Which photo are they looking at?

A ☐   B ☐   C ☐

6 Which T-shirt is Beth wearing?

 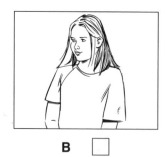 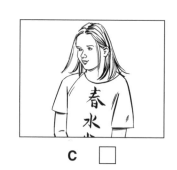

A ☐   B ☐   C ☐

7 Where is the man?

A ☐   B ☐   C ☐

Part 2

Questions 8–13

You will hear part of a radio programme called *What's On*.
For each question, put a tick (✓) in the correct box.

---

8   The competition this year is to find the best

      A actor. ☐

      B dancer. ☐

      C singer. ☐

9   You can enter the competition if you

      A send your entry by post. ☐

      B live less than five miles from the city centre. ☐

      C phone any time after Saturday. ☐

10 To find out more about the theatre group, you should phone

      A the theatre. ☐

      B Saint Paul's School. ☐

      C the secretary of the group. ☐

11 What is different about the arrangements at the sports hall this week?

      A The closing time is later than usual. ☐

      B It is not possible to hire the football pitch. ☐

      C All activities must be booked in advance. ☐

12 What information are we given about the new swimming pool?

      A It will open next month. ☐

      B It will be free for one week. ☐

      C It is bigger than the old one. ☐

13 What are we told about the rock group *Switch*?

      A They were all born in Westfield. ☐

      B They all live in Westfield. ☐

      C They are doing two concerts in Westfield. ☐

Part 3

You will hear someone talking about the city of Cork.
For each question, fill in the missing information in the numbered space.

Cork

The population is **(14)** ....

Drivers find the number of **(15)** .... confusing.

St Patrick Street – on one side are old buildings, on the other side are

(16) .... and shops.

Market – **(17)** .... and fruit are recommended today.

Café in the **(18)** .... is good for lunch.

Public Museum is closed on **(19)** ....

Part 4

Questions 20–25

Look at the six sentences for this part.
You will hear a conversation between a woman, Kim, and a man, Rob, who live in the same block of flats.
Decide if each sentence is correct or incorrect.
If it is correct, put a tick (✓) in the box under **A** for **YES**. If it is not correct, put a tick (✓) in the box under **B** for **NO**.

		A YES	B NO
20	Kim gave a party last night.	☐	☐
21	Rob could hear music from Kim's flat.	☐	☐
22	Rob apologises for disturbing Kim's visitors.	☐	☐
23	Rob plays music when he has visitors.	☐	☐
24	Kim dislikes working in silence.	☐	☐
25	Kim prefers to work during the day.	☐	☐

Part 1

General conversation: saying who you are, giving personal information, spelling

Take turns to be the examiner. Ask your partner questions to find out some information about each other.

Ask each other at least four of these questions:

- What's your name?
- Can you tell me about your family?
- Are you the oldest, the youngest or in the middle?
- Where exactly do you live?
- How long does it take you to get to school?
- Can you spell the name of your street for me, please?

Part 2

Simulated situation: giving opinions and making suggestions

The examiner gives you both a picture. You do a task together.

You are planning to go out with your classmates for an evening to celebrate the end of term. Look at page 165. Decide together where to go.

Ask and answer questions like these:

- Which place would people prefer?
- Is it better to do something indoors or outdoors?
- Do people want to sit and talk?
- How much will people want to spend?

Part 3

Responding to photographs: describing where people and animals are and what they are doing

You take turns to tell each other about a photograph.

Candidate A: look at Photograph 4A on page 169.
Candidate B: look at Photograph 4B on page 172.

Think about your photograph for a few seconds. Describe it to your partner for about one minute.

Tell your partner about these things:

- what kind of place it is
- what part of the world it might be
- what animals and people there are
- how the people are dressed
- what they are doing.

Part 4

General conversation about the photographs: talking about likes, dislikes and preferences

The examiner asks you to talk to your partner. You give your opinion about something and explain what you prefer.

Tell each other about animals you like.

Use these ideas:

- Say if you like horses.
- Say if you have ever been horse-riding. Where?
- Say if you would like to. Explain why / why not.
- Say if you have any pets at home.
- Say what other animals you like.
- Say if you know of any unusual pets.

TEST 5

Reading

Part 1

Questions 1–5

Look at the text in each question.
What does it say?
Mark the correct letter **A**, **B** or **C** on your answer sheet.

Example:

0

> IT IS FORBIDDEN TO
> MOVE COMPUTERS FROM
> THIS ROOM WITHOUT
> PERMISSION FROM
> THE HEADTEACHER

A   You mustn't take the computers out of this room without asking the headteacher.

B   You should check with the headteacher before using the computers in this room.

C   You must ask the headteacher for permission to move the computers into this room.

Answer:

0	A	B	C

1

> Students who are late must sign this book before going to their class.

A   Students will not be allowed to enter their class if they are late.

B   Students should sign their names in this book if they expect to be late.

C   Students who arrive late should not go to class before signing this book.

2

> Hi everyone! When exams are over, what about trying the new club in Green Street? I haven't been there yet, so I'd like to know what it's like. Mack

A   Mack recommends a new club to his friends.

B   Mack wants to go clubbing before the exams.

C   Mack suggests going to a club after the exams.

[Turn over

3

> Pete ~ Would you mind collecting my things from dry cleaners? Ticket is on hall table. Thanks, Emma

A   Emma wants Pete to bring her clothes home.

B   Emma wants Pete to give her a lift to the dry cleaners.

C   Emma has forgotten her ticket and wants Pete to collect it for her.

4

> PARENTS ARE REMINDED THAT THIS IS **NOT** A PLAYGROUND – **PLEASE KEEP CHILDREN OFF SCULPTURES!**

A   Families can only watch sports events in this park.

B   Children must not climb on the sculptures.

C   Some of the sculptures are unsuitable for children.

5

> **PASSENGERS FOR INTERNATIONAL FLIGHTS – CHECK LUGGAGE IN HERE**

A   Passengers arriving from abroad must check in their luggage here.

B   Travellers from other countries have to check in their own luggage here.

C   This is where you check in your luggage if you are going abroad.

Part 2

Questions 6–10

The people below all want to visit a museum in the Kington area.
On the opposite page there are descriptions of eight museums.
Decide which museum would be most suitable for the following people.
For questions **6–10**, mark the correct letter **(A–H)** on your answer sheet.

6

Tina is going to art college soon. She wants to spend an afternoon looking at some modern art. She would like to have lunch and buy some art books.

7

Karen needs to buy a special present for a friend and wants to get her some jewellery or pottery made locally. She can only go shopping after five o'clock in the evening.

8  Stefan has just moved to Kington. He would like to find out more about life in the area over the last hundred years. He is only free on Saturdays.

9  Gareth and Sue want to spend Sunday outdoors. Their children want to learn about how people used to live in the past. The family are looking for somewhere which has a playground.

10  Jack is studying art and is particularly interested in the development of painting over the last three hundred years. He is free every afternoon and would like to stop and have a snack in the museum.

Museums and galleries around Kington

A Most of the machines in this interesting museum are indoors, but some of the larger farming equipment is outside. A lot of the machines still work and you can try using them. It is especially suitable for school groups and families and is open Monday to Saturday from 10 a.m. till 6 p.m.

B This museum changes its exhibitions regularly. At the moment it is showing paintings by artists who all live in the area. The excellent bookshop and café are above the gallery. The café is open for lunch from 12 till 2.30, and the gallery and bookshop from 11 till 6 every day.

C The Kington area was once very important industrially, and this museum tells the history of the local industries of shipbuilding and pottery. There is a large car park at the front and a playground at the back. The museum is open Monday–Friday 10–5.

D All the exhibits in this attractive little museum were produced in the region over the last 100 years. There is a good range of jewellery, clothes and pictures for sale, all produced in Kington. The museum is open Thursday–Sunday from 2 p.m. till 9 p.m. and the tearoom from 2 p.m. till 5 p.m.

E The best art collection in the area is here, and there is a separate room for each century, including a small one for twentieth-century paintings. There is a shop selling posters, postcards and cards. The coffee shop is open for lunch and afternoon tea from midday Tuesday–Saturday. The museum is open from 11 a.m. till 7 p.m. Tuesday–Saturday.

F This museum shows family life in Kington during the twentieth century. There are rooms furnished exactly as they were in 1920, 1940 and 1960, a 1920s garage and two shops – a 1950s general store and a 1930s jeweller's. There is a large playground outside. Open every day from 10 a.m. till 6 p.m.

G There was a village on this site 500 years ago and it is now completely rebuilt. You can walk around the fields and along the paths to see how people lived and worked all those years ago. There is a car park and a large playground. Open every day from 9 a.m. till 5.30 p.m.

H This museum is very small but is full of interesting objects, including jewellery, weapons, pottery, cooking equipment and other household items. They were all found on an ancient site outside the town and they are all over 1,000 years old. The museum is open on Saturdays and Sundays only.

Part 3

Look at the sentences below about the facilities in a hotel.
Read the text on the opposite page to decide if each sentence is correct or incorrect.
If it is correct, mark **A** on your answer sheet. ·
If it is not correct, mark **B** on your answer sheet.

___

11   Breakfast in the dining room costs the same whatever you eat.

12   The dining room closes at 9 p.m.

13   The Coffee Shop is open at the same times as the swimming pool.

14   The receptionist will bring you a newspaper with your breakfast if you want.

15   You can unlock the front door for yourself if you return to the hotel very late.

16   To telephone a room in the hotel, you press 9 followed by the room number.

17   Children may only use the swimming pool when a member of staff is present.

18   You can use the hotel laundry facilities any afternoon.

19   The hotel will look after your money for you while you are out.

20   You must tell the receptionist if you are going out in the evening.

GERALD'S HOTEL Information

Meals

Breakfast is served in the dining room 7.30–9.30 a.m. (10.00 a.m. on Sundays). Help yourself from our buffet or order a full cooked breakfast at no extra charge. A light breakfast can be served in your room if preferred (see Room Service below).
Dinner is served in the dining room from 7.30 p.m. (Last orders by 9 p.m. please.)

A children's dinner menu is available until 8 p.m. at a reduced charge.

The Coffee Shop at the swimming pool is open from 10 a.m. serving a range of drinks, snacks and light meals.

Room service

24-hour room service is not available, but we are happy to bring light meals and snacks to your room for a small extra charge when the Coffee Shop is open. Light breakfasts are also available from 7 a.m. Please inform reception the previous evening if you would like breakfast in your room.

Newspapers can be ordered from Reception and will be on your breakfast table.

We do not have a **night porter**. If you are likely to come back to the hotel after midnight, please ask the receptionist for a front-door key.

The **telephone** in your room can be used to make calls within the hotel by dialling the number as shown on the list beside it. For calls outside, dial 9 followed by the number. Calls are charged at normal price for the first two minutes, then double after that.

The **swimming pool** is open from 7 a.m. to 10 p.m. Please collect swimming towels from Reception. Do not use the towels in your bathroom.
Please note that children must be with a responsible adult at all times when using the pool. The hotel does not have staff available to do this and can take no responsibility for accidents.

There is a washing machine (£1.50 required) and drier (50p required). These are in the **laundry room**, opposite Room 17, and are available for guests to use after 1.30 p.m. every day. An iron and ironing board is also available. The hotel also offers a laundry service, which takes a minimum of twenty-four hours, from Monday to Friday. Prices are available from Reception.

Cash and items of value can be locked away in the hotel office if you wish to avoid carrying them with you to the beach, etc. Please ask at Reception. There is normally no charge for this service.

Please leave your room by 10 a.m. on the day of your **departure** to give us time to prepare for the next guests. If you would like to leave luggage with us for part of the day, please tell the receptionist the evening before.

Part 4

Read the text and questions below.
For each question, mark the correct letter **A**, **B**, **C** or **D** on your answer sheet.

Waiter!

I went to the cinema last week and laughed all the way through the new film *Waiter!* which is set in a restaurant. American actor Tom Waters plays the worst cook the world has ever seen and he employs one of the worst waiters, played by Joe Vermont.

The London restaurant where the filming took place does actually exist. Jane Connors, the owner, runs a successful business with many regular customers. However, although she thinks *Waiter!* is a good film, she is very annoyed with the director. When she agreed to the filming, she wasn't told that the film is about a restaurant where everything goes wrong and the food is disgusting. Although the film might make Jane's restaurant famous if it is a success, she is afraid that people will stop coming because they will think the food and service is terrible – like it is in the film. Jane is worried she will lose business and may even have to close and start again with a new restaurant.

Having seen the film, I agree that she has a problem. The film company paid her a very small fee, and she has since asked for more. The best solution, though, is for her to contact the newspapers. I am sure they will be interested in her story and it will actually help her business in the end.

21 What is the writer trying to do in the text?

    A   advertise a restaurant

    B   review a film

    C   explain someone's problem

    D   take someone's advice

22 What do we learn about Jane's restaurant?

    A   It is very popular.

    B   The food is not good.

    C   It is in a beautiful building.

    D   The waiters are unhelpful.

23 What did the director not tell Jane?

    A   that the film would be a success

    B   that the restaurant in the film would be very bad

    C   that she would not be paid

    D   that she would need to employ extra staff

24 What does the writer think Jane ought to do?

    A   open a new restaurant

    B   ask the film company for more money

    C   improve the quality of the food in her restaurant

    D   write to the newspapers

25 Which of these is an advert for the film?

A

> ## *Waiter!*
> Comedy film set in a typical American town.
> Laugh at the mistakes of crazy cook (Tom Waters) and
> mad waiter (Joe Vermont).

B

> ## *Waiter!*
> Learn how to cook and be amused at the same
> time at this film made specially for television by
> well-known cook, Tom Waters.

C

> ## *WAITER!*
> *All the action takes place in a famous London
> restaurant. Find out the truth about what happens
> in the kitchens.*

D

> ## *Waiter!*
> Sit back and enjoy the performances of Tom
> Waters and Joe Vermont in this comedy filmed
> in a London restaurant.

Part 5

Questions 26–35

Read the text below and choose the correct word for each space.
For each question, mark the correct letter **A**, **B**, **C** or **D** on your answer sheet.

Example:

0   **A** are   **B** made   **C** got   **D** were

Answer: | 0 | A ■ | B ☐ | C ☐ | D ☐ |

Modigliani – an Italian artist

Nowadays cards and posters of pictures by Amedeo Modigliani **(0)** .... popular
with people all **(26)** .... the world, but the artist himself did not have an easy life.
He **(27)** .... born in Livorno, Italy, in 1884. His father was a businessman who did
not make **(28)** .... money, and his mother **(29)** .... a school.

Modigliani went to art school in Florence and Venice, before moving to Paris **(30)** ....
he painted and made sculptures. His work was **(31)** .... by art from Africa which he
saw in museums. He was very poor and not very strong, and after a **(32)** .... years he
gave up making sculptures. He painted people in a gentle, thoughtful style.

Many of his most beautiful paintings **(33)** .... Jeanne, the woman he loved. Often
the people in his paintings look sad or tired. Perhaps Modigliani was painting his own
feelings. **(34)** .... in the end he began to **(35)** .... a little money, he was
never very successful in his lifetime.

26	**A** over	**B** on	**C** through	**D** along
27	**A** been	**B** has	**C** was	**D** is
28	**A** many	**B** much	**C** lot	**D** very
29	**A** held	**B** taught	**C** ran	**D** gave
30	**A** that	**B** which	**C** when	**D** where
31	**A** felt	**B** influenced	**C** suggested	**D** discovered
32	**A** few	**B** several	**C** short	**D** number
33	**A** see	**B** give	**C** show	**D** realise
34	**A** Therefore	**B** However	**C** But	**D** Although
35	**A** earn	**B** take	**C** bring	**D** win

Writing

Part 1

Questions 1–5

Here are some sentences about a new sports centre.
For each question, complete the second sentence so that it means the same as the first.
Use no more than three words.
Write only the missing words on your answer sheet.
You may use this page for any rough work.

Example:

0   A famous tennis player opened the new sports centre.

   The new sports centre .... **a famous tennis player.**

Answer: | **0** | *was opened by* |

---

1   The facilities are excellent.

   It .... **excellent facilities.**

2   It's better than the old one.

   The old one wasn't .... **this one.**

3   I prefer doing sport to watching it on TV.

   I like doing sport .... **watching it on TV.**

4   The pool is used by people of all ages.

   People of all ages .... **the pool.**

5   It's possible to go swimming early in the morning.

   You .... **go swimming early in the morning.**

Part 2

Question 6

Yesterday you arranged to go the cinema with Selina, an English friend.
Unfortunately, you didn't get to the cinema on time and missed her.

Write a note to Selina. In your note, you should

- apologise for not meeting her
- explain why you were late
- suggest meeting another time.

Write **35–45 words** on your answer sheet.

Part 3

Write an answer to **one** of the questions (**7** or **8**) in this part.
Write your answer in about **100 words** on your answer sheet.
Put the question number in the box at the top of your answer sheet.

Question 7

- Last week you went to a birthday party. This is part of a letter you have received from your English penfriend, Annabel.

> In your last letter you said you were going to a birthday party. Please tell me what you did at the party. What present did you take for your friend? Did everyone enjoy themselves?

- Now write a letter to Annabel answering her questions.

- Write your **letter** on your answer sheet.

Question 8

- Your English teacher has asked you to write a story.

- Your story must begin with these words:

    I had just finished getting dressed when the doorbell rang.

- Write your **story** on your answer sheet.

Part 1

Questions 1–7

There are seven questions in this part.
For each question, there are three pictures and a short recording.
Choose the correct picture and put a tick (✓) in the box below it.

Example: What will the boy take back to the shop?

A ✓

B ☐

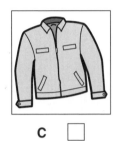

C ☐

---

1 Which band did the boy watch last night?

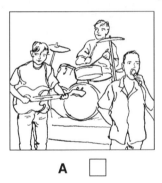

A ☐

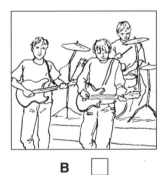

B ☐

C ☐

2 Where is the woman's new flat?

A ☐

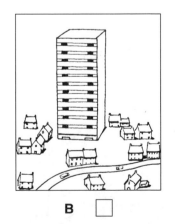

B ☐

C ☐

[Turn over

3 Where is the magazine?

A ☐

B ☐

C ☐

4 Which is the boy's teacher?

A ☐

B ☐

C ☐

5 What did the man receive in the post?

A ☐

B ☐

C ☐

6 What time is the flight from New York expected?

A ☐

B ☐

C ☐

7 What was the boy doing when the phone rang?

A ☐

B ☐

C ☐

Part 2

Questions 8–13

You will hear a woman talking to an evening class about carpentry.
For each question, put a tick (✓) in the correct box.

8 The speaker says that when she was at school, girls

    A were taught separately from boys. ☐

    B could do carpentry if they wanted to. ☐

    C were not allowed to do carpentry. ☐

9 Making her chest of drawers took

    A eighteen months. ☐

    B six months. ☐

    C two months. ☐

10 She first planned to put the chest of drawers

    A in the sitting room. ☐

    B in the bedroom. ☐

    C in the hall. ☐

11 What advice does she give about electric tools?

    A They are useful for some people. ☐

    B They are necessary for beginners. ☐

    C Only lazy people use them. ☐

12 She suggests that the first job should be something

    A small and simple. ☐

    B for a friend. ☐

    C which practises many skills. ☐

13 What does she suggest that the class should do first?

    A choose who they will work with ☐

    B decide what they need for one job ☐

    C discuss what they should do ☐

Part 3

You will hear someone talking on the radio about a fashion show.
For each question, fill in the missing information in the numbered space.

Fashion Show

Place: sports stadium

Date: (14) ....

Time: 7.30

Colour of clothes: grey or (15) ....

Talk: at 6.30 by a (16) ....

Clothes for sale: everything except (17) ....

Prize for best design: (18) ....

Buses: depart at 6 p.m. and 7 p.m. from outside (19) ....

Part 4

Questions 20–25

Look at the six sentences for this part.
You will hear a conversation between a boy, Ian, and a girl, Zoe, about a holiday.
Decide if each sentence is correct or incorrect.
If it is correct, put a tick (✓) in the box under **A** for **YES**.
If it is not correct, put a tick (✓) in the box under **B** for **NO**.

		A YES	B NO
20	Ian is going to visit relatives who live in Africa.	☐	☐
21	Zoe believes Namibia is a good place to visit.	☐	☐
22	Ian's parents insist he must go on holiday with them.	☐	☐
23	Zoe's father is unemployed.	☐	☐
24	Zoe's mother dislikes flying.	☐	☐
25	Ian suggests Zoe should visit Namibia with him.	☐	☐

Part 1

Take turns to be the examiner. Ask your partner questions to find out some information about each other.

Ask each other at least four of these questions:

- What's your name? Can you spell your surname for me?
- Where do you live?
- Is that near the city centre?
- Do you live in a house or a flat?
- Is it very old? Do you know when it was built?
- How many rooms does it have?
- Have you always lived there?

Part 2

Simulated situation: exchanging opinions, saying what you think other people would like

The examiner gives you both a picture. You do a task together.

Your class is on a trip to London for the day. Daniel, one of your classmates, couldn't come with you and you decide to take him a souvenir. Look at page 166. There are some ideas of souvenirs you could buy. Decide together what you will take. You can only take one thing.

Ask and answer questions like these:

- What do you think he would like?
- Would he prefer something to wear or something to look at?
- Would he like something to read?
- Would that be too heavy/expensive/easily broken?

Part 3

Responding to photographs: describing a place and what is happening

You take turns to tell each other about a photograph.

Candidate A: look at Photograph 5A on page 170.
Candidate B: look at Photograph 5B on page 173.

Think about your photograph for a few seconds. Describe it to your partner for about one minute.

Tell your partner about these things:

- what kind of place it is
- what the people are watching
- what the people are wearing
- whether they look comfortable/happy/excited
- what you can guess about the music.

Part 4

General conversation about the photographs: talking about music – likes and dislikes

The examiner asks you to talk to your partner.

Tell each other about the kind of music you like.

Use these ideas:

- talk about your favourite singer/band.
- say if you have ever seen them in a concert.
- say where you usually listen to music.
- say what kind of music you don't like.
- say if you play any instruments or sing or dance yourself.

TEST 6

Reading

Part 1

Questions 1–5

Look at the text in each question.
What does it say?
Mark the correct letter **A**, **B** or **C** on your answer sheet.

Example:

0

To	John
From	Nell

Can you call the cinema from home and check film time before leaving? Let me know what time we should get there.

John should

A   contact Nell after phoning the cinema.

B   ring Nell after arriving at the cinema.

C   go to the cinema to check when the film starts.

Answer: | 0 | **A** ▬ | **B** ▭ | **C** ▭ |

1

To	Jen
From	Angus

I've had a problem with the car. Can you get a taxi from the station and ring when you get to your hotel?

A   Angus wants Jen to telephone him from her hotel.

B   Angus wants Jen to take him to the hotel in a taxi.

C   Angus wants Jen to collect him from the station.

2

DO NOT USE EQUIPMENT IN THIS BOX BEFORE READING INSTRUCTIONS

A   Do not remove the equipment from the box before reading the instructions.

B   Read the instructions before using the equipment.

C   Put the equipment in the box after using it.

[Turn over

3

351 Bunting Ave, Trifford TR6 1AG
We're having a sale this weekend before moving house. Any reasonable offers accepted for unwanted furniture, washing machine, etc., toys and bikes.
10 – 5 Sat & Sun

A These people are selling things to get money for travelling.

B These people sell toys, furniture and bicycles.

C These people don't want to take all their furniture to their new home.

4

THE BUS DRIVER TAKES CASH ONLY.

THE TICKET OFFICE TAKES

CREDIT CARDS OR CASH.

A You cannot pay the bus driver with a credit card.

B The ticket office can give you change for the bus.

C It is not possible to buy a ticket with a credit card.

5

Mum, I wanted to wash my red jeans to wear tomorrow but they've disappeared. Did you do them? If you did, thanks but where have you put

A Tammie wants her mother to wash her jeans for her.

B Tammie is asking her mother where her jeans are.

C Tammie's mother promised to wash her jeans for her.

Part 2

Questions 6–10

The people below all want to find a summer holiday job.
On the opposite page there are advertisements for eight jobs.
Decide which job would be most suitable for the following people.
For questions **6–10**, mark the correct letter **(A–H)** on your answer sheet.

6  Tom is going abroad to learn German and French in October. He wants to spend July working for a newspaper or magazine. He would prefer to be in a large town or city.

7 Martha would like a job working with children under twelve. A friend is coming to stay for two weeks in early July, so she must be free then. She's happy to travel and can work until the autumn.

8 Sindy is looking for work in the evenings this summer. She enjoys talking to people, but she doesn't want to stand up all the time, as she already works in a restaurant during the day.

9 Aidan wants to find a job which provides a room to live in. He doesn't mind working long hours, but he must be free on Saturdays when he takes part in swimming competitions.

10  Nick needs a job for at least two months which pays well. He speaks English, Italian and Swedish and would like the chance to use them. He starts university on 5 October.

Summer jobs special

A **Dambury Journal** is looking for a keen young reporter to work full-time Tuesday–Sunday from our office in this picturesque little town for the summer. An opportunity to learn about journalism on this local newspaper which covers country life and events throughout the area. Accommodation can be arranged.

B ## Enjoy meeting new people?
Good with children?
You could be a travel guide for American tourists in Southern Europe and Scandinavia.
Newcaston Travel Ltd looks after small groups of children and teenagers and also families travelling in groups of up to twenty.
Excellent rates of pay (extra for foreign-language speakers).
Minimum six weeks, starting mid July.

C **Hotel Ferdinand, Dambury**, requires kitchen and dining-room staff for the summer. Six days per week (any day off by arrangement except Fridays). Hours from 2 p.m. till 10 p.m. or from 6 a.m. till 2 p.m. Also some part-time work (evenings only). Meals provided and some accommodation available if required.

D **Newcaston This Week ★ ★ ★**
The best new *What's On* guide to Newcaston needs lively young people to work at its main office, right in the centre of this great city, for one or two months this summer. Hours 10–6.
Experience in magazine journalism not necessary, but enthusiasm is! Ideal for students and school leavers.

E Friendly Australian family living near Newcaston requires help from mid-July to September. Four girls aged three to eleven, baby boy. We'll want you to spend about one month in France with us. Own room and bathroom. Two free days per week, some evening and weekend work. Good pay.

F **Dambury Summer Play Scheme** needs helpers from 8.30 a.m. till 5.30 p.m. Monday–Friday for nine weeks in July and August. You must be energetic, friendly and get on well with children. Cooking ability useful. Some days we will take trips to the seaside and return late evening. Good pay.

G **Newcaston University Summer School Hostel**
We are looking for a friendly efficient person to answer phone and e-mail enquiries, check application forms and occasionally show new visitors round. Daytime or evening (Monday–Saturday) until end of summer. Some accommodation may be available if required.

H **Teen Wheels Magazine** is looking for foreign language speakers to work in the telephone sales department from late August. You can earn lots of money selling advertising to companies in Europe and the US. Possibility of permanent job if required. Office in suburbs of Newcaston, easy access city centre.

Part 3

Look at the sentences below about unusual women of the past.
Read the text on the opposite page to decide if each sentence is correct or incorrect.
If it is correct, mark **A** on your answer sheet.
If it is not correct, mark **B** on your answer sheet.

---

11   The writer says many women joined armies before the twentieth century.

12   Christian Walsh wanted to marry a soldier.

13   Kit Cavanagh spent thirteen years in the army.

14   Kit fought the doctors when they tried to operate.

15   Anne Bonney went to the Bahamas to find John Rackham.

16   Anne helped John to get a fast ship.

17   Mary was already working on a ship before she met Anne.

18   Mary joined the army in order to be with her husband.

19   Anne and Mary went to prison after John Rackham.

20   It is uncertain what happened to Anne and Mary in the end.

Unusual women of the past

You may think that no women went to sea or joined the army until the twentieth century, but this is not true. Although they usually had to pretend to be men, there are a few true stories of woman who fought for both good reasons and bad ones.

One English woman soldier in the seventeenth century was Christian Walsh, the wife of a man who was made to join the army, although he did not want to be a soldier. Christian refused to accept the situation, unlike most women in those days. She cut off her hair, dressed as a man and joined the army, calling herself Kit Cavanagh, in order to look for her husband. It was thirteen years before she found him and during that time she fought in several different countries. She was only discovered to be a woman when doctors were operating on her for an injury she had received while fighting.

A rather different example, from around the same time, is Anne Bonney. It is not certain why she left Ireland, where she was born, and went to the islands which are now called the Bahamas. However, we know that when she got there, she fell in love with a sailor called John Rackham. She worked with John to steal a ship from the local port. They obviously chose the ship carefully, because it was the fastest one in the port at the time. For the next ten years they sailed round the Caribbean, attacking other ships and stealing everything valuable from them, as well as taking sailors to help on their own ship.

One day, Anne was surprised to discover that a boy they had taken off another ship in this way was really a young woman. She told Anne her name was Mary Read. She said she had dressed like a man to increase her opportunities, because in those days of course most women were expected to stay at home. Earlier, Mary had fought in the army, but had stopped pretending to be a man for a short time when she married a soldier who had realised that she was a woman. Unfortunately her husband died, and so Mary started to dress as a man once again and became a sailor.

Anne and Mary continued their criminal career with John Rackham, but in the end their ship was caught by the navy. The two women went on fighting even after all the men were taken prisoner, but they avoided punishment and disappeared. Nobody knows what happened to them after that. Perhaps they pretended to be men and joined another ship, or maybe they got married.

Part 4

Questions 21–25

Read the text and questions below.
For each question, mark the correct letter **A**, **B**, **C** or **D** on your answer sheet.

Living in the Ice Age

I'm a scientist and I arrived here in Antarctica three months ago in December. The temperature is cold but not unpleasant yet. Since arriving, I've worked with about 60 other people getting everything ready for the Antarctic winter. It's been a lot of hard work, but it was fun too. However, a few days ago the ship left taking most of the staff with it, and it won't be back to fetch us until next December. So the hardest thing to get used to is that there are now just fourteen of us because I'm used to working in a large company.

I'm living on the same work station I was on ten years ago. It was new then and it's still in good condition and unchanged. The dried food we get is also the same – you forget what real food tastes like after a few weeks. The people working here with me are all different from then, but I'm always happy getting to know new people. Ten years ago, we were able to send faxes to friends and family once a month, but today we can send e-mails and talk on the phone so we don't feel so far away.

Last week we went out exploring for a few days. We slept in our very thick sleeping bags to keep the cold out. We always have to wear the right clothes and boots for walking on ice and snow. We were joined together by a rope all the time in case we fell into any holes in the ice. They're too deep to climb out of. The skies were clear and I was reminded how lucky I am to be here. Soon we will get amazing sunsets too.

21 What is the writer trying to do?

   A   persuade people to work in Antarctica

   B   complain about his life in Antarctica

   C   describe his own experiences in Antarctica

   D   suggest ways of improving life in Antarctica

22 What is difficult for the writer at the moment?

   A   He is working with a small number of people.

   B   There is too much work to do.

   C   The weather is too cold.

   D   The ship won't return for months.

23 In the writer's opinion, what has improved since ten years ago?

   A   The living accommodation is better.

   B   The food is more tasty.

   C   Communications have improved.

   D   His colleagues are easier to work with.

24 What particular danger was there when they were exploring?

   A   the cold

   B   the holes in the ice

   C   getting lost

   D   slipping on the ice

25 Which of the following e-mails did the writer send to a friend?

A

> I'm getting used to being in Antarctica. Although people had told me what it was like, it's still a shock to experience it myself.

B

> There hasn't been much to do here yet, so I've spent the time getting to know my colleagues and relaxing.

C

> It's good to be back here. I'd forgotten how beautiful it is. I'm looking forward to seeing some wonderful sunsets.

D

> I'll send you my news as often as I can. It won't be long till I'm home, as I've already been here nearly a year.

Part 5

Questions 26–35

Read the text below and choose the correct word for each space.
For each question, mark the correct letter **A**, **B**, **C** or **D** on your answer sheet.

Example:

0 **A** doubt   **B** chance   **C** way   **D** matter

Answer:

0	A	B	C	D
	■	☐	☐	☐

Fashions go round and round

Fashions have always changed with time. No **(0)** .... Roman girls worried
about having the latest hairstyle and boys in Ancient Egypt wanted to have sandals
(26) .... were cool and not the sensible ones their mothers preferred.

Looking **(27)** .... over recent times, there seem to be two main differences in the
(28) .... fashions have changed compared to earlier times. Firstly, **(29)** ....
more people have a choice of clothes available to them. There are few places
(30) .... the world where the trainers, the caps or the T-shirts of teenagers do not
change from one year to the next. Secondly, styles are **(31)** .... within a much
shorter time than they **(32)** .... to be. For instance, in the 1960s, **(33)** .... had
the same low waists and narrow skirts as forty years before.

In the early years of the 21st century, the shops are **(34)** .... of long skirts and
coloured scarves like the ones in fashion only thirty years before. Soon, we will find that
the really fashionable people look no different from the **(35)** .... of us, because it is
only ten years since their clothes were in fashion before!

26	**A** they	**B** that	**C** these	**D** those
27	**A** about	**B** round	**C** back	**D** behind
28	**A** sort	**B** kind	**C** type	**D** way
29	**A** some	**B** much	**C** far	**D** even
30	**A** in	**B** on	**C** of	**D** through
31	**A** accepted	**B** returned	**C** exchanged	**D** repeated
32	**A** wanted	**B** needed	**C** used	**D** had
33	**A** dresses	**B** jackets	**C** trousers	**D** blouses
34	**A** filling	**B** filled	**C** full	**D** fuller
35	**A** other	**B** most	**C** rest	**D** all

Writing

Part 1

Questions 1–5

Here are some sentences about a new pop group.
For each question, complete the second sentence so that it means the same as the first.
Use no more than three words.
Write only the missing words on your answer sheet.
You may use this page for any rough work.

Example:

0   The group is called *Fireworks*.

   The name of .... *Fireworks*.

Answer: | **0** | the group is |
---

1   The new pop group was discovered by a television producer.

   A television producer .... **the new pop group.**

2   The singer was a waiter before he joined this group.

   Before .... **this group, the singer was a waiter.**

3   The women aren't such good musicians as the men.

   The men are .... **musicians than the women.**

4   The women all dance brilliantly.

   The women .... **dancers.**

5   I couldn't afford a ticket for their concert.

   The tickets for their concert cost .... **for me.**

Part 2

Question 6

You have an English friend called Lee. You are both going to another friend's birthday party next week.

Write an e-mail to Lee. In your e-mail, you should

- say how you will get there
- suggest you go together
- ask him for advice about a present.

Write **35–45 words** on your answer sheet.

Part 3

Write an answer to **one** of the questions (**7** or **8**) in this part.
Write your answer in about **100 words** on your answer sheet.
Put the question number in the box at the top of your answer sheet.

Question 7

- This is part of a letter you receive from an English penfriend.

> *I always go shopping with my friends at the weekend. What do you like buying when you go shopping? What kind of shops are there near where you live?*

- Now write a letter answering your penfriend's questions.

- Write your **letter** on your answer sheet.

Question 8

- Your English teacher has asked you to write a story.

- Your story must begin with this sentence:

  I got off the train and waved to my brother, who was waiting on the platform.

- Write your **story** on your answer sheet.

Part 1

Questions 1–7

There are seven questions in this part.
For each question, there are three pictures and a short recording.
Choose the correct picture and put a tick (✓) in the box below it.

Example: What will the boy take back to the shop?

A ✓   B ☐   C ☐

---

1 Which instrument is the girl learning now?

A ☐   B ☐   C ☐

2 What will they buy for Lucy?

A ☐   B ☐   C ☐

[Turn over

3 What will the weather be like on Sunday?

A ☐

B ☐

C ☐

4 What did the boy leave in the girl's house?

A ☐

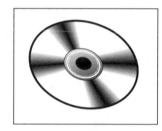

B ☐

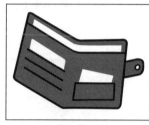

C ☐

5 What will the boy get from the shop?

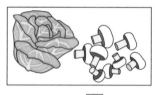

A ☐

B ☐

C ☐

6 Which sport is unavailable today?

A ☐

B ☐

C ☐

7 What is the girl wearing?

A ☐

B ☐

C ☐

Part 2

Questions 8–13

You will hear a radio interview with a teenage boy called Matthew who has invented a game.
For each question, put a tick (✓) in the correct box.

8 How old was Matthew when his game
   was first sold?

   A ten ☐

   B thirteen ☐

   C fourteen ☐

9 When Matthew tried to sell his idea to companies,

   A he had no replies. ☐

   B some companies asked to see the game. ☐

   C none of them was interested. ☐

10 Matthew borrowed money from

   A a bank. ☐

   B some relatives. ☐

   C a businessman. ☐

11 How did Matthew get his idea for a
   second product?

   A An American company made a suggestion. ☐

   B Some other children told him about it. ☐

   C He watched his sisters playing. ☐

12 According to Matthew, most ten-year-olds
   are interested in

   A games which test what they know. ☐

   B games which are about their everyday lives. ☐

   C games which use their imagination. ☐

13 When Matthew leaves school, he wants to

   A run his own business. ☐

   B do a course in business studies. ☐

   C continue inventing games. ☐

Part 3

You will hear a radio announcer giving some information about a cycling holiday with Pathway Holidays. For each question, fill in the missing information in the numbered space.

Pathway Holidays

<u>Monday 12 June – Saturday 17 June</u>

Cycle from Whitehaven to Sunderland in England

The total length of the ride is **(14)** .... kms.

The highest place on the ride is **(15)** .... Hill.

The price includes accommodation, food, luggage transport and a

(16) ....

It is recommended that you bring your own **(17)** ....

On Friday evening there is a **(18)** ....

Information available from the **(19)** ....

Part 4

Questions 20–25

Look at the six sentences for this part.
You will hear a conversation between a girl, Jane, and her mother about where Jane will work next month.
Decide if each sentence is correct or incorrect.
If it is correct, put a tick (✓) in the box under **A** for **YES**.
If it is not correct, put a tick (✓) in the box under **B** for **NO**.

	A YES	B NO
20 Jane is leaving school next week.	☐	☐
21 Jane's mother is unhappy about Jane working in her office.	☐	☐
22 Jane has met her mother's colleagues before.	☐	☐
23 Jane is uncertain about what career she wants.	☐	☐
24 Jane is interested in working in a school with her friends.	☐	☐
25 In the end, Jane's mother agrees to take her to work.	☐	☐

PAPER 3 Speaking Test (10–12 minutes)

Part 1

General conversation: saying who you are, giving personal information, spelling

Take turns to be the examiner. Ask your partner questions to find out some information about each other.

Ask each other at least four of these questions:

- What's your name?
- What do you like doing at weekends?
- What do you do when you have free time at home?
- Where do you go to meet your friends?
- How often do you go shopping?
- Who helps you to choose your clothes?
- Can you spell the name of your favourite shop for me, please?

Part 2

Simulated situation: exchanging information and giving opinions

The examiner gives you both a picture. You do a task together.

You've won a competition to learn a new skill. You're going to do a course together for one week. Look at page 167. You have a choice of seven courses. Decide together which one you will choose. Think about what you can do already and what you would like to learn.

Ask and answer questions like these:

- Can you do any of these things already?
- Which of these things would you like to learn?
- Which courses do you not want to do?
- Which course would be most useful/fun/interesting?

Part 3

Responding to photographs: describing where people are and what they are doing.

You take turns to tell each other about a photograph.

Candidate A: look at Photograph 6A on page 170.
Candidate B: look at Photograph 6B on page 173.

Think about your photograph for a few seconds. Describe it to your partner for about one minute.

Tell your partner about these things:

- what kind of place it is
- what you can see there
- what the people look like
- what the people are doing/buying
- whether they are all enjoying what they are doing.

Part 4

General conversation about the photographs: talking about likes, dislikes and preferences

The examiner asks you to talk to your partner. You give your opinion about something and explain what you prefer.

Talk to each other about earning money.

Use these ideas:

- Say whether you have a job or have ever had one.
- Say what you do (or did) and what you feel about doing it.
- Say what kind of job you would like to have.
- Say why you think you would enjoy it.
- Say how you would spend the money you earn.

Extra practice for Writing Part 1

Here are some sentences about a motorbike.
For each question, complete the second sentence so that it means the same as the first.
Use no more than three words.
Write only the missing words on your answer sheet.
You may use this page for any rough work.

Example:

0   This is my brother's motorbike.

   This motorbike .... **my brother.**

Answer:

0	belongs to

---

1   He's only had it for two weeks.

   He only .... **two weeks ago.**

2   One of his friends sold it to him.

   A friend .... **sold it to him.**

3   It wasn't very expensive.

   It didn't .... **much.**

4   I asked him if I could have a ride on it.

   I said ' .... **a ride on it?'**

5   It's essential to wear a helmet when you ride it.

   You .... **a helmet when you ride it.**

Here are some sentences about a winter holiday.
For each question, complete the second sentence so that it means the same as the first.
Use no more than three words.
Write only the missing words on your answer sheet.
You may use this page for any rough work.

6   Sunbathing isn't as much fun as skiing.

   Skiing is .... **sunbathing.**

7   I was taught to ski by my mother.

   My mother .... **to ski.**

8   She advised me to do some exercises first.

   She said, 'You .... **do some exercises first.'**

9   My father doesn't ski now, but he did when he was young.

   My father .... **ski when he was young.**

10 He says he doesn't have enough time to come with us.

   He says he's too .... **to come with us.**

Extra language for all parts of the Speaking Test

1 When you don't understand:

Could you say that again, please?

Could you repeat that, please?

Please can you explain what you want me to do?

I'm afraid I don't understand what you want me/us to do.

I'm sorry, what does .... mean?

I'm sorry, I don't understand what you mean.

2 When you don't know the name of something:

I don't know the word for this in English.

It's like a box.

It's similar to a CD.

You use it to make a hole in a wall.

3 Giving yourself time to think what to say:

Well, I suppose, my opinion is that . . .

I'm not really sure what to say, but . . .

It's difficult to say, but . . .

Let me think for a moment . . .

Extra language for Part 1 of the Speaking Test

4 Introducing yourself:

I'm Maria Gonzalez.

My name's Maria Gonzalez.

I'm called Maria Gonzalez.

But my friends call me Mari.

5 Giving information about yourself:

Your family:

I'm from a large/small family.

I have two (younger) brothers and a(n older) sister.

I'm an only child.

Your home:

We live in a flat/house in ....

My grandmother also lives with us.

I share a flat with some other students.

Your job/studies:

I live/work/go to school in . . .

I'm studying at high school/university.

I'm training to be an engineer.

I'm a nurse.

Your free time:

In my spare time I play computer games.

I do a lot of sport.

My hobby is photography.

I don't have much free time, but when I do I like to . . .

Extra language for Part 2 of the Speaking Test

6 Making suggestions:

What about going clubbing?

Shall we buy a ticket?

We could hire bicycles.

I think we should catch a bus.

It would be a good idea to take our mobiles.

Why don't we take a picnic?

Let's have a party.

Would you like to go to the cinema?

7 Agreeing:

I agree with you.

I completely agree.

That's (probably) right.

You could be right.

Definitely!

Sure!

8 Disagreeing:

I can't agree with that.

In my opinion, that's quite wrong.

I don't really agree with you about that.

I see what you mean, but I think . . .

9 Asking someone else for their ideas:

What about you?

So, what do you think?

Do you agree?

How do you feel about this?

10 Accepting that your opinion is different from someone else's:

I don't think we can agree about this.

We both have our own opinions about it.

My opinion/experience isn't the same as yours.

Let's agree to disagree about that.

Extra language for Part 3 of the Speaking Test

11 Saying where a place is:

It's near/not far from/a long way from here.

It's in the city/in the country/in the mountains/on the coast.

It's north of here.

It's about twenty kilometres south of here.

It's in the west of the country.

12 Saying where something is in a picture:

It's in the background/foreground/the middle.

It's on the left/right.

It's at the top/bottom.

13 Saying where people are:

They're in a shop/in a café/in a hotel/in the city centre/in a taxi.

They're on a bus/train/plane.

They're at home/at work/at school/at the theatre/at the beach.

14 Describing people:

He's (quite/very) tall/short/fat/thin.

He's got dark hair.

She's wearing blue jeans.

15 Making guesses:

They look happy to me.

They look like brothers.

They could be friends.

They may be students.

They seem bored.

Perhaps they've lost something.

Maybe they need a lift.

It's possible that they're strangers.

They're probably enjoying themselves.

16 Explaining your opinion:

I (don't) think/believe he's happy because he's (not) smiling.

She must be tired because she's yawning.

Extra language for Part 4 of the Speaking Test

17 Saying what you like:

I like/love watching music videos.

I prefer swimming to cycling.

I'd rather play volleyball than write a letter.

My favourite colour is pink.

and dislike:

I don't really like cooking.

I'm not very keen on westerns.

I hate doing housework.

I never enjoy long journeys.

18 Talking about plans:

I want to go to university.

I'm planning to travel abroad.

I'm hoping to become a teacher.

I'm going to study engineering.

I think I'll probably get a job.

I'm not sure what I'm going to do.

Visuals for Speaking Test

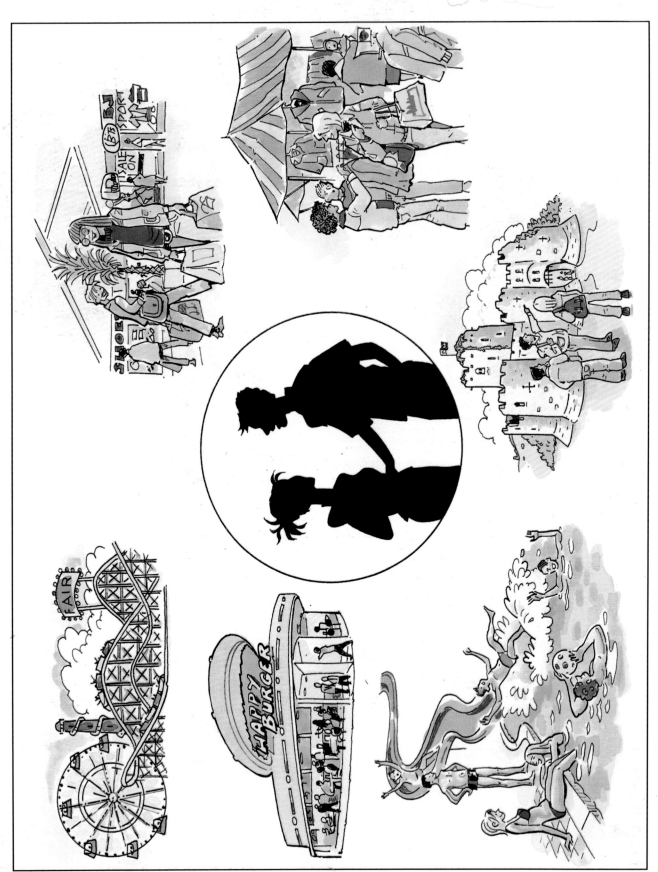

Test 1, Part 2

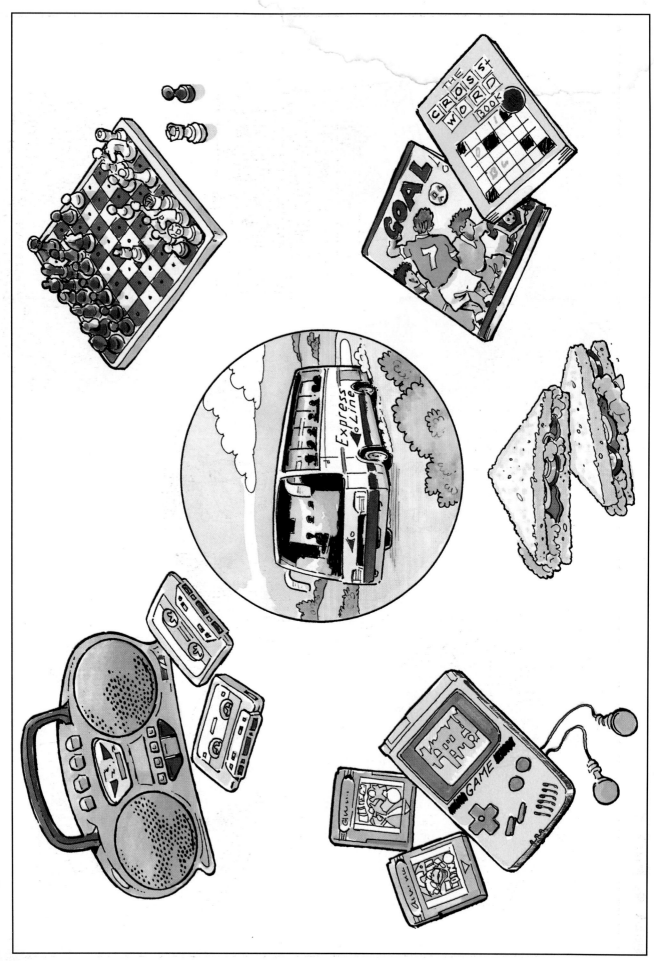

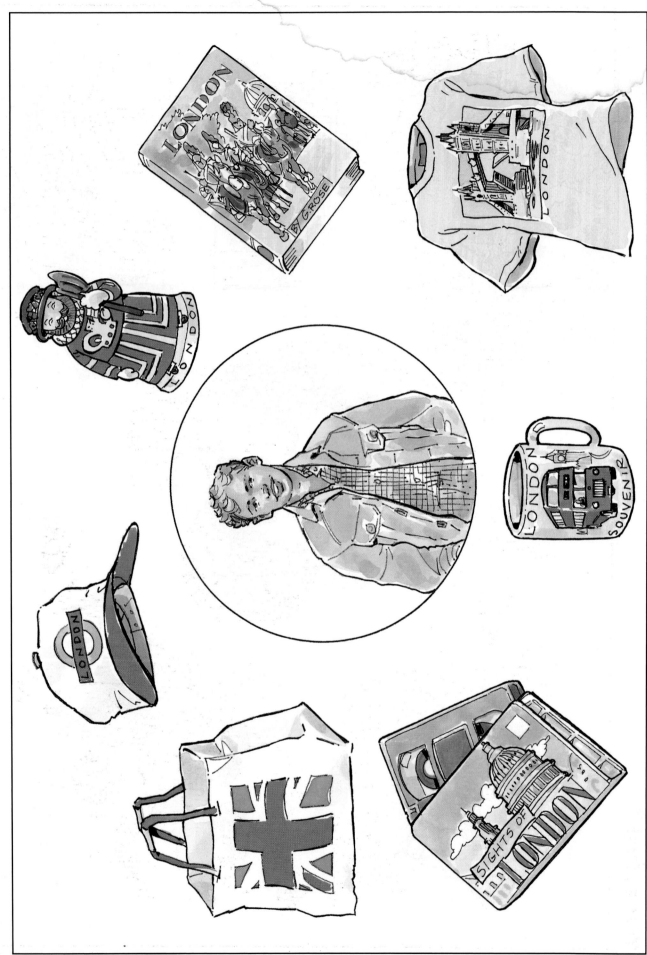

Test 1, Part 3, Photograph 1A

Test 2, Part 3, Photograph 2A

Test 3, Part 3, Photograph 3A

Test 4, Part 3, Photograph 4A

Test 5, Part 3, Photograph 5A

Test 6, Part 3, Photograph 6A

Test 1, Part 3, Photograph 1B

Test 2, Part 3, Photograph 2B

Test 3, Part 3, Photograph 3B

Test 4, Part 3, Photograph 4B

Test 5, Part 3, Photograph 5B

Test 6, Part 3, Photograph 6B

Candidate Name
If not already printed, write name in CAPITALS and complete the Candidate No. grid (in pencil).

Candidate Signature ....

Examination Title

Centre

Supervisor:
If the candidate is ABSENT or has WITHDRAWN shade here ☐

Centre No.

Candidate No.

Examination Details

SAMPLE

PET Paper 1 Reading and Writing Candidate Answer Sheet 1

Instructions

Use a PENCIL (B or HB).

Rub out any answer you want to change with an eraser.

For Reading:
Mark ONE letter for each question.
For example, if you think **A** is the right answer to the question, mark your answer sheet like this:

0 ⟨A⟩ B C D

Part 1	Part 2	Part 3	Part 4	Part 5
1 A B C	6 A B C D E F G H	11 A B	21 A B C D	26 A B C D
2 A B C	7 A B C D E F G H	12 A B	22 A B C D	27 A B C D
3 A B C	8 A B C D E F G H	13 A B	23 A B C D	28 A B C D
4 A B C	9 A B C D E F G H	14 A B	24 A B C D	29 A B C D
5 A B C	10 A B C D E F G H	15 A B	25 A B C D	30 A B C D
		16 A B		31 A B C D
		17 A B		32 A B C D
		18 A B		33 A B C D
		19 A B		34 A B C D
		20 A B		35 A B C D

Continue on the other side of this sheet →

 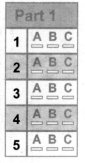

SAMPLE

Part 3: Mark the number of the question you are answering here → Q7 ☐ or Q8 ☐
Write your answer below.

Do not write below this line

This section for use by SECOND Examiner only

Mark:

0	1.1	1.2	1.3	2.1	2.2	2.3	3.1	3.2	3.3	4.1	4.2	4.3	5.1	5.2	5.3

Examiner Number:

| 0 1 2 3 4 5 6 7 8 9 |
| 0 1 2 3 4 5 6 7 8 9 |
| 0 1 2 3 4 5 6 7 8 9 |
| 0 1 2 3 4 5 6 7 8 9 |

SAMPLE

For **Writing** (Parts 1 and 2):

Write your answers clearly in the spaces provided.

Part 1: Write your answers below.

Do not write here

1	1 1 0
2	1 2 0
3	1 3 0
4	1 4 0
5	1 5 0

Part 2 (Question 6): Write your answer below.

Put your answer to Writing Part 3 on Answer Sheet 2 →

Do not write below (Examiner use only)

0	1	2	3	4	5

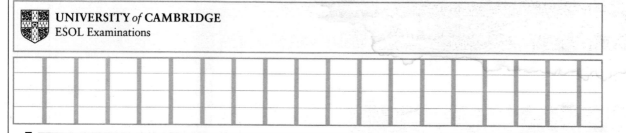

Candidate Name
If not already printed, write name
in CAPITALS and complete the
Candidate No. grid (in pencil).

Candidate Signature

Examination Title

Centre

Supervisor:

If the candidate is ABSENT or has WITHDRAWN the h...

Centre No.

Candidate No.

Examination Details

SAMPLE

PET Paper 2 Listening Candidate Answer Sheet

You must transfer all your answers from the Listening Question Paper to this answer sheet.

Instructions

Use a PENCIL (B or HB).

Rub out any answer you want to change with an eraser.

For **Parts 1, 2** and **4:**
Mark ONE letter for each question.
For example, if you think **A** is the right answer to the question, mark your answer sheet like this:

| 0 | A̶ B C |

For **Part 3:**
Write your answers clearly in the spaces next
to the numbers (14 to 19) like this:

| 0 | example |

Part 1	Part 2	Part 3	Do not write here	Part 4
1 A B C	8 A B C	14	1 14 0	20 A B
2 A B C	9 A B C	15	1 15 0	21 A B
3 A B C	10 A B C	16	1 16 0	22 A B
4 A B C	11 A B C	17	1 17 0	23 A B
5 A B C	12 A B C	18	1 18 0	24 A B
6 A B C	13 A B C	19	1 19 0	25 A B
7 A B C				

PET L   Print Director Limited 01384 241442   DP493/391

©UCLES   Photocopiable

Teacher's guide and answer key

Test 1

PAPER 1 Reading

Part 1

Teacher's notes

- In Part 1, the texts are signs, notices, labels, e-mails, phone messages, handwritten notes, messages on Post-it notes or postcards. The signs and notices are mostly ones seen in public places, for example in shops, libraries, stations, hotels, theatres, museums, schools, etc. and on public vehicles such as buses and trains. Sometimes there is a label from a bottle or packet or a notice on a school or public noticeboard.
- The signs often give instructions, warnings or information.
- Language in signs is usually quite formal, but certain words like *the*, *a(n)* and the auxiliary verb *to be* are often omitted.
- The messages are informal and usually make or change arrangements, ask someone to do something, ask for information, etc.

A photocopiable answer sheet is on page 174.

Strategy

1
1 five
2 what each text says
3 on the answer sheet (but see second Exam tip!)

2
1 b) a sign.
2 In a room in a school.
3 *You mustn't; out of this room; without asking.*
4 Because the sign is about *moving* computers, not using them.
5 Because it's about moving them *from* the room, not into it.

3
1 a) an e-mail .
2 no
3 yes – she says *I've found my card.*
4 to bring her student card because her ticket will cost less
5 no, at the ticket office before they get on the train
6 in the ticket queue
7 C means the same as the message. *See you in queue at ticket office* tells you they will meet before they get on the train.
8 A Katie tells Emily to bring her student card so Emily can buy her own ticket. Katie says she will meet Emily in the queue so she isn't going to buy Emily's ticket.
   B Katie's train ticket will cost the same as Emily's if they both have their student cards. If Emily forgets her card, her ticket will cost more than Katie's because Katie has found her card.

Reading Part 1 key

1 C
2 C *for use by visiting team only* = members of the local swimming team can't use these lockers
3 A *ring him before six* = she phones James by six
4 C *staff* = people who work here; *after 5 p.m.* = in the evening
5 B *can you ring Mum and ask her?* = find out; *then please post it* = send the letter

Language practice: Reading Part 1

1 Grammar: modal verbs *(may, must/mustn't, should/shouldn't, needn't)*
c) 1 must
   2 mustn't
   3 needn't
   4 should
   5 may
   6 shouldn't

2 Writing: words left out
1 In **an** emergency, use **the** telephone in **the** hall to call **the** hostel manager.
2 Don't forget to take **your** towel with you to **(the)** football practice tonight.
3 Read **the** instructions before **the** equipment is switched on.
4 **We're/I'm** having **a** lovely time in Spain. **The** weather **is** wonderful.
5 If **a** receipt **is** needed, ask **the** assistant when **you are** paying.

3 Grammar: *if/unless* sentences (real situations)
a) 1 present; future
   2 future; present
   3 future; present
   unless = if not

b) 1 b
   2 e
   3 f
   4 a
   5 c
   6 d

c) *Suggested answers:*
   1 there's a good film on.
   2 I won't get a good mark.
   3 you like it.
   4 we'll go to the café.
   5 I'll be tired tomorrow.

Part 2

Teacher's notes

- Part 2 tests students' detailed comprehension of factual information.
- The eight short texts are about one topic. They may be from tourist brochures, information leaflets, catalogues, etc.
- There are always three texts which are not needed.
- There is only one answer to each question.
- Each text can be used only once as an answer.

- The pictures are there to help students understand the descriptions.
- Students should be advised not to write on the answer sheet until they have answered all the questions in case they change their minds.

A photocopiable answer sheet is on page 174.

Strategy

1
1 five
2 to find somewhere to stay
3 hotels
4 eight
5 which hotel would be most suitable for each of the people
6 on the answer sheet (but see Teacher's note above)

2
6 a young couple and their son
7 a young man
8 a middle-aged woman
9 a young couple
10 a couple with 3 children

3
1 in the city centre near the railway station
2 No, they're with their one-year-old son.
3 walk everywhere
4 in restaurants

b)
7 Giorgos wants to be able to <u>swim</u> but is <u>not</u> interested in <u>other sports</u>. He'd like to spend the weekend somewhere <u>quiet</u> in the <u>country</u>. The hotel must have a <u>car park</u>.
8 Monica would like to stay somewhere in the <u>countryside</u> where there are <u>organised activities</u> so that she can meet other people. As she has some work to do, <u>e-mail</u> facilities must be available.
9 Julia and Robert are travelling by <u>car</u> and want to <u>park</u> at their hotel. They <u>don't want</u> to be <u>further than ten kilometres</u> from the city. They want to <u>swim</u> every day and have <u>dinner at the hotel</u>.
10 Adam and Barbara need to stay somewhere in the <u>city</u> which provides <u>lunch and dinner</u> and has a <u>car park</u>. Their three <u>children</u> all enjoy <u>sport</u>.
(Now students can see which people want to stay in the city and which people want to stay in the country. They can also see which facilities the people want.)

4
a) 1 D, E, G
   2 G It's near the railway station, near restaurants and is a family hotel.

Reading Part 2 key
6 G
7 F middle of the hills; peaceful; swimming pool; car park
8 B between two farms; dances and other events; popular with people travelling alone; internet cafe
9 D one kilometre from city centre; car park; swimming pool in the next street; dinner is available
10 A a five-minute drive from the city centre; gym, tennis courts; guests can eat all their meals here; car park

---

Language practice: Reading Part 2

1 Vocabulary: hotel facilities
1 swimming pool
2 television in room
3 car park
4 tennis courts
5 telephone in room
6 bicycles for hire
7 lift
8 restaurant
9 entertainment
10 gym
11 garden
12 golf
13 railway station – 5 mins
14 city centre – 3 kms

2 Grammar: linking words
a) 1 B
   2 A
   3 A
   4 C
   5 B
   6 B

b) 1 Parking is available in the street, but it is sometimes difficult to find a space. / Although parking is available in the street, it is sometimes difficult to find a space.
   2 The rooms at the front are very popular because / since / as they have lovely views of the sea.
   3 I like to eat dinner in my hotel, so I choose hotels which have a restaurant
   4 Hotels usually offer lunch and dinner, while guesthouses often serve only breakfast.

3 Vocabulary: prepositions
1 on; of
2 near
3 in
4 between
5 from
6 of; in
7 with
8 in

4 Grammar: present perfect and past simple
a) 1 a week
   2 every day
   3 twice
   4 no
   5 two days ago

b) 1 c
   2 a
   3 b

c) 1 we've/we have stayed
   2 've/have been
   3 've/have never ridden
   4 I played
   5 haven't had

Part 3
Teacher's notes

- In Part 3, students' ability to scan a text is tested.
- The text may give information, for example about a holiday or a course, or it may be a set of instructions.
- The sentences come in the same order as the information in the text.
- Students do not need to understand everything to answer the questions. For example, they may not know the word *deposit*, but this sentence is not tested.

- Students can sometimes guess the meaning of a word by reading the words around it. For example, they may not know *squash racket*, but from the sentence they can guess that it is used for an indoor sport.

A photocopiable answer sheet is on page 174.

Strategy

1
1 ten
2 a company which organises sports camps
3 the text
4 if each sentence is correct or incorrect
5 if the sentence is correct
6 if the sentence is incorrect

2
a) 17   f) 18
b) 15   g) 11
c) 20   h) 16
d) 12   i) 19
e) 14   j) 13

Reading Part 3 key

11 B
12 A
13 B *sport for all, not just for those who are brilliant at athletics.*
14 B *unnecessary to bring any equipment*
15 A *we do all come together for social activities and meals.*
16 A *but some of the assistants ... are students*
17 B *Most of the places are recommended to us, but not all, so we are not responsible for the quality*
18 B *one month before your camp.*
19 A *you are charged 2.5% extra by us if you pay with your credit card.*
20 A *Fifty per cent of the fee is refunded if a cancellation is made up to two weeks before*

Language practice: Reading Part 3

1 Vocabulary: negative adjectives
b) 1 Some of the staff are unqualified.
   2 It is impossible for us to arrange other accommodation.
   3 Luxury accommodation is unavailable near our camps.
   4 Some of the other guests were untidy people.
   5 It's unsafe to go on a boat if you can't swim.
   6 His answer was incorrect.

2 Vocabulary: words with similar meanings
1 shut – closed
2 staff – employees
3 return – take back
4 reserve – book
5 cheaper – less expensive
6 forbidden – not allowed
7 complete – fill in
8 recommends – advises

3 Grammar: the passive
b) 1 invite bands from all over the world.
   2 attend the festival every year.
   3 sells tickets.
   4 gave me a ticket.
   5 offered me a lift in his car.

c) 1 were told where to put our tent (by a man).
   2 was provided by the campsite owner.
   3 wasn't spoiled by the bad weather.
   4 were asked to take all our rubbish away with us (by the organisers).
   5 were woken up too early by the people in the next tent.

4 Vocabulary: sports
a) 1 table tennis
   2 sailing
   3 windsurfing
   4 climbing
   5 volleyball
   6 horse-riding

b) boat – sailing
   rope – climbing
   board – windsurfing
   bat – table tennis
   net – volleyball
   hat – horse-riding

5 Speaking: your experiences (2)
a)

	staff	accommodation	activities	weather
boring	✔		✔	
cold				✔
comfortable		✔		
warm				✔
helpful	✔			
interesting			✔	
rainy				✔
sunny				✔
friendly	✔			

b) uncomfortable, unhelpful, uninteresting, unfriendly

Part 4
Teacher's notes

- In Part 4, the text always gives an opinion as well as information.
- Some of the questions ask about the whole text and some ask about one part of the text. For each question, help students to decide how much of the text they need to look at in order to find the answer.
- The questions are not in the same order as the information in the text.
- Question 21 is always a general question.
- Questions 22, 23 and 24 ask about a detail in the text or the opinion of the writer or someone else who is mentioned.
- Question 25 is general. It can sometimes be a picture, poster, etc.
- Encourage students to read the text quickly to get an idea what it is about before looking at the questions. Then students should read the text again much more carefully.

A photocopiable answer sheet is on page 174.

Strategy

1
1 the text and questions
2 mark the correct letter, A, B, C or D
3 on your answer sheet

2
1 He's an artist.
2 He works at home.
3 No.

3
1 why
2 feelings
3 thoughts
4 usually does
5 might do

Language practice: Reading Part 4

1 Language focus: feelings
1 +   2 +   3 –   4 +   5 –   6 –   7 –   8 –   9 –   10 +

2 Grammar: expressions with -ing
Suggested answers:
1 going to clubs.
2 doing my homework.
3 watching television.
4 going out at the weekend.
5 tidying my bedroom.
6 doing grammar exercises.
7 passing my exams.
8 learning languages.
9 getting up early.
10 finishing this exercise.

4 Vocabulary: jobs
a) 1 postman/woman
    2 shop assistant
    3 disc jockey
    4 chef
    5 footballer
    6 architect

b) 2 A shop assistant serves customers.
    3 A disc jockey plays records.
    4 A chef cooks meals.
    5 A footballer scores goals.
    6 An architect designs buildings.

Part 5

Teacher's notes

- The questions in Part 5 test either lexical or structural knowledge.
- Students should be advised to write their answers in the spaces in the text first, as this will help them to grasp the overall meaning. They can transfer their answers when they have read the whole text and checked their answers.
- Point out that there can only be one word which fits each space. For example, in Question 32, *a variety* makes sense, but *variety* on its own does not make sense, so B is wrong.
- Sometimes an English word may look like a similar word in another language but mean something different, so students should look carefully at all four options. If they choose too quickly, they might make mistakes.
- Students should check that they have chosen the right kind of word for each space. In Question 30, a comparative form is needed because *than* comes later in the sentence, so only *more* will fit.
- They can mark A, B, C or D on the exam paper and copy them to the answer sheet later.

A photocopiable answer sheet is on page 174.

Strategy

1
1 the text
2 the correct word for each space
3 on the answer sheet (but see Teacher's note above)

2
It will probably include 2, 4 and 6.
It may also talk about 1.
It's unlikely to mention 3 and 5.

3
The reviewer mentions everything except 1, 3 and 5.

4
1 A
2 Only *enjoyed* can be followed by *reading it*. The other three words would be used to describe someone's feelings: *I was pleased/amused/delighted by the book.*

Language practice: Reading Part 5

1 Vocabulary: similar meanings
1	A	6	B
2	D	7	D
3	A	8	A
4	C	9	C
5	B	10	C

2 Grammar: comparative forms
a) 1 than
    2 more
    3 as/so ... as
    4 less ... than
    5 much

b) 1 less friendly than
    2 as often/much as
    3 more exciting than
    4 more expensive than
    5 more than

3 Grammar: *too/very/enough*; *so/such ... that*
a) 1 very
    2 too/very
    3 too
    4 enough
    5 enough

b) 1 d
    2 e
    3 a
    4 c
    5 b

c) 1 enough money
    2 so good
    3 so noisy
    4 too warm
    5 loud enough

4 Vocabulary: books

a)
1	NF	6	NF
2	F	7	F
3	NF	8	NF
4	NF	9	F
5	F		

PAPER 1 Writing

Part 1

Teacher's notes

- In Part 1, students have to rewrite five sentences using different structural patterns but retaining the same meaning.
- The answer may require one, two or three words. One or two-word answers are common, and students should understand that three words will be wrong in some cases.
- The five sentences and the example are always about the same topic.
- It is extremely important that grammar and spelling are completely correct in this part.
- Remind students not to forget punctuation in names, etc.
- Encourage students to write straight onto the answer sheet if they feel confident, as this will save time and avoid copying errors. If they prefer, they can try out their ideas on the exam paper first.
- If students want to change something they have written, they should cross it out tidily rather than using (brackets).
- Encourage students to read through and check their work when they have finished.

A photocopiable answer sheet is on page 175.

Strategy

1
1 five (and an example)
2 a guesthouse
3 complete the second sentence so that it means the same as the first
4 no more than three
5 on the answer sheet (but see Teacher's note above)
6 only the missing words
7 on the exam paper

2
1 It tells us that there is a games room in the guesthouse.
2 Yes, it does. The first sentence uses *There is*, the second sentence uses *has*, but the information is the same.

3
1 what the guesthouse is called
2 *The name ... is 'Sunshine Cottage'.*
3 of the guesthouse

Writing Part 1 key	
1	of the guesthouse
2	I've/I have stayed
3	told me
4	must book
5	as/so big as

Language practice: Writing Part 1

1 Grammar: matching patterns
a) and **b)**
2,8 = d)
3,5 = a)
4,9 = b)
6,11 = c)
10,12 = e)

c)
1 needn't pay
2 gave her
3 should rest
4 have/'ve never been
5 has
6 delayed
7 was called
8 doesn't have/hasn't got
9 heavier
10 as/so interesting as

2 Correcting mistakes
1 This car isn't **big enough** for my family. (word order)
2 My uncle **owns** that factory. (tense – the first sentence is present simple passive)
3 There **are** several pleasant parks in the town. (plural verb)
4 This is the first time **I've visited** an internet café. (tense after *first time*)
5 You **needn't** book a ticket for this show. (wrong verb giving wrong meaning)

Part 2

For a marking guide, see page 202.

Teacher's notes

- In Part 2, students write a short note or e-mail. If students are not used to e-mail, they should be reassured that as far as PET is concerned, it means the same as a note.
- The instructions always say who they are writing to, why they are writing and what they must say.
- There are always three things they must mention to get full marks.
- Suggest that students practise writing 35–45 words as they lose marks if they write a very short answer – fewer than 25 words.
- Encourage students to write straight onto the answer sheet if they feel confident, as this will save time and avoid copying errors. If they prefer, they can try out their ideas on the exam paper first.
- If students want to change something they have written, they should cross it out tidily rather than using (brackets).
- Encourage students to read through and check their work when they have finished.

A photocopiable answer sheet is on page 175.

Strategy

1
1 an e-mail
2 an English friend called Charlie
3 three
4 between 35 and 45
5 on the answer sheet (but see Teacher's note above)

2
1 go clubbing
2 next Saturday
3 Dear Charlie
4 *suggested answer:* because I'm going out with my family
5 *suggested answer:* at the swimming pool on Sunday afternoon

3
1 B includes all three points and is the right length
2 C is too short
  A doesn't follow the instructions

4
Thank you for asking me ~~coming~~ **to come** with you to the city centre on Tuesday. ~~I sorry~~ **I'm sorry** but I can't come because ~~I go~~ **I'm going** to the dentist ~~this~~ **that** afternoon. What about ~~we meet~~ **meeting** ~~on~~ – another time? ~~Do~~ **Would** you like to go ~~the~~ **on** Friday afternoon?

Language practice: Writing Part 2

1 Grammar: future plans
a) 1 B
   2 A
   3 B
   4 C

b) 1 arrives
   2 I'll have
   3 'm meeting
   4 're not going to catch
   5 finishes
   6 I'll phone
   7 'm going to do/'m not getting

2 Function: different kinds of messages
1 g   6 e
2 d   7 h
3 b   8 f
4 i   9 c
5 a

3 Exam Task

Writing Part 2
Suggested answer:
Dear Hannah,
It's great that you're coming here on Saturday. Would you like to meet? I can wait for you outside the bus station and show you some of my favourite places. What time does your bus arrive?
Best wishes
Vera

Part 3

Teacher's notes

For a marking guide, see page 202.

- In Part 3, students have to choose one of two tasks: either a letter to an English-speaking friend, or a story for which they are given a title or the opening words.
- The instructions for the letter always say why they are writing and tell them what to write about. It is important that they include everything required by the instructions in their answer or they will lose marks.
- The subject to be written about in the letter is always a general one so everyone has something to say about it. Students can use their imagination as much as they like.

- The story can be anything which fits the title or beginning given. It can be an everyday incident or a fantasy, provided that it is complete and fits the task given.
- Students should remember to keep their story simple so that it can be completed within the word limit. An incomplete or very overlength story is unlikely to get full marks.
- About 100 words = between 85 and 120 words, so students need not worry if they do not write exactly 100. (See *Exam tip!*)
- They get marks for writing an appropriate answer to the question and for using correct English.
- Students should be encouraged to make notes and a plan on the exam paper, but write their answer directly on the answer sheet to save time and avoid copying errors.
- If students want to change something they have written, they should cross it out tidily rather than using (brackets).
- Students should be encouraged to use a range of vocabulary and a variety of sentence structures.
- Encourage students to read through and check their work when they have finished.

A photocopiable answer sheet is on page 175.

Strategy
1
1 only one
2 about 100
3 on your answer sheet
4 in the box at the top of your answer sheet

Strategy: letter
1
1 an English penfriend
2 what you like doing in your free time and whether you stay at home or like going out
3 on your answer sheet

2
c) 1 e
   2 f
   3 d
   4 b
   5 a
   6 c
beginning: 1, 3, 6
end: 2, 4, 5

3
1 A (*I've been at school today and it was boring. I don't like Thursdays because we do sport in the afternoon and I have to play volleyball. I'm not very tall, so I never get the ball. I prefer swimming, but we don't do that.*)
2 B (A few words more or less than 100 doesn't matter, but A is much too long and extra words do not gain extra marks.)
3 B (A starts with words more appropriate to the end of a letter.)
4 A (Copying verbatim is a bad exam strategy and should not be encouraged. Compare how B re-words part of the question and incorporates it in a natural manner *You want to know what I like doing in my free time.*)
5 B (A doesn't mention staying at home and spends too much time talking about school and holidays, and possible future activities rather than what she usually does in her free time at present.)

6 B (Good beginning and ending; right length; answers the question; no unnecessary material; good organisation.)

7 I don't enjoy **stay** at home; **There's café** in the park; **On** the evening.

Strategy: Story

1
1 At six o'clock in the morning, the telephone rang.
2 On your answer sheet

3
1 A is better because it describes what happened in a more logical sequence.
2 In B, 'Who's that?' I said. should come before *It was my brother Sami*, and the writer explains why his brother was at the airport too late in the story. There are also grammatical mistakes.
3 *I told* needs an object; *at a party*, not *in*; While I ~~have driven~~ *was driving* to the airport. I realised that I had ~~forgot~~ *forgotten*. He ~~went~~ *had gone/been* to Paris.

Language practice: Writing Part 3

1 Grammar: narrative tenses
a) A 1 *rang; ran* 2 *fell* 3 *reached* 5 *started* 6 *walked*
   7 *answered; was*
   B 4 *was crying*
   C 2 *was running* 5 *was talking*
   D 3 *had stopped* 4 *had woken* 8 *had … forgotten; had agreed*

b) 1 was walking; saw
   2 had already seen
   3 were standing; arrived
   4 waited
   5 came; put
   6 had sold
   7 had waited; felt
   8 hadn't they/he told

Writing Part 3
Suggested answers:
7
Dear John,
In your last letter you asked me whether I ever go to concerts and whether I collect CDs. I don't go to concerts very often because the town where I live is quite small, so we don't get many good groups here. But I do collect CDs. I like several kinds of music, for example I like singers like Norah Jones. Do you know her? I think she's American. And I also listen to my dad's old Beatles tapes. We listen to them on long journeys in the car.
What about you? What kind of music do you like? .
Best wishes
Ida

8
I checked that my ticket was in my bag and locked the front door. At the airport I went to the check-in desk.
'This ticket is for yesterday.' said the man. I looked at it. He was right. Why hadn't I checked the date when I got my ticket?
'What can I do?' I asked.
'There may be a seat today,' he said. 'But you must wait.'
I waited anxiously for twenty minutes and watched the passengers checking in. At last the clerk told me there was one spare seat.
I will never forget to check the date on a ticket again!

PAPER 2 Listening

Part 1

Teacher's notes

- In Part 1, there are seven recordings. For each one, there is either one speaker or two.
- First, students hear the instructions. They are the same as what they read.
- Each recording has a question and three pictures.
- Students should tick the picture, A, B or C on the exam paper, which best represents the answer to the question.
- The recording for each question is repeated before students hear the next recording.
- Students are given six minutes to check their answers and transfer them to the answer sheet at the end of the Listening Test.
- Before attempting Question 4 of Listening strategy Part 1, it would be a good idea to revise telling the time with the class.

A photocopiable answer sheet is on page 176.

Strategy

1
1 four
2 twice
3 on the question paper
4 copy your answers onto the answer sheet
5 six minutes

2
1 seven
2 three
3 choose the correct picture and put a tick in the box below it

3
1 What will the boy take back to the shop?
2 A
3 the box under A is ticked

4
1 the time that Paula will pick Julie up
2 A seven twenty/twenty past seven
   B seven forty/twenty to eight
   C eight fifteen/(a) quarter past eight
3 eight fifteen; twenty past seven; twenty to eight.
4 See key.
5 That is the time Paula will leave home.
6 That is the time the film starts.
7 Paula says, *I'll be at your house at twenty to eight*, so this is the time she will pick Julie up.

Listening Part 1 key
1 B
2 C They will get a film first, then go for trainers and lastly fruit.
3 B She didn't leave them on the hall table and she is going to look for them in the car when the man finds them in the kitchen.
4 A The woman suggests fish and chips or chicken or a chicken sandwich but he chooses salad and a roll.
5 C 10.15 is her old appointment. She is offered 2.45 or 4.15 and she chooses 4.15.
6 B There was a coach but they had to take a helicopter because the ferry was cancelled.
7 A He didn't enjoy the football match because they lost and he didn't enjoy the film because it wasn't as good as he expected. He had a great time in the bookshops and music shops.

Language practice: Listening Part 1

1 Vocabulary: word sets
Parts of the body: neck, ankle, stomach, thumb, shoulder
Money words: cheque, credit cards, purse, wallet, coin
Animals: horse, duck, chicken, sheep, turkey
Sports: football, tennis, volleyball, swimming, cycling

2 Grammar: saying when things happen
a) 1 while
   2 after
   3 before
   4 since
   5 during
   6 as soon as

b) 1 until
   2 since
   3 as soon as
   4 after
   5 before

Part 2
Teacher's notes

- Part 2 usually consists of someone giving factual information or telling a story, often about something that has happened to them.
- There is only one main speaker, although sometimes there is a short introduction by another speaker, or an interviewer asks questions.
- The instructions are the same on the recording and the exam paper.
- There is quite a lot to read in Part 2, so students have 45 seconds to read the questions before they listen.
- The questions come in the same order as the information on the recording.
- Students should mark the answers on the exam paper and copy them onto the answer sheet later.
- A beep on the recording indicates where the tape should be paused.

A photocopiable answer sheet is on page 176.

Strategy
1
1 six
2 a woman called Vanessa
3 a journey she made
4 her husband
5 her baby
6 put a tick in the correct box for each question
7 twice

2 *Suggested answers:*
2, 3, 4, 5

3
a) clue = *sail*
b) clue = *anxious*

Listening Part 2 key

8 B   *last year we gave up our jobs and decided to sail back to England.*

9 C   *... was most anxious about our health, particularly the baby ... .*

10 A *I considered flying home to England*

11 B *My father-in-law was very happy to take care of the baby while we sailed the boat.*

12 B *he wants us to play with him all the time now.*

13 C *as long as they have plenty to do on board.*

Language practice: Listening Part 2

1 Vocabulary: -*ing* and -*ed* adjectives
a) *we were getting* **bored**

b) 1 amazing   6 interested
   2 amazed   7 tired
   3 surprised   8 tiring
   4 surprising   9 exciting
   5 interesting 10 excited

2 Grammar: verbs followed by *to* + infinitive
b) 1 to swim   6 to reply
   2 to come   7 to play
   3 to travel   8 to tell
   4 to study   9 to buy
   5 to paint 10 to meet

Part 3
Teacher's notes

- In Part 3, there is only one main speaker. Sometimes there is also a short introduction by another speaker.
- The instructions are the same on the recording and the exam paper.
- The questions may be in a list, a note or a notice.
- The information comes in the right order for students to answer the questions.
- Students do not need to understand everything they hear, but should only listen for the answers to the questions as there will be words they do not know. Reassure them that they do not have to worry about this, as the answers are always common words.
- Students should write the answers on the exam paper and copy them to the answer sheet later.
- A beep on the recording indicates where the tape should be paused.

A photocopiable answer sheet is on page 176.

Strategy
1
1 six
2 Willingham is a name (probably a place). It begins with a capital letter. (Point out to students that words with capital letters are usually names of people or places, so they need not worry if they do not recognise them.)
3 someone talking on the radio; the Willingham Museum
4 fill in the missing information in the numbered space for each question

2
1 A noun. In (14) it has *a* and 19th-century before the space.
In (15) the answer is something which could be the subject of an exhibition because it says *an exhibition about.*
In (17) the answer is a kind of building. The gap has *a* before it.
In (18) the answer is a place or a building. It has *the* before it and it is something which can be outside the town.
2 (16) a day or a date because it says *on.*
3 (19) must be an adjective because it has *the* before and *signs* (a noun) after it.

5
one or two (It is possible that students may need to write three words, but this is very unusual.)

Language practice: Listening Part 3

1 Grammar: prepositions

1	around	6	in
2	outside	7	in
3	from	8	of
4	to	9	until
5	in	10	on

2 Vocabulary: compound nouns

a) *dining* is made from *dine + ing – dine* becomes *din* when we add *-ing*

b) 1 driving
   2 swimming
   3 sleeping
   4 washing
   5 waiting
   6 frying
   7 writing
   8 walking

3 Vocabulary: places to visit
1 paintings
2 sculptures
3 café
4 exhibition
5 guided tour
6 old books
7 souvenirs
8 gift shop

Part 4

Teacher's notes

- Part 4 is always a conversation between two people. Both of them usually give their opinions about something and agree or disagree.
- The instructions are the same on the recording and the exam paper.
- The questions come in the same order as the information on the recording.
- Encourage students to read through the questions before they listen to get a good idea of what they are going to hear.
- Students should mark the answers on the exam paper and copy them onto the answer sheet later.
- A beep on the recording indicates where the tape should be paused.

A photocopiable answer sheet is on page 176.

Strategy

1
1 six
2 two
3 William
4 Sophie
5 in a music shop
6 decide if each sentence is correct or incorrect and tick the box under A for *yes* or under B for *no*

3 *Suggested answers:*
mother; shopping; Birmingham; band; CD; birthday

Language practice: Listening Part 4

1 Vocabulary: words with similar meanings

b) 1 feels
   2 prefers
   3 suggests
   4 thinks
   5 is keen
   6 recommends
   7 is disappointed
   8 persuade

2 Grammar: *if* sentences (unreal situations)

b) 1 d
   2 a
   3 b
   4 e
   5 f
   6 c

c) *Suggested answers:*
1 I'd/I would buy a sports car.
2 I'd/I would go to lots of parties.
3 I'd live on an island.
4 I'd/I would invite him/her for dinner.
5 I'd/I would be really happy.
6 I'd/I would wear a hat all the time.

PAPER 3 Speaking

For notes and a guide to assessment, see page 203.

Teacher's notes

- The Speaking Test is taken in pairs, although if there is an odd number of students, the final three candidates may go in together.
- There are always two examiners, but only one will interact with the students. The other will make notes. Reassure students that they should not worry about this.
- In Part 1 the examiner will address each student separately; in Parts 2–4 the students talk mainly to each other.
- It is essential that students practise in pairs. The exercises are designed to help students get experience of this. It is important for students to know how to ask questions and respond to answers, as well as being able to give information and opinions.
- It is very sensible for students to learn useful expressions and vocabulary, but it is not advisable for them to prepare whole speeches as they will be penalised for this.
- Candidates are assessed on their general ability to communicate. This includes pronunciation of sounds, intonation and stress. They are not assessed on their general knowledge or educational level and should be reassured about this. Students should be prepared to talk about everyday subjects in a relaxed atmosphere. They will not be expected to discuss anything outside their own experience.

- The sample Speaking Test is intended to illustrate the format of the test in a realistic way. It offers only an example of the content and scope of possible answers and can be used as a pedagogical tool. Students should not be encouraged to learn the conversations by heart, but should be aware of what to expect. It does not contain any student errors in order that it can be used as a model. Students should be reassured that they do not have to speak as fast as these candidates and that they can get very good marks even if they make some grammatical, lexical or phonological errors. This sample test would get full marks.

Part 1

Teacher's notes

- Part 1 requires students to respond to questions from the examiner about themselves.
- Students will be asked to spell something.

1 Sample interview

Play the recording of Part 1.

a) The examiner might ask any of these questions, but not all of the same student.

1 ✔
2 ✔ The examiner uses the word *surname* but the question means the same.
3 ✔
4 ✔
5 ✗
6 ✔
7 ✔
8 ✔
9 ✗ The examiner asks about the previous evening
10 ✔

b) 1 the candidates' mark sheets (they will have been given these just before they go into the exam room)
2 Michael, the other examiner
3 their surnames
4 *I'm sorry, I don't understand. Can you repeat that, please?*
5 *I'm at school. /... and then I watched a football match on television.*

2 Spelling

a) 1

I	/aɪ/	H	/eɪtʃ/
E	/iː/	R	/ɑː/
X	/eks/	A	/eɪ/
K	/keɪ/	Z	/zed/
Q	/kjuː/	S	/es/
U	/juː/	C	/siː/
O	/əʊ/	G	/dʒiː/
V	/viː/	J	/dʒeɪ/
W	/dʌbəljuː/	Y	/waɪ/

2 *double* + name of letter, e.g. *double em*

b) Students do not ask each other questions at this stage in the actual exam, but working in this way will give them plenty of practice and help to understand what they are asked by the examiner.

Part 2

Teacher's notes

- In Part 2, students take part in a simulated discussion. They are asked to make and respond to suggestions, discuss different possibilities and agree or disagree.
- It is not necessary for students to agree about everything as long as they have a sensible discussion.
- They are given line drawings as a prop to give them

ideas.
- Point out to students that the examiner may offer to repeat the instructions and they will not be penalised if they say 'yes'.

1 Sample interview

Play the recording for Part 2.

a) You are going to make some plans for a day out together. Talk together about which three places you'll go to. Decide which one you will go to first.

b) market, mall, swimming pool

2 Functions: making plans

a)

1	✔	6	✔	11	✗
2	✗	7	✔	12	✔
3	✔	8	✔	13	✗
4	✗	9	✔	14	✔
5	✔	10	✔	15	✔

b)

2	e	9	b
3	b	10	b
4	a	11	d
5	c	12	c
6	d	13	c
7	a	14	d
8	a	15	e

c)

1	about	7	shall/can
2	do/see	8	Let's
3	sure	9	idea
4	would	10	like
5	about	11	Let's
6	see/do		

Part 3

Teacher's notes

- In Part 3, the students are each given a colour photograph which they are asked to describe.

1 Describing where things are in a picture

a) *Suggested answers:*
Picture B is probably a room in a school or a club.
Picture C shows a boy and a girl watching TV.

b)

1	bookcase	7	table football	13	rug
2	bed	8	cupboard	14	cushion
3	chest of drawers	9	noticeboard	15	sofa
4	mirror	10	curtains	16	lamp
5	wardrobe	11	television		
6	shelf	12	video		

2 Describing people

a) 1 In Picture A, a boy is sitting at the table. I think he's about 15 years old. There's a book open in front of him, but he isn't studying. He's looking at something else. He's wearing a dark jumper. There's a lamp on the table.
2 In Picture B, a boy and a girl are playing table football. The boy's on the left and he's wearing a striped sweater and jeans. The girl's wearing a T-shirt and shorts. There's a noticeboard on the wall.

c) In Picture C, a girl and a boy are sitting on the sofa watching TV. They're both laughing so probably they're watching a funny programme. There's a lamp in the corner and a cushion on the floor.

4 Sample interview
a) talk about them

b)
	Carlo	Anna
what kind of room it is	✔	✔
what people he/she can see	✔	✔
what the people are wearing		
where the people are in the room	✔	
what things he/she can see	✔	✔
his/her opinion about the things	✔	
what the people are doing	✔	✔
how the people are feeling		✔

Part 4

Teacher's notes

- In Part 4, students are asked to respond to situations in the photographs, to talk about likes and dislikes, experiences and give opinions.

1 Sample interview
Play the recording of Part 4.

a) talk together about the kind of places you prefer to study in – find out how you each like to organise your work

b) Anna: Do you prefer to study alone Carlo?
Carlo: What about you?

c)
1	✔	5	✗
2	✔	6	✔
3	✔	7	✗
4	✗	8	✔

Test 2

PAPER 1 Reading

Part 1

For Teacher's notes, see page 177.

A photocopiable answer sheet is on page 174.

Strategy
1
1 five
2 what each text says
3 on the answer sheet (but if students prefer, they can mark their answers on the exam paper and copy them when they have finished this part)

2
1 c
2 on someone's computer
3 *call the cinema*
Let me know
4 *before they go to the cinema*
5 he should *call* (= phone) the cinema, not go to the cinema

3
1 b
2 in a railway station; *tickets, train*
3 yes
4 yes; *any train after that* = trains later than 10.15
5 no
6 A *can be used on, any train after that*
7 B cost isn't mentioned
C the message says that saver tickets can be used on other trains

Language practice: Reading Part 1

1 Grammar: time words and phrases
a) before, after, when, then, until, at present, at the moment, in advance, later, the same day, twenty-four hours a day, within the next two days

b) 1 I'm on holiday until Tuesday.
2 That film is no longer showing.
3 The museum is closed for lunch, but it will be open later.
4 There's a tram from here to the city centre every fifteen minutes.
5 I promise I'll reply to your request within a fortnight.
6 Harry's not here at the moment, can I take a message?
7 We need to know how many people are coming to the performance in advance.
8 You must be here in time to catch the ferry.

2 Vocabulary: words you see in signs
a) 1 out of order; assistant
2 urgent; reception
3 discount; credit card
4 on time; cancelled
5 available; emergency
6 arrival; responsible
7 forbidden; permitted
8 security; staff

b) *Suggested answers:*
1 shop, station, etc.
2 office
3 travel agent, station, etc.
4 station
5 surgery
6 school sports centre
7 university
8 airport, station, factory

3 Grammar: *before/after + -ing*
b) 1 You must take a shower before using the swimming pool.
2 Please clear the table after eating a meal.
3 You'll have to ask permission before using this telephone.
4 Don't forget to pick up your rubbish after finishing your picnic.
5 Employees must wash their hands before preparing a meal.
6 Remember to lock the door after putting out the rubbish.
7 Passengers must buy a ticket before getting on the train.
8 Switch off your mobile before entering the theatre.

4 Vocabulary: money words
1	credit card	6	correct money
2	cheaper	7	expensive
3	discount	8	sell
4	change	9	cost extra
5	pay		

Part 2

For Teacher's notes, see pages 177–178.

A photocopiable answer sheet is on page 174.

Strategy

1
1 five
2 They want to watch a film on TV.
3 films
4 eight
5 which film would be most suitable for the five people
6 on the answer sheet (Students should be advised not to write on the answer sheet until they have answered all the questions in case they change their minds.)

3
a) 1 No, he likes old-fashioned ones.
   2 comedies
   3 famous ones
   4 musicals and thrillers

b) 7 Tom's hobby is reading and he enjoys watching films on TV whose <u>stories are taken from literature</u>. His favourite books are those by <u>famous authors of the past</u>. He reads books about the cinema too and likes watching <u>famous actors</u>.
   8 Elena likes to relax by watching the <u>latest romantic films</u> on TV, especially if they make her <u>laugh</u>. She particularly likes those which have some <u>music</u> in them.
   9 Belinda enjoys watching <u>thrillers</u>. She prefers adventures which actually happened to people in <u>real life</u>, as she is interested in the lives of other people.
   10 Carol loves listening to <u>pop music</u> and reading magazines about it. She doesn't mind what sort of film she sees, if it's a <u>new one about pop stars or their music</u>.

4
a) 1 A, E
   2 E

+---+
| **Reading Part 2 key** |
| **6** E |
| **7** D *novel written two hundred years ago* |
| **8** B *fall in love ... songs ... amusing parts* |
| **9** F *adventure film ... this actually happened* |
| **10** C *music of this group ... everyone's favourite* |
+---+

Language practice: Reading Part 2

1 Vocabulary: expressions with similar meanings
1 g
2 c
3 f
4 d
5 a
6 e
7 b

2 Grammar: present perfect
a) 1 c
   2 a
   3 d
   4 f
   5 g
   6 b
   7 e

b) yet; already; just; still; recently

c) 1 ago; still
   2 in/during; during/in
   3 already; just
   4 yet; later
   5 last month; for

3 Grammar: time expressions
1 's/has been
2 since she wrote
3 started
4 's/has just
5 is

4 Vocabulary: word sets

Film	Music	Magazine	Computer
actor	<u>CD</u>	article	<u>CD</u>
camera	concert	contents	game
cinema	drummer	crossword	<u>keyboard</u>
director	guitarist	headline	mouse
make-up	<u>keyboard</u>	photograph	<u>movie</u>
<u>movie</u>	musician	<u>story</u>	program
screen	rock		<u>screen</u>
<u>story</u>			software
			website

b) see underlined words above

c) 1 headline
   2 websites
   3 movie
   4 contents
   5 director

6 Writing: an e-mail or letter about a film
1 about
2 keen
3 prefer
4 favourite
5 funny
6 like
7 best/funniest
8 when
9 just
10 actors

Part 3

For Teacher's notes, see pages 178–179.

A photocopiable answer sheet is on page 174.

Strategy

1
1 ten
2 advice for new students at a university
3 the text on the opposite page
4 if each sentence is correct or incorrect
5 if the sentence is correct
6 if the sentence is not correct

2
b 18   g 19
c 11   h 17
d 12   i 14
e 13   j 15
f 20

3

As a new student, you've arrived two days before term starts to look around and get settled in before your course begins and the place fills up. Here is some information to make all that a bit easier (we hope!).

The Student Welfare Office is normally open from 4 p.m. till 8 p.m. Monday to Friday. Today and tomorrow it will be open all day, from about 9 a.m. This is the place to come if you have any problems, for example about money or accommodation (we have a list of rental agencies and also advertise any rooms which become available in the university hostels at the end of term). We also give out the university identity cards which you need to join the library and which allow you to get discounts at a number of local shops (including bookshops) and places of entertainment, such as clubs and cinemas.

On Monday and Tuesday of next week, second-year students will be running a book sale in the canteen from 10–3. Many of the books on your first-year reading list will be available, and we suggest you should look here first before spending too much on new books.

The university canteen (open from 7.30 a.m. till 7.30 p.m.) sells hot meals fairly cheaply, as well as snacks and drinks, but it'll save you money to cook at least some of your own meals. There is a basic cookery course starting next week (run by students for students, so it's really practical). If you don't know how to boil an egg, this is for you. It's always full, so get your name on the list in the Welfare Office NOW!

The sports centre is open from today. Look on the noticeboards there for information about athletics, swimming, team games, and so on. It is also possible to join some local city clubs, such as golf or squash, at a discount (show them your card) if you can play at a reasonable level. Addresses in the sports centre office.

The Music School welcomes all members of the university, whatever their main subject of study, for part-time courses. Why not take the opportunity to start learning the guitar, violin or piano while you're here? Many advanced students offer really cheap lessons. There are also open evenings when anyone can take the chance to perform in front of an audience. Look out for notices advertising times and dates.

Reading Part 3 key

11	B	*you've arrived two days before term starts*
12	A	*the Student Welfare Office is normally open from 4 p.m. till 8 p.m.*
13	B	*we have a list of rental agencies and also advertise any rooms ... in the university hostels*
14	A	*to get discounts at a number of local shops (including bookshops)*
15	B	*second-year students will be running a book sale*
16	B	*it'll save you money to cook at least some of your own meals*
17	A	*It's always full*
18	B	*if you can play at a reasonable level* (Point out that *take up = play for the first time*.)
19	B	*start learning the guitar.* (So you don't need to play reasonably well.)
20	A	*anyone can take the chance to perform*

Language practice: Reading Part 3

1 Vocabulary: student life
1 rent
2 welfare office
3 student card
4 canteen
5 club
6 part-time course
7 full-time course
8 hostel
9 reading list
10 sports centre
11 noticeboard
12 advanced

3 Grammar: adverbs of frequency (*how often?*)
a) *Suggested answers:*

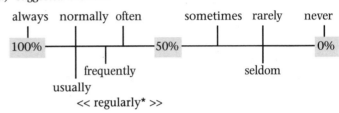

(* You may wish to point out that this can mean at very infrequent, but regular, intervals.)

5 Grammar: relative clauses
b) 1 which
   2 where
   3 who
   4 which
   5 when

c) 1 A group of students share this flat which Keith's father owns.
   2 We often have a party at weekends when we don't have classes.
   3 Most students live in hostels where parties aren't allowed.
   4 This is my penfriend who's coming to stay next month.
   5 I usually study in the college library where most of my friends study too.
   6 It's a pity we have exams in the summer when the weather is very hot.

d) 1 where
   2 where I
   3 which was
   4 a person/someone/somebody who
   5 (some) mornings when

Part 4

For Teacher's notes, see page 179.

A photocopiable answer sheet is on page 174.

Strategy
1
1 the text and questions
2 mark the correct letter, A, B, C or D
3 on your answer sheet

2
1 a lake
2 because it's his favourite place for watersports
3 the valley was filled with water

3
1 why
2 a person
3 information
4 opinions
5 persuading people to visit

Reading Part 4 key

21 A The text reports what people think all the way through.
22 D she runs a shop on the edge of the lake
23 C *the number of visitors ... continues to increase*
24 B *It is a shame*
25 C It mentions watersports, the café and car-parking space.

Language practice: Reading Part 4

1 Function: expressing attitudes

1	a	5	c
2	d	6	b
3	b	7	b
4	c	8	b

2 Grammar: reported speech
a) The pronoun changes; the verb goes back a tense

b) 1 He said <u>he would</u> visit <u>them the next day</u>.
<u>I'll</u> visit <u>you tomorrow</u>.
2 She said <u>she could</u> help <u>us</u> with <u>our</u> luggage.
<u>I can</u> help <u>you</u> with <u>your</u> luggage.
3 They told us <u>they weren't</u> going to leave <u>that</u> evening.
<u>We aren't</u> going to leave <u>this</u> evening.
4 We told them we <u>had</u> already locked the door.
We <u>have</u> already locked the door.
5 I said I <u>hadn't been there the day before</u>.
I <u>wasn't here yesterday</u>.

c) 1 is
2 usually work here
3 I'm/I am going
4 I/We expect
5 'll/will help
6 have to pay
7 'll/will phone tomorrow
8 can speak
9 Your sister has

3 Grammar: patterns after reporting verbs
1 should
2 you like
3 forget
4 will not/won't
5 I'm/I am sorry (that)

4 Vocabulary: *get*
a) 1 d
2 a
3 b
4 c

b) a) 3
b) 1
c) 4
d) 2

c) 1 get to school
2 got to the sports club
3 get it back
4 get any e-mails
5 get out of bed
6 getting off
7 get a lift
8 get married
9 get home
10 get to know

Part 5

For Teacher's notes, see page 180.

A photocopiable answer sheet is on page 174.

Strategy
1
1 the text on the opposite page
2 the correct word for each space
3 on the answer sheet (Students should be advised to write their answers in the spaces in the text first, as this will help them to grasp the overall meaning. They can transfer their answers when they have read the whole text and checked their answers.)

4
1 A
2 B is not the answer because it's wrong to say *went his home*. We must say *went away from*.
C is not the answer because *removed* cannot be used with *home* here.
D is not the answer because it is wrong to say *departed his home*. We do not use *depart* with *home*.

Reading Part 5 key

26 C (lexical)
27 B (structural)
28 A (lexical)
29 D (lexical)
30 A (lexical)
31 B (structural)
32 C (structural)
33 D (structural)
34 B (lexical)
35 C (lexical/structural)

Language practice: Reading Part 5

1 Grammar: preposition or no preposition after a verb
1 *no preposition*
2 *no preposition*
3 for
4 *no preposition*
5 *no preposition*
6 with
7 off/from
8 *no preposition*
9 at
10 *no preposition*

2 Grammar: words that describe *how much* and *how many*
a) 1 a few
2 some
3 a
4 some; a little
5 any
6 much

b) 1 of
2 of
3 –
4 –
5 of
6 –

3 Vocabulary: *like/as*

1	like	6	like
2	as	7	as
3	like	8	like
4	like	9	as
5	as	10	as

4 Vocabulary: at the airport

a) *Suggested answers:*

baggage hall – This is the place where you collect your bags when you arrive.

check-in desk – This is the place where you show your passport and get your seat number.

customs officer – This is someone who checks your bags for illegal things.

departure lounge – This is the place where people wait until their plane is ready to leave.

duty-free shop – This is the place where you can buy things without paying tax on them.

flight attendant – This is the person who looks after people on the plane.

information desk – This is the place where you can find out the times of trains, buses, etc.

passenger – This is the person who travels in a plane (or bus, train, etc.)

pilot – This is someone who flies planes.

snack bar – This is the place where you can buy sandwiches, drinks, etc.

c) *Suggested answer:*

... go to the snack bar for a drink. Then you go to the duty-free shop and then to the departure lounge. When you arrive, you go to the baggage hall and finally you go to the information desk.

5 Vocabulary: words that go together

a) cash some traveller's cheques
cross the border
fasten your seat belt
miss the flight
pack your suitcase
reach your destination
reserve a seat

b) 1 crossed the border
2 cash some traveller's cheques
3 reserve a seat
4 pack your suitcase
5 fasten your seat belt
6 reach your destination

PAPER 1 Writing

Part 1

For Teacher's notes, see page 181.

A photocopiable answer sheet is on page 175.

Strategy

1
1 five (and an example)
2 a cinema
3 complete the second sentence so that it means the same as the first
4 up to three
5 on the answer sheet (but students can try out their ideas on the exam paper first)
6 only the missing words
7 on the exam paper

2
1 It is near the shopping mall.
2 yes

3
1 when it opened
2 *The cinema ... here for two years*
3 *has been*

Language practice: Writing Part 1

1 Grammar: matching patterns

a) 2,5
3,10
4,11
6,9
8,12

b) a 4,11
b 2,5
c 6,9
d 3,10
e 8,12

c) 1 under(neath) mine   6 unless
2 are looking for   7 favourite
3 don't you   8 eat
4 too dirty to   9 far from
5 open   10 haven't got any

2 Correcting mistakes
1 My flat is smaller **than** yours.
2 My brother **belongs** to the tennis club.
3 'Why **don't** you come swimming with me?' suggested my sister.
4 You **can't** get a table if you don't book.
5 I prefer modern shops **to** old ones.

Part 2

For Teacher's notes, see page 181.

For a marking guide, see page 202.

A photocopiable answer sheet is on page 175.

Strategy

1
1 a note
2 a friend called Eva
3 three
4 between 35 and 45
5 on the answer sheet

2
1 your rucksack
2 two weeks ago
3 Hi Eva
4 Return your rucksack
5 *Suggested answer:* because you want to use it this weekend

3
1 B is the best answer because it includes all three points and is the right length.
2 A doesn't follow the instructions.
C has misunderstood the question.

4
a) Do you remember **camping** in Wales last year? Would you like **to come** to Ireland with me **next month**? My **exams** finish **in** two weeks and my cousins have invited me **to go** with them. We can use my **brother's** tent because he **doesn't need** it.

Language practice: Writing Part 2

1 Grammar: possessives
a) 1 *Students* is plural, *sister* is singular.
   2 *Children* is plural.
   3 It is irregular (compare *people, sheep*).

b) 1 I have two brothers and two sisters – my brothers'
      school is near our house, but my sisters' school is
      three kilometres away.
   2 I looked through all the women's clothes in the
      shop, but there was nothing suitable.
   3 I tried not to laugh when I saw Jane's new hairstyle.
   4 Her friends' parents all agreed that the party should
      finish at eleven.
   5 I don't like borrowing other people's clothes.

2 Grammar: verbs followed by *-ing* or infinitive
   1 to learn
   2 to arrive
   3 to phone
   4 driving
   5 to buy
   6 to tidy
   7 talking
   8 applying
   9 to know
  10 leaving

Writing Part 2
Suggested answer:
Dear Saskia
I'm very pleased you're coming here next Sunday. You'll meet my
parents and my sister Nellie. We'll all have a barbecue lunch
together. What would you like to do in the afternoon? We could go
to the swimming pool, if you like.
Love,
Angie

Part 3

For Teacher's notes, see page 182.

A photocopiable answer sheet is on page 175.

Strategy: letter
1
1 an English-speaking friend
2 your new home
3 on the answer sheet

3
1 B. Although both letters are the right length and cover
   the content, the language in B is more accurate.
2 A has eight grammatical errors.
3 Dear Marco
   Thanks for your letter. You want to know **what the
   new flat is like**. Well, I love it! It's **in** a block of flats
   near ~~of~~ the city centre, but it's in a quiet street. It's
   not so small **as** our old one, so I don't **have** to share
   a room with my brother. I've got plenty of space for
   my computer. I painted my room before we **moved** in.
   But the **best** thing about this flat is the balcony. It's
   really big and we **have** breakfast there every morning.
   I hope you'll come and see it soon.
   All the best
   Alex

Language practice: Writing Part 3

1 Vocabulary: describing houses and flats
   1 window
   2 first floor
   3 garage
   4 ground floor
   5 path
   6 front door
   7 gate
   8 hedge
   9 basement
  10 balcony

Strategy: story
1
1 The surprise
2 on your answer sheet

3
1 B is the best answer.
2 A has five grammar mistakes. It also has too many
   short simple sentences.
3 I knew a boy called Timmy. He used to steal~~ing~~ things
   from shops. He had lots **of** money. Nobody liked him.
   He told his friends he stole things. They weren't
   interested ~~in~~.
   One day he was talking to some other boys in a café.
   A young man came in. He sat at the same table. He
   said **to** Timmy, 'I don't believe you really steal things.'
   Timmy showed him a CD. He'd stolen the CD that
   morning. 'Do you believe me now?' he asked.
   'Yes,' said the young man. 'I'm arresting you. I'm **a**
   policeman'.
   Timmy was very surprised. He didn't know what to say.

Language practice: Writing Part 3

1 Improving your story: using linking words
1 who
2 Although
3 but
4 when
5 and
6 which
7 so
8 that

2 Improving your story: adding information
a) 1 c
   2 b
   3 a
   4 e
   5 d

b) *Suggested answers:*
   1 was at the top of an old house.
   2 he was on holiday in Brazil.
   3 very loudly
   4 everyone had a good time.
   5 tells lots of funny stories.

Writing Part 3
Suggested answers:

7

Dear Jacob,

You want to know about my cousins' home? Well, they live in a flat near the sea. It's great because it's only five minutes from the harbour. My uncle has a sailing boat which my cousins and I can use. Sailing is quite hard work, but we have a lot of fun. We also go swimming, but not in the harbour because the water is rather dirty. We cycle to a little bay outside the town. The town is quite old and it's popular with tourists. Perhaps you'll come there with me one year.

Best wishes

Fred

8

Last year I was ill for two months. I didn't feel very bad, but I was always tired and sometimes I felt depressed. One day my brother came home with a large cardboard box. There were some holes in the top of it. 'This is for you,' he said.

I couldn't guess what was inside. He put the box on my bed. I realised that there was an animal in it. It was a little cat. I decided to call her Milly. I could play with her all day and I felt quite happy. I soon got better after she arrived.

PAPER 2 Listening

Part 1

For Teacher's notes, see page 183.

A photocopiable answer sheet is on page 176.

Strategy

1
1   four
2   twice
3   on the question paper
4   copy your answers onto the answer sheet.
5   six minutes

2
1   seven
2   three
3   choose the correct picture and put a tick in the box below it

3
1   What will the boy take back to the shop?
2   A
3   the box under A is ticked

4
1   where they will meet
2   A library B swimming pool C café
3   all of them
4   See key.
5   It is where the woman is going.
6   It is near the café.
7   The woman says *When you've parked the car, I'll see you in the café*, so this is where they will meet.

Listening Part 1 Key
1   C
2   C   She is looking for a coat with a wide belt, large collar and two big pockets on the front.
3   B   The photo is of the village from the top of the mountain before they reached the forest. He took some of the sea, but they were no good.
4   C   The boy says: *Take the first turning on the right, then the second turning on the left. My flat is just before the roundabout on the right.*

5   A   Her aunt is coming and she's bringing the girl's twin cousins – they're six. The girl says: *My uncle has to stay behind because he has to work and Joe, their teenage son, has decided to stay with him, so they aren't coming.*

6   B   It was sunny when they left home, but cloudy on the holiday. It didn't rain and had been foggy the week before, but not while they were there.

7   A   The desk is now under the little window opposite, not behind the door. It used to be behind the door and she tried it under the big window, but it was too sunny.

Language practice: Listening Part 1

1   Vocabulary: weather
Suggested answers:
1   It's snowing.
2   It's windy.
3   It's cloudy.
4   It's raining. / It's damp. / It's wet.
5   It's freezing. / It's frosty. / It's icy.
6   It's misty. / It's foggy.
7   It's icy. / It's freezing. / It's frosty.
8   It's sunny.

2   Functions: giving and understanding directions
a)   1   library
     2   theatre

3   Vocabulary: clothes
a)   *Suggested answers:*

skirt	coat	jacket	dress	shirt	boots
belt	belt	belt	belt		
				V-neck	
silk	silk	silk	silk	silk	
knee-length	knee-length	knee-length	knee-length		knee-length
pockets	pockets	pockets	pockets	pockets	
	collar	collar	collar	collar	
		short sleeves	short sleeves	short sleeves	
buttons	buttons	buttons	buttons	buttons	
zip	zip	zip	zip		zip
			round neck	round neck	
leather	leather	leather			leather
					high heels
			sleeveless	sleeveless	
wool	wool	wool	wool	wool	
cotton	cotton	cotton	cotton	cotton	

b)   *Suggested answers:*
     1   zip
     2   pockets
     3   leather
     4   belt

Part 2

For Teacher's notes, see page 184.

A photocopiable answer sheet is on page 176.

Strategy

1
1   six
2   a tour guide
3   a group of tourists
4   a coach trip
5   put a tick in the correct box for each question
6   twice

2

The following should be ticked:
1 They will come back to the hotel in the early evening.
2 They will visit a town.
4 Something about the trip has changed.
6 They will stop in the countryside for a drink.
7 They will visit a wildlife park.

> **Listening Part 2 key**
> **8** C *But today, because we have a lot of children here this week, we're also going to a wildlife park.*
> **9** A *In the next valley we'll have a break for coffee. There's a café near a beautiful waterfall.*
> **10** B *it's the university that made the town famous*
> **11** A *we'll see lions in the park*
> **12** B *we'll return to the hotel at a quarter to seven*
> **13** C *if anyone wants to ask any questions, I'll try to answer them*

Language practice: Listening Part 2

1 Grammar: possessives
1 neighbour of mine
2 of my brother's
3 of mine
4 student of hers
5 cousin of theirs
6 of Sally's

2 Grammar: reported questions
b) 1 when the match starts
   2 what the time is
   3 how far it is to the cinema
   4 if Paula is busy tonight
   5 where the nearest bus stop is
   6 if they are coming to the cinema

c) 1 do you live
   2 Can we sit
   3 will
   4 Are there
   5 does Clare
   6 didn't you phone

3 Vocabulary: the environment
1 D
2 C
3 A
4 B
5 C
6 B

Part 3

For Teacher's notes, see page 184.

A photocopiable answer sheet is on page 176.

Strategy
1
1 six
2 a woman talking on the radio about a competition
3 fill in the missing information in the numbered space for each question

2
1 a word which describes *printer* (14) (Remind students that this could be a noun or an adjective, e.g. we can say *a new printer* (adjective) or *a colour printer* (noun).); a word which describes *a story* (16).
2 a number
3 a time or place because it says *takes place in*
4 a noun because it is the last thing in a list of nouns
5 a day or date

5
1 one or two (It is possible that students may need to write three words, but this is very unusual.)

> **Listening Part 3 key**
> **14** colour
> **15** 1,500
> **16** crime
> **17** the future
> **18** age
> **19** 8(th) March

Language practice: Listening Part 3

1 Writing dates and numbers
a) a date – Question 19
   a number – Question 15

b) (You can write dates in different ways. British English usually puts the day first, whereas American English normally puts the month first.)
   Suggested answers:
   1 21(st) February 2002 / February 21(st) 2002
   2 Wednesday 2(nd) March 2005 / Wednesday March 2(nd) 2005
   3 4(th) September 2009 / September 4(th) 2009
   4 Thursday 19(th) April 2020 / Thursday April 19(th) 2020

c) 1 seven and a quarter
   2 one third / a third
   3 first
   4 second
   5 third
   6 fourth
   7 seventy-five per cent
   8 nought point three five
   9 one thousand five hundred and eighty
   10 two hundred thousand

2 Grammar: expressions of purpose
a) 1 c   4 e
   2 f   5 a
   3 b   6 d

3 Vocabulary: computer words

K	T	W	F	E	S	U	O	M	G
B	E	N	M	A	O	X	C	V	F
V	N	Y	K	U	F	I	O	Q	R
G	R	J	B	U	T	N	R	W	E
M	E	I	E	O	W	E	E	R	K
W	T	M	T	J	A	E	F	T	A
E	N	C	A	F	R	R	C	H	E
R	I	V	Y	I	E	C	D	N	P
N	A	J	T	D	L	S	Z	B	S
L	R	E	T	N	I	R	P	I	P

keyboard, mouse, internet, speaker, printer, software, e-mail, screen

1 internet
2 software
3 speaker
4 mouse
5 e-mail

Part 4

For Teacher's notes, see page 185.

A photocopiable answer sheet is on page 176.

Strategy

1
1 six
2 two
3 Marcus
4 Cora
5 They work in the same office.
6 decide if each statement is correct or incorrect and tick the box under A for *yes* or under B for *no*

3
Suggested answers:
late; traffic jams; cycling; buses; tomorrow; lazy
(These words give the students the idea that the conversation is about different ways of travelling to work and why people use one method of transport or another.)

Listening Part 4 key

20	A	*Only a few minutes today. But you're never exactly early, are you?*
21	A	*But that's where you're wrong. It's the cars that make traffic jams.*
22	B	*I just don't accept that.*
23	B	*employers should pay part of people's bus fares. He doesn't say they should provide buses.*
24	B	*tomorrow's my day off*
25	A	*I sometimes wonder how you manage to get out of bed in the mornings!*

Language practice: Listening Part 4

1 Functions: agreeing and disagreeing
a) 2 D
    3 A
    4 A
    5 D
    6 D
    7 D
    8 A

2 Vocabulary: traffic problems
1 car park
2 traffic lights; pedestrians
3 motorway; speed limit
4 traffic jam
5 petrol
6 pavement
7 tunnel

PAPER 3 Speaking

For Teacher's notes, see pages 185–186.

For notes and a guide to assessment, see page 203.

Part 1

For Teacher's notes, see page 186.

1 Giving personal information
a) 1 b   5 g
    2 h   6 e
    3 d   7 a
    4 f   8 c

b) 1 No (complete sentences would be unnatural)
    2 a and d

2 Vocabulary and pronunciation: school subjects
b) <u>ph</u>ysics, en<u>v</u>ironmental <u>sc</u>ience, <u>g</u>eography, <u>h</u>istory, philosophy, <u>m</u>usic, com<u>p</u>uting, re<u>lig</u>ion, <u>mo</u>dern <u>lang</u>uages, <u>li</u>terature

Part 2

For Teacher's notes, see page 186.

2 Functions: choosing a present
a) 1 a
    2 c
    3 a
    4 b
    5 a/b
    6 b/c
    7 a

b) 1 kind/sort
    2 sure
    3 idea
    4 because/as
    5 might/may
    6 going
    7 about
    8 better

Part 3

For Teacher's notes, see page 186.

2 Describing photos
a) B

Part 4

For Teacher's notes, see page 187.

1 Talking about your own or other people's experiences
1 c
2 e
3 a
4 b
5 d

2 Talking about some of the people in a group
a) 1 All of
    2 Two of
    3 Both of
    4 One of
    5 None of
    6 All of

Test 3

Photocopiable answer sheets are on pages 174–176.

Reading

Part 1

1. B *you'd be back* = arrive home
2. A *to be left at reception* = give ... to the receptionist
3. C *exchange goods* = change things
4. B *having her computer repaired* = someone is doing it for her, so she won't get e-mails
5. C *every 15 minutes* = regularly

Part 2

6. F *one-, two- or three-month courses; January; improve particular language skills*
7. H *during the morning; three weeks; minimum age eighteen; all levels*
8. A *up to age sixteen; learning fun and safe; a month; many ... activities*
9. C *aimed at beginners; English to buy tickets ... make new friends; two weeks*
10. D *three-month courses preparing for a certificate*

Part 3

11. A *St Michael's little sister, St Margaret*
12. A *in 1960 the last person left ... in 1991 two families moved back*
13. B *Three miles across the water from the town of Blascott lies the group of islands; restaurants in Blascott*
14. B *range of perfumes made from the wild flowers*
15. B *the same path which continues to climb to the highest point*
16. A *Priory Beach ... is safe for swimming; Sandtop Bay ... swimming is not advised here*
17. B *boat trips which depart from Blascott harbour in summer, Monday-Friday*
18. A *The charge for landing*
19. A *The crossing takes thirty minutes*
20. B *Before you set off ... visit the exhibition centre*

Part 4

21. A He describes the situation in the whole text and we know it is a problem because he asks: *How can I show ... without causing a family quarrel?*
22. B The text says: '*... with my grandparents ... a few aunts and uncles*'.
23. C *I was happy to have a friend in a strange place.*
24. A *she can't behave so badly towards me*
25. B The writer of the answer doesn't know James (James introduces himself at the beginning of the text, so this must be a letter to a magazine). A and C would have to come from one of his friends. D is incorrect because James's relatives aren't quarrelling, it is only James and his cousin Sophie.

Part 5

26. A (lexical)
27. C (lexical/structural)
28. B (structural)
29. C (lexical)
30. D (structural)
31. A (lexical)
32. B (structural)
33. D (lexical)
34. C (lexical)
35. B (structural)

Total reading marks = 35
These marks are weighted to 25.

Writing

Part 1

1. had
2. do you want
3. his own
4. can't afford
5. good at

Part 2

For a marking guide, see page 202.

6

Sample answer:

Hi Jimmy
Thanks for the great T-shirt. I really like it. Where did you get it? I'm going to wear it when I go clubbing at the weekend. Everyone will be so jealous!
All the best
Pietro

Part 3

For a marking guide, see page 202.

7

Sample answer 1:

I went to Tenerife with my parents and my brother. It's an island in the Atlantic. The weather is warm and sunny there and it's very popular with people from northern Europe. My brother and I swam every day and played tennis. We also went on a tour of the island with my parents. In the evenings we went to the disco in our hotel. The hotel was very big, with lots of sports facilities and two swimming pools. I shared a room with my brother. We had a view of the sea. It was a great holiday. Wouldn't you like to go there one day?
Best wishes,
Kurt

Sample answer 2:

I went camping with some friends from my English class. We went to a village near the sea. We had three tents for seven people. Luckily one tent was quite big. The place was very pretty, but the weather was not very good. It was cloudy on several days and sometimes it rained. But we had a good time in spite of the weather. We did some walking and on two days we went diving with a local club. It was very exciting. There was an old ship under the water that we could explore.
Was your holiday good? Write soon.
Love
Bettina

8

Sample answer 1:

Last Wednesday started really badly for me. I woke up late and I had to leave the house without any breakfast. At school, I realised I had forgotten my books, so I ran home between lessons to fetch them. I was one minute late for the next lesson.
The teacher asked me why I was late and I explained. He was surprised because he knows where I live. 'If you can run that fast, you should come and play football on Saturday.' I did, and I was amazed when he offered me a place on the team.
So Wednesday was a lucky day for me!

Sample answer 2:
My lucky day was a few weeks ago. I needed 50 euros to buy a new CD player, but I had saved only 40. I decided to go to the city centre to find a cheaper one. The tram costs 3 euros, but there was a problem with the ticket machine. I got on the tram, but I didn't have to pay. Then I went to the music store and saw that the CD player I wanted was cheaper than before, only 37 euros. So I was able to buy it, and I had enough money for the tram home.

Total writing marks = 25

Listening

Part 1

1 B Her house has bushes and flowers, no tree (that is next door) and the bus stop is on the other side of the road.
2 B There is a huge queue of cars at the roundabout.
3 C He says, *the plates I've bought for them*. The other things are what he suggests the woman should get.
4 A He says, *on foot*. He complains because he couldn't get a bus or taxi.
5 B He says *I've hurt my knee*.
6 A He says *Her hair's white now and she doesn't wear glasses any more*.
7 B She has put all the information at the bottom; she's forgotten to put the name of the school at the top; she chose the drawing of the violin.

Part 2

8 A *I was a typical student, passed enough exams and so on.*
9 B *I had to do a year's business course first.*
10 B *I learnt a lot there ... by watching people, I realised what you can and can't do with different types of cloth.*
11 C *I stayed at home until I won a prize.*
12 C *I went on to spend three wonderful years in Milan.*
13 A *I was too far away from my family.*

Part 3

14 first floor
15 map
16 fountain
17 lifts
18 a quarter past two / 2.15 / 14.15 / 2.15 p.m.
19 Whitmarsh

Part 4

20 A *under the big oak tree in the garden today as it's too hot inside.*
21 B *Miss Hayes ... says my voice isn't loud enough ... she's not giving me another chance.*
22 B *You've got a louder voice than most of the other people.*
23 B *It won't help.*
24 B *You can't persuade me ... I'm going to offer to do the scenery instead.*
25 A *They're still looking for someone to do that.* i.e. the scenery.

Total listening marks = 25

Speaking

For assessment and marking guide, see page 203.

Test 4

Photocopiable answer sheets are on pages 174–176.

Reading

Part 1

1 A *if they're closed* = even when the shop is closed
2 B *you are given* = free
3 C *lost property* = things people have lost; *left here after two weeks* = we keep ... for a maximum of two weeks
4 B *bring it to your house* = return it
5 A *serve yourself* = do your photocopying; *on way out* = when you leave

Part 2

6 H *amusing novel; a famous fashion house; written by a former model; the modern fashion world's secrets*
7 C *autobiography of the international gymnastics star*
8 D *beautifully written; lively descriptions of some of the great cities (of Europe) and their inhabitants, past and present.*
9 G *fast-moving adventure story, set in an imagined world of international football stars*
10 A *nineteenth century; won the hearts of young men;... silk dresses, the beautiful rooms ... world of palaces and gardens*

Part 3

11 A *light traffic*
12 B *services may only run once daily.*
13 B *it should not be too difficult to arrange things as you go*
14 B *There is no maximum or minimum number of hotel tickets you can buy*
15 A *Ruby being the most basic*
16 B *if ... Taz have no hotels, then we will find other ... accommodation ... in exchange for your Taz tickets.*
17 B *Later the scenery becomes even more amazing*
18 B *a half-day cruise* (i.e. in a boat) *... Then ... a leisurely drive*
19 A *from where there are wonderful views of the mountain itself*
20 A *Return to the airport*

Part 4

21 D The text mentions his general behaviour, but does not describe his business methods. However, at the end, it does suggest what he will do next in business, i.e. take over another company.
22 B *a colleague from his paper* = a journalist. The colleague was female (*her*).
23 D The waiter had heard of Parrish, but he didn't recognise him.
24 A The writer says *of course* because he agrees that Parrish doesn't look like the owner of one of the world's most successful computer companies.
25 C This headline summarises the writer's idea about Parrish's future.

Part 5

26 B (structural)
27 C (structural)
28 C (lexical)
29 A (lexical)
30 D (lexical)
31 B (structural)
32 C (lexical)
33 A (structural/lexical)
34 B (structural)
35 C (lexical)

Total reading marks = 35
These marks are weighted to 25.

Writing

Part 1

1 moved (in)
2 to live
3 We don't
4 bought them
5 don't have /need

Part 2

For a marking guide, see page 202.
Sample answer:
Dear Leo
Thanks very much for asking me to come to the match with you on Saturday. I'm really looking forward to it. I'm sure it'll be exciting. Would you like to come back to my house for a meal afterwards?
Hossein

Part 3

For a marking guide, see page 202.
7
Sample answer 1:
I am sixteen and I go to school here in Bern. I am studying a lot of different subjects, but my favourites are languages and biology.
In my free time I like to go swimming, and of course skiing in the winter. I'm also keen on reading, especially detective novels. When I have time, I like to look around the shops with my friends because we enjoy trying on new clothes.
I'm looking forward to coming to England and meeting you all. I hope I'll be able to visit some different cities in England, including London.
Thank you for inviting me.
Yours sincerely,
Ursula Haupt

Sample answer 2:
It's very kind of you to invite me to stay with you. I suppose you'd like to know something about me. I'm nineteen and I live and work in Malaga. I'm one of the receptionists at a hotel. I meet lots of English tourists, so I'm looking forward to seeing England.
In my free time I do watersports and I go horse-riding. I enjoy playing the guitar and singing, too.
I'd like to try some real English food while I'm in England. I'd also be interested to visit some famous historical places, such as Stonehenge, if that's possible.
Is there anything special I can bring you from Spain?
With best wishes,
Miguel

8
Sample answer:
Children were afraid of our neighbour Jordan Jenkins because he never spoke, but my mother said he was lonely and she sometimes invited him to dinner.
One week, my homework was to find out about the Second World War.
'Ask Jordan,' said my mother. 'He was a soldier.'
At first I was frightened, but in the end I went to see him. We had a very interesting conversation. He showed me photos and let me try on his army cap and helped me to write my homework. I realised that he was shy, not unfriendly. Now we're friends and I often visit him.

Total writing marks = 25

Listening

Part 1

1 B *what I always wanted to,* i.e. to be a nurse
2 C *I'll wait for you by the bus station*
3 A *Take the second turning on the right. The car park is on the left-hand side.*
4 A Brian will be twenty years old on the 15th.
5 C *He only had two children then.*
6 B *this plain one that I'm wearing*
7 C He's just got off the train and is still on the platform. He'll go to the café soon.

Part 2

8 C *This year we're looking for the best singer*
9 B *you must live within five miles of the city centre.*
10 C *you need to contact the theatre group's secretary*
11 A *10.30 p.m. instead of 9*
12 B *there will be no charge for swimmers for the whole of the first week*
13 B *all four of them now live here*

Part 3

14 420,000
15 bridges
16 (modern) offices
17 bread
18 (art) gallery
19 Saturday(s)

Part 4

20 B She has too much college work, she was listening to music while she studied.
21 A *It was loud enough for me to be able to listen to it*
22 B Kim didn't have visitors, Rob thought she had. *I was feeling sorry for myself* i.e. he was feeling sad.
23 A *I like something quiet in the background*
24 A She says the traffic noise disturbs her if it's too quiet.
25 B *I'm useless in the mornings* i.e. she can't work then.

Total listening marks = 25

Speaking

For a guide to assessment and marking, see page 203.

Test 5

Photocopiable answer sheets are on pages 174–176.

Reading

Part 1

1 C *students arriving late* = students who are late; *must sign ... before going* = should not go ... before signing
2 C *exams are over* = after their exams; *what about trying* = suggests going to
3 A *collecting my things* = bring her clothes home
4 B *keep children off* = children must not climb on
5 C *passengers for international flights* = if you (people) are going abroad

Part 2

6 B *artists who all live* (i.e. they are painting nowadays); *the café is open for lunch; the excellent bookshop*
7 D It has jewellery, etc. produced in Kington (= locally) and it is open until 9 p.m.
8 F *during the twentieth century* = over the last hundred years; *open every day*
9 G This is a rebuilt village which you can walk around, so it is outdoors. The children can learn about life 500 years ago and there is a playground.
10 E *a separate room for each century*, i.e. the museum contains paintings from past centuries (including over the last 300 years). It's open in the afternoon and there is a coffee shop.

Part 3

11 A *a full cooked breakfast at no extra charge*
12 B Last orders are taken at 9 p.m., but the dining room will be open after that for people to finish their meals.
13 B The Coffee Shop opens at 10 a.m., but the swimming pool is open from 7 p.m..
14 B Newspapers can be ordered at reception, but they are put in the dining room before you have breakfast.
15 A You can ask for a key and let yourself in.
16 B *For calls outside, dial 9*
17 B Children must be with an adult, there are no staff available for this.
18 A *after 1.30 p.m. every day*
19 A *Cash ... can be locked away*
20 B This is not mentioned.

Part 4

21 C The first two paragraphs explain the situation and in the third, the writer says that Jane has a problem.
22 A *a successful business with regular customers*
23 B *she wasn't told that the film is about a restaurant where everything goes wrong and the food is disgusting.*
24 D *The best solution ... is for her to contact the newspapers.*
25 D The film is a comedy and it was filmed in a London restaurant. It doesn't claim to be the truth and it will not teach you to cook.

Part 5

26 A (structural)
27 C (structural)
28 B (structural)
29 C (lexical)
30 D (lexical)
31 B (lexical)
32 A (structural)
33 C (lexical)
34 D (lexical/structural)
35 A (lexical)

Total reading marks = 35
These marks are weighted to 25.

Writing

Part 1

1 has
2 as good as
3 better/more than
4 use
5 can

Part 2

For a marking guide, see page 202.
Sample answer:
Dear Selina
I'm so sorry I didn't get to the cinema on time yesterday. There was an accident on the main road and terrible traffic jams everywhere. I hope you aren't too angry with me. What about meeting next Saturday?
Love,
Tanya

Part 3

For a marking guide, see page 202.
7
Sample answer 1:
Dear Annabel
It was my friend Bobby's 21st birthday. His parents hired a room in a hotel and paid for a disco. I danced for four hours! I took Bobby a cowboy hat as a present. It's a real one I bought in America. I guess he liked it because he wore it all evening.
There were about 60 people there. I knew most of them and they all seemed to enjoy themselves very much. I met one girl who I really liked. I'm going to see her again next weekend.
In my opinion, it was a great party.
All the best,
Simon

Sample answer 2:
Dear Annabel
You wanted to know about my friend Luisa's birthday. We listened to some music and then we watched a video. The music was great. It was a CD Luisa got for her birthday, but the film was very silly. Luisa's older sister Martina was there and Martina's boyfriend and four other friends. I hadn't met Martina before. She's very pretty, and her boyfriend told some good jokes. They are both at university and they talked about that. We all had a good time. I took Luisa some expensive handcream and soap. She said she really liked it. Write back soon.
Love from
Carla

8
Sample answer:
I had just finished getting dressed when the doorbell rang. I ran downstairs and got into the taxi. The driver took me to the television company's offices.
'I'm here for the music competition,' I told the receptionist.
I was taken to a waiting room. There were several other people there, some of them had musical instruments.

We could hear a singer in the studio next door. I was so nervous that I was shaking.
At last it was time for me to perform.
I sang well, but I wasn't good enough to win. However, I made some new friends while I was waiting and we've started our own band. One day we'll be famous.

Total writing marks = 25

Listening
Part 1

1   A   *they've only got one singer; The guitarist and the drummer*
2   C   She says the four blocks are close together, but hers is much taller, and she says the main road is no problem.
3   A   *And you'd better look in that pile of magazines by the bin. I'm going to throw them away. Yes! I asked you just in time.*
4   B   This is how he looks now. *hasn't got much hair and it's grey ... beard ... wears glasses*
5   A   She says *two letters and a postcard* but only one of the letters is for the man and there's also a parcel
6   C   It was due at 9.20 and it is now 9.35, which is why the woman is making enquiries. It is expected at 10.55, but the woman guesses she won't leave until later than that.
7   C   He was going to babysit, but he didn't have to, and he had already done his homework earlier.

Part 2

8   C   *a boys' subject*
9   C   *I've spent the past couple of months*
10   B   *my original plan was to use it in my bedroom*
11   A   *if you aren't very strong, the power of electric tools can be a real help.*
12   A   *don't expect to make anything very big or difficult for the first few months*
13   B   *begin with a list of everything that's going to be necessary*

Part 3

14   26(th) October
15   blue
16   (top) hairdresser
17   shoes
18   (a) computer
19   (the) cinema

Part 4

20   B   *my uncle and aunt are going ... and they've asked me to go with them.* They don't live there.
21   A   *It's a really brilliant place for a trip, I've heard.*
22   B   They don't insist, although they really want him to spend his holiday with them.
23   B   *he's out at work all year,* i.e. away from the house
24   A   *isn't keen on planes*
25   A   *What about my uncle and aunt's trip? If you came, it'd be even better.*

Total listening marks = 25

Speaking

For assessment and marking guide, see page 203.

Test 6

Photocopiable answer sheets are on pages 174–176.

Reading
Part 1

1   A   *ring when you get to your hotel* = Angus wants Jen to telephone him from her hotel
2   B   *Do not use... before reading* = read before using
3   C   *before moving house* = to their new home; *unwanted furniture* = don't want to take all their furniture
4   A   *cash only* = you cannot pay with a credit card
5   B   *where have you put them* = is asking her mother where her jeans are

Part 2

6   D   *in the centre of this great city; one or two months this summer; magazine journalism*
7   E   *mid-July to September;, four girls aged three to eleven baby boy; one month in France*
8   G   *answer phone and e-mail enquiries, check application forms and occasionally show new visitors round; evening; until end of summer*
9   C   *Six days per week (any day off by arrangement except Fridays). Hours from 2 p.m. till 10 p.m. or from 6 a.m. till 2 p.m.; accommodation available if required*
10   B   *in Southern Europe and Scandinavia; Excellent rates of pay (extra for foreign language speakers); Minimum six weeks, starting mid July.*

Part 3

11   B   *there are a few true stories*
12   B   *the wife of a man who was made to join the army*
13   A   *joined the army .... it was thirteen years before she found him*
14   B   *doctors were operating on her for an injury she had received while fighting*
15   B   *it's not certain why she left Ireland ... and went to the islands... when she got there she fell in love*
16   A   *she worked with John to steal a ship*
17   A   *a boy they had taken off another ship ... was Mary Reed*
18   B   *Mary had fought in the army but had stopped pretending to be a man ... when she married*
19   B   *the men were taken prisoner but they avoided punishment*
20   A   *Nobody knows what happened to them*

Part 4

21   C   The writer discusses what Antarctica is like for him – his aim isn't to persuade other people to go there, to complain (he says he is lucky) or to suggest ways of improving life there
22   A   *So the hardest thing to get used to is that there are now just fourteen of us because I'm used to working in a large company.*
23   C   *Ten years ago, we were able to send faxes to friends and family once a month but today we can send e-mails and talk on the phone so we don't feel so far away.*
24   B   *We were joined together by a rope all the time in case we fell into any holes in the ice. They're too deep to climb out of.*
25   C   *I was reminded how lucky I am to be here. Soon we will get amazing sunsets too.* A is wrong because he's been there before. B is wrong because he's worked hard. D is wrong because he's only been there three months.

Part 5

26 B (structural)
27 C (lexical)
28 D (lexical)
29 C (structural)
30 A (structural)
31 D (lexical)
32 C (lexical/structural)
33 A (lexical)
34 C (structural)
35 C (lexical/structural)

Total reading marks = 25

Writing
Part 1

1 discovered
2 joining
3 better
4 are all brilliant
5 too much

Part 2

For a marking guide, see page 202.
Sample answer:
Dear Lee
I'm going to the party next week by bus. Why don't we go together? We can meet at the bus stop near my flat. Have you decided what present to take? I can't decide. Have you got any ideas?

Part 3

For a marking guide, see page 202.
7
Sample answer 1:
I always go shopping on Saturdays. I get up late, then I meet my friends in the town centre. Sometimes we go to a café first, then we look at all the shops in the shopping centre. I like buying clothes best, but I also look for CDs. Sometimes there are sales. I'm happy then because I don't have much money to spend. There are lots of different shops in my town selling everything you need. We have plenty of good clothes shops, but there aren't many good shops for buying shoes.

Sample answer 2:
I live in a village which has only three shops – a baker's, a butcher's and a very small supermarket. I sometimes do the shopping for my mother there. At the weekend I often catch the bus with my friends to the town and we spend the day there because there are lots of shops. A lot of them sell food, but we like looking at the sports shops. When I have some money, I like to buy sports equipment and trainers. I sometimes buy CDs or clothes, but the clothes in my favourite shop are very expensive.

8
Sample answer:
I got off the train and waved to my brother, who was waiting on the platform. He called to me. 'Hurry' he said 'I've come in the car so we can get home quickly.' I couldn't understand why he wanted to hurry because I was looking forward to having a rest at home. 'Why do we need to hurry?' I asked. But he didn't tell me. When we went into the flat I noticed several suitcases in the hall. Then my mother told me. She had won a holiday in

Greece in a radio competition. She told me not to unpack because there was no time. So instead of relaxing at home, I had a lovely holiday on the beach in Greece.

Total writing marks = 25

Listening
Part 1

1 A She's teaching herself the keyboard. Her violin teacher moved away, and her brother is looking for a drummer.
2 B *How about a book about painting? She's just started some art classes; I think my idea was best. She doesn't want to borrow her mum's books all the time*
3 C *On Sunday it will be cloudy. It won't rain until Monday*
4 C *see if I left my wallet in your house*
5 A *could you go out and get a lettuce; get some mushrooms*
6 C *you won't be able to play tennis today*
7 B *but aren't the sleeves a bit long – only the blouse has sleeves*

Part 2

8   B *the game didn't actually go on sale until the day after my thirteenth birthday*
9   C *None of them let me show them the game.*
10 B *Then we talked to my grandmother and my great aunt who are quite rich. They were happy to lend us enough to make the first thousand games.*
11 C *I was watching my sisters playing one day and I got the idea from them.*
12 A *'Then between ten and twelve, they enjoy games based on knowledge – quizzes and things like that.*
13 B *I'd like to learn how to run a business so that's what I'll study at college.*

Part 3

14 210
15 Black / black
16 guide
17 bicycle /bike
18 party
19 website

Part 4

20 B *a week going to work instead of going to school.*
21 A *Do you think it's a good idea? I'm so busy.*
22 B *I don't even know what they look like.*
23 A *then I'll decide*
24 B *I think it's better to try something you don't know about.*
25 A *I'll do it.*

Total listening marks = 25

Speaking

For a guide to assessment and marking, see page 203.

Extra practice for Writing Part 1

1 got/bought it
2 of his
3 cost very
4 Can I have
5 must wear
6 more fun than
7 taught me
8 should
9 used to
10 busy

Assessment and marking guide

Writing Part 2

Mark	Criteria
5	All content elements covered appropriately. Message clearly communicated to reader.
4	All content elements adequately dealt with. Message communicated successfully, on the whole.
3	All content elements attempted. Message requires some effort by the reader. **or** One content element omitted but others clearly communicated.
2	Two content elements omitted, or unsuccessfully dealt with. Message only partly communicated to reader. **or** Script may be slightly short (20–25 words).
1	Little relevant content and/or message requires excessive effort by the reader, or short (10–19 words).
0	Totally irrelevant or totally incomprehensible or too short (under 10 words).

Writing Part 3

Mark	Criteria
5	Very good attempt: • Confident and ambitious use of language. • Wide range of structures and vocabulary within the task set. • Well organised and coherent, through use of simple linking devices. • Errors are minor, due to ambition, and non-impeding. • Requires no effort by the reader.
4	Good attempt: • Fairly ambitious use of language. • More than adequate range of structures and vocabulary within the task set. • Evidence of organisation and some linking of sentences. • Some errors, generally non-impeding. • Requires only a little effort by the reader.
3	Adequate attempt: • Language is unambitious, or if ambitious, flawed. • Adequate range of structures and vocabulary. • Some attempt at organisation; linking of sentences not always maintained. • A number of errors may be present, but are mostly non-impeding. • Requires some effort by the reader.
2	Inadequate attempt: • Language is simplistic/limited/repetitive. • Inadequate range of structures and vocabulary. • Some incoherence; erratic punctuation. • Numerous errors, which sometimes impede communication. • Requires considerable effort by the reader.
1	Poor attempt: • Severely restricted command of language. • No evidence of range of structures and vocabulary. • Seriously incoherent; absence of punctuation. • Very poor control; difficult to understand. • Requires excessive effort by the reader.
0	Achieves nothing: language impossible to understand, or totally irrelevant to task.

Speaking Test

Throughout the test, candidates are assessed on their language skills, not their personality, intelligence, or knowledge of the world. They must, however, be prepared to develop the conversation, where appropriate, and respond to the tasks set. Prepared speeches are not acceptable. Candidates are assessed on their own individual performance and not in relation to each other. Both examiners assess the candidates according to criteria which are interpreted at PET level. The interlocutor awards a mark for global achievement, whilst the assessor awards marks according to four analytical criteria:

- Grammar and Vocabulary
- Discourse Management
- Pronunciation
- Interactive Communication.

Grammar and Vocabulary – This scale refers to the accurate and appropriate use of grammatical forms and vocabulary, It also includes the range of both grammatical forms and vocabulary. Performance is viewed in terms of the overall effectiveness of the language used in dealing with the tasks.

Discourse Management – This scale refers to the coherence, extent and relevance of each candidate's individual contribution. On this scale, the candidate's ability to maintain a coherent flow of language is assessed, either within a single utterance or over a string of utterances. Also assessed here is how relevant the contributions are to what has gone before.

Pronunciation – This scale refers to the candidate's ability to produce comprehensible utterances to fulfil the task requirements. This includes stress, rhythm and intonation, as well as individual sounds. Examiners put themselves in the position of the non-language specialist and assess the overall impact of the pronunciation and the degree of effort required to understand the candidate. Different varieties of English, e.g. British, North American, Australian etc., are acceptable, provided they are used consistently throughout the test.

Interactive Communication – This scale refers to the candidate's ability to use language to achieve meaningful communication. This includes initiating and responding without undue hesitation, the ability to use interactive strategies to maintain or repair communication, and sensitivity to the norms of turn-taking.

Global Achievement – This scale refers to the candidate's overall effectiveness in dealing with the tasks in the four separate parts of the PET Speaking Test. The global mark is an independent impression mark which reflects the assessment of the candidate's performance from the interlocutor's perspective. The interlocutor gives one global mark for each candidate's performance across all parts of the test.

Marking – As mentioned above, assessment is based on performance in the whole test, and is not related to performance in particular parts of the test. The assessor awards marks for each of the four criteria listed above. The interlocutor awards each candidate one global mark.

Tapescripts

Test 1

PAPER 2 Listening

There are four parts to the test. You will hear each part twice. For each part of the test there will be time for you to look through the questions and time for you to check your answers.

Write your answers on the question paper. You will have six minutes at the end of the test to copy your answers onto the answer sheet.

Part 1

There are seven questions in this part. For each question, there are three pictures and a short recording. Choose the correct picture and put a tick in the box below it.

Before we start, here is an example.

What will the boy take back to the shop?

Girl: Did you get everything you wanted?

Boy: I did. In fact I only needed to go into one shop. I'd seen a T-shirt in the window and I got the last one in the sale. And some shorts to match. I bought this jacket too but I'm not sure if I like it.

Girl: Oh, it looks great. I'd keep it. But those shorts are a horrible colour. I should change them.

Boy: You're right. They looked different in the shop.

The first picture is correct so there is a tick in box A.

Look at the three pictures for question 1 now.

Now we are ready to start. Listen carefully. You will hear each recording twice.

1 *What time will Paula pick Julie up?*

Woman: Hi Julie. This is Paula. I'm ringing to remind you that I'll pick you up tonight. The film doesn't start until eight fifteen, so we can go a bit later than I thought. I'll leave here at about twenty past seven so I'll be at your house at twenty to eight. We need to allow time to park the car and I want to get good seats. See you later then. Give me a ring if there's a problem.

Now listen again.

2 *What will they get first?*

Girl: The most important thing I need is new trainers. I know exactly which ones I want. They're in the shop by the library. Let's go straight there.

Woman: Just a minute. That's the opposite end of town. I want to get a film for my camera in this shop while we're here.

Girl: Don't forget we need some fruit.

Woman: We'll get that last, after we've bought your trainers, because it'll be heavy.

Now listen again.

3 *Where did the woman leave her keys?*

Woman: Oh, I'm in a hurry and I can't find my keys. I always leave them on the hall table.

Man: Let's see. You didn't leave them in the car, did you? That's what I did last week.

Woman: I'll go and look.

Man: There are some keys in the kitchen but I don't think they're yours. I'll get them.

Woman: Those are mine. Thanks.

Now listen again.

4 *What does the man decide to eat?*

Woman: What will you have? How about fish and chips? It's really good here.

Man: Actually I think I'll just have a drink.

Woman: You must have more than that. It's hours since we had lunch. What about chicken then or a chicken sandwich?

Man: If they have salad, I'll have some with a roll.

Now listen again.

5 *What time is the woman's new appointment?*

Woman 1: Good morning. Dr Clarke's surgery.

Woman 2: Hello. Could I change the appointment I have for tomorrow, please? It's in the morning and I can't come till the afternoon. The name's Joanna Saunders.

Woman 1: Certainly. I'll have a look and see if Dr Clarke is free. ... So you can't come at a quarter past ten. Erm ... quarter to three is available or a quarter past four.

Woman 2: I'll take the later one, thank you. Goodbye.

Now listen again.

6 *What was cancelled?*

Woman: We missed the first day of our holiday because of the bad weather.

Man: Oh! Was your plane cancelled?

Woman: That wasn't the problem. And the coach was waiting to take us to the port, but the sea was so rough we had to wait till the next day and take a helicopter to the island. It was much more expensive and I was looking forward to the ferry crossing.

Now listen again.

7 *What did Jason enjoy doing on Saturday?*

Girl: Hi, Jason. Did you have a good day yesterday? Did you have a football match?

Boy: Yes, but we lost, so we all felt a bit miserable. The score was 5-0.

Girl: I went shopping with Sally. We really enjoyed ourselves. But I know you don't like shopping.

Boy: Well, actually I spent Saturday afternoon looking for a birthday present for my sister, and I had a great time in the bookshops and music shops. I got her a book and a CD. Then I went to the cinema to see *Road to the Stars*. I was really looking forward to it, but it wasn't as good as I expected.

Now listen again.

That is the end of Part 1.

Part 2

You will hear a woman, Vanessa, talking about a journey she made with her husband, Robert, and her baby, Ben. For each question, put a tick in the correct box.

You now have 45 seconds to look at the questions for Part 2.

Now we are ready to start. Listen carefully. You will hear the recording twice.

Interviewer: Good evening Vanessa. You're going to tell us about your journey. Where was it from and to?

Vanessa: Well, my husband, Robert, and I had worked in Hong Kong for years. We got married there six years ago and had a baby there. But last year, we gave up our jobs and decided to sail back to England, with the baby.

Interviewer: And how long did it take you to get ready for the trip?

Vanessa: We had six months to buy a boat and make sure we had everything we needed. My friends didn't believe I could live in such a small space, but I was happy about that. I was most anxious about our health, particularly the baby, and I started collecting medicines in case we needed them.

Interviewer: And your first stop was Singapore?

Vanessa: Yes. The first part of the journey was the worst – we were sick all the time. I hadn't expected to hit bad weather so soon. We'd no worries about the boat, which had already been round the world once. In fact, when we reached Singapore, I wasn't sure about spending six more months on the boat and I considered flying home to England, but luckily decided not to. We spent six long boring weeks in Singapore waiting for the weather to improve.

Interviewer: And you were joined by your father-in-law?

Vanessa: On the next part of the journey, my father-in-law joined us with a friend of his, who's a cook. It was wonderful to have a cook to prepare meals. This gave Robert and me more time. My father-in-law was very happy to take care of the baby while we sailed the boat.

Interviewer: And did the baby enjoy the trip?

Vanessa: He did, I think. He loved climbing up the steps in the boat. He spent the first year of his life at sea. While he was awake we played with him because it was dangerous to leave him alone. I'm sure this is why he wants us to play with him all the time now. I worried that he wouldn't learn to walk, but he had no problems. He'll only eat particular foods, but all children are like that, whether they've been on a boat or not.

Interviewer: And do you have any advice for other people sailing with children?

Vanessa: Children are happy on long journeys as long as they have plenty to do on board. It's dangerous otherwise. We just had one child with us, but it might be better with two or three who can play together.

Interviewer: Well, has anyone got any questions?

Now listen again.

That is the end of Part 2.

Part 3

You will hear someone talking on the radio about the Willingham Museum. For each question, fill in the missing information in the numbered space.

You now have 20 seconds to look at Part 3.

Now we are ready to start. Listen carefully. You will hear the recording twice.

Radio presenter: And to finish our programme about the area, I must advise you to visit Willingham. Cars aren't allowed into the centre, so it's very pleasant to walk around. Your first stop should be the museum, where history is brought to life. Go back to the nineteenth century and walk along a street which looks just like it did then. There's even a horse and cart that you can ride on. The part of the museum which really interested me was a 1950s dining room. It was just like my grandmother's house when I was a child. And there's plenty more – toys, pottery, jewellery.

If you can wait, there's a new exhibition opening soon. Willingham is famous for one thing in particular – something all of us wear – shoes. People have made them in Willingham for hundreds of years, and in this exhibition you can see how they were made. But don't go yet because it doesn't start until the 14th of July.

Allow at least half a day to visit the museum. It's on a hill in a very old building which used to be a prison. It's a much happier place now than it was then, I can tell you. One room describes the history of the building itself.

You can't miss the museum. It's not in the town centre itself – it's just in front of the castle, and you can see that from wherever you are in the town.

Have a look round the town of Willingham too while you're there. If you start in the main square and follow the green signs, they'll take you to the museum. And you'll see lots of other interesting things on the way too. Well, that's all for today ...

Now listen again.

That is the end of Part 3.

Part 4

Look at the six sentences for this part. You will hear a conversation between a boy, William, and a girl, Sophie, in a music shop. Decide if each sentence is correct or incorrect. If it is correct, put a tick in the box under A for YES. If it is not correct, put a tick in the box under B for NO.

You now have 20 seconds to look at the questions for Part 4.

Now we are ready to start. Listen carefully. You will hear the recording twice.

Sophie: Hi, William.

William: Oh, hi, Sophie.

Sophie: This is a good music shop, isn't it? Before it opened, I had to ask my mum to buy me what I wanted in Birmingham because there wasn't a good shop here.

William: Your mum went all the way to Birmingham to buy what you wanted? It's about twenty kilometres from here!

Sophie: No, silly. She works there.

William: So do you go with her sometimes in the holidays and spend the day shopping in Birmingham?

Sophie: Well, I find the city centre a bit big, so I get anxious about getting lost. I'd rather tell my mum what I want and she gets it for me. She doesn't mind.

William: Well, next time you go I could come with you. If we had a map, it wouldn't be a problem for me.

Sophie: Yes, if we were together, it'd be OK. That CD you had in your hand when I came in … are you going to buy it?

William: I already have. Why?

Sophie: Oh, I was thinking of getting it too. It's the new one by that band 521, isn't it? I didn't use to like them much, but their music has got a lot better recently.

William: Mmm. Don't get the same one. You can borrow mine. If you got a different one by the same band, then you could lend that to me.

Sophie: Well ...

William: I don't think this one's very good anyway actually. Look at these others – they've got much better songs on them.

Sophie: Mmm, I hadn't seen that one. But I'm going to get the one I planned to buy – that's what I really want.

William: Well, here you are then. Happy birthday! I've just bought it for you.

Sophie: Oh, thank you, but my birthday's not till next week. I really prefer surprises.

William: Well, you spoilt the surprise. I had to give it to you now to stop you buying it.

Now listen again.

That is the end of Part 4.

You now have six minutes to check and copy your answers on to the answer sheet.

That is the end of the test.

Speaking
Part 1

Sample interview

Examiner: Good morning. Can I have your mark sheets please? I'm Mary, and this is Michael. He's just going to listen to us. Now, what is your name?

Carlo: I'm Carlo.

Examiner: Thank you. And what is your name?

Anna: Anna.

Examiner: Thank you. What's your surname, Carlo?

Carlo: Bianchi.

Examiner: How do you spell it?

Carlo: B-I-A-N-C-H-I

Examiner: And Anna, what's your family name?

Anna: Rimini.

Examiner: How do you spell that?

Anna: R-I-M-I-N-I.

Examiner: Where do you come from, Carlo?

Carlo: Italy.

Examiner: And do you work or are you a student in Italy?

Carlo: I'm a student.

Examiner: What do you study?

Carlo: Er, in Italy?

Examiner: Yes. What subjects do you study in Italy?

Carlo: Oh. Er ... lots of subjects. I'm at school.

Examiner: Yes, I see, thank you. Anna, where do you come from?

Anna: I'm from Italy too. My home's in Milan.

Examiner: What do you do there?

Anna: I work in an office. I'm a secretary.

Examiner: Thank you. What do you enjoy doing in your free time?

Anna: Er ... I'm sorry, I don't understand. Can you repeat that please?

Examiner: What do you enjoy doing when you're not working?

Anna: I like going out with my friends and I also like cooking.

Examiner: Really? And what did you do yesterday evening?

Anna: I did my homework for my English teacher, and I visited a friend.

Examiner: OK. Thank you. And what about you, Carlo? What did you do yesterday evening?

Carlo: I did some homework too and then I watched a football match on TV.

Examiner: Do you enjoy studying English?

Carlo: Um, sometimes.

Examiner: Do you think English will be useful for you in the future?

Carlo: Yes.

Examiner: Why?

Carlo: Er, because, um, it's useful for, um, it's useful, it can help me to get a job, I think.

Examiner: Thank you.

Part 2

Sample interview

Examiner: Now I'm going to describe a situation to you. You are going to make some plans for a day out together. I'll give you some pictures of places you can visit. Talk together about which three places you'll go to. Decide which you will go to first. Here are the pictures. Just think for few seconds and I'll say that again.

You are going to make some plans for a day out together. Talk together about which three places you'll go to. Decide which one you will go to first. Ready? Anna, would you like to start?

Anna: Where would you like to go, Carlo? There's an old castle ... What do you think?

Carlo: Well, can we try something else? I'd prefer to go to the swimming pool because ... because ... I like swimming and diving and er, because I like taking exercise and ... What do you want to do?

Anna: Er ... I'd prefer to go somewhere for shopping, like the mall or the market ... yeah, I think the market has some interesting clothes. OK ... so, shall we go to one place that you want – like the swimming pool – and one place that I want – like the market?

Carlo: Yes, that sounds good. Let's do that. Let's go to the market, and you can look at the clothes, and then the swimming pool. What shall we do for lunch?

Anna: Well, how about, how about going to the burger bar for lunch? It's probably OK.

Carlo: I'm not so sure about that. I'd prefer to eat in a restaurant. Perhaps we can find a restaurant in the mall and eat there.

Anna: That's a great idea. So, shall we go to the mall after the market?

Carlo: All right. Let's do that. I'd like to go there too. Then we can relax at the swimming pool all the afternoon.

Anna: That's a great idea.

Examiner: Thank you.

Part 3

Sample interview

Examiner: Now I'm going to give each of you a photograph of people indoors. Carlo, here's yours.

Carlo: Thank you.

Examiner: Would you show it to Anna and talk about it, please? Anna, I'll give you a photograph in a moment. Carlo, would you start now?

Carlo: OK, so, it's a bedroom, I think. There's a girl. She's sitting on a sofa, no perhaps it's a bed. I'm not sure. She's studying. She's got some books. Er … The television is on, but she's not looking at it. Perhaps she can hear it. Um …

Examiner: The room's not very tidy.

Carlo: No, it isn't. Um, there's a – I don't know the word in English, um, it's like a box, beside her. It's full of paper and, it's for rubbish? And there's a toy, a bear. I don't like er, this room, very much.

Examiner: Thank you. Now Anna, here's your photo. Would you show it to Carlo and tell him about it, please.

Anna: Thank you. Well, there's a girl in the photo. She's in a room, it could be her bedroom, I can't see, but it's got a computer in it. There are two photos behind her, and a toy animal, a tiger.

Carlo: Yes.

Anna: It's night, I think, because the light is on.

Examiner: Mmm.

Anna: She's listening to, um, she's, er, on the phone. She looks bored, I think. Er, I think she was working when the phone rang. She's looking at the computer. Maybe her friend phoned about homework, to talk about their homework.

Examiner: Thank you. May I have the photographs back? Thank you.

Part 4

Sample interview

Examiner: Um, your photographs showed people studying. Now, I'd like you to talk together about the kind of places you prefer to study in – find out how you each like to organise your work.

Carlo: Yes.

Anna: Do you prefer to study alone, Carlo?

Carlo: Er, sometimes. If I have to write something, I like to be alone. What about you?

Anna: Me too. I can't work when there are other people in the room with me. But sometimes if the work is hard, I want to be with my friend.

Carlo: What do you mean?

Anna: You know, we can help each other, give each other some ideas …

Carlo: Um, yes, that's OK sometimes. And when you want to learn something, some vocabulary, something …

Anna: Oh, yes.

Carlo: Because that's sometimes boring.

Anna: Yes, I sometimes work with my friend and we make games to help remember words. But I don't want other people there, you know, who are doing different things, like watching television.

Carlo: No.

Anna: Because I can't work if they are talking.

Carlo: Yes. And if I'm bored I listen to music as well.

Anna: I agree. I often listen to music when I'm studying.

Carlo: Very loud.

Anna: Oh, yes. But not the radio because they talk too much.

Carlo: No. That's, um, that's annoying.

Anna: Yes …

Examiner: So, do either of you use a computer for your studies?

Carlo: Yes. I have a laptop and I write on it. It's good for my spelling.

Anna: Yes. I haven't got a computer, but there are some computers in my school. Sometimes I use the internet.

Carlo: Yes. But it's difficult to find things sometimes.

Anna: You're right, but my teacher helps me.

Carlo: That's good for you, but my school doesn't have enough computers.

Anna: No?

Carlo: We have to share.

Examiner: Thank you both. That's the end of the test.

Anna: Thank you.

Carlo: Thank you.

Test 2

PAPER 2 Listening

There are four parts to the test. You will hear each part twice. For each part of the test there will be time for you to look through the questions and time for you to check your answers.

Write your answers on the question paper. You will have six minutes at the end of the test to copy your answers onto the answer sheet.

Part 1

There are seven questions in this part. For each question, there are three pictures and a short recording. Choose the correct picture and put a tick in the box below it.

Before we start, here is an example.

What will the boy take back to the shop?

Girl: Did you get everything you wanted?

Boy: I did. In fact I only needed to go into one shop. I'd seen a T-shirt in the window and I got the last one in the sale. And some shorts to match. I bought this jacket too but I'm not sure if I like it.

Girl: Oh, it looks great. I'd keep it. But those shorts are a horrible colour. I should change them.

Boy: You're right. They looked different in the shop.

The first picture is correct so there is a tick in box A.

Look at the three pictures for question 1 now.

Now we are ready to start. Listen carefully. You will hear each recording twice.

1 Where will they meet?

Woman: Oh, I'm tired of sitting in this traffic queue. Do you mind if I get out here, because I want to go to the library. When you've parked the car, I'll see you in the café. You know, the one next to the swimming pool.

Man: OK, I think I'll try the car park behind the swimming pool. Then I won't have far to walk back. See you later then.

Woman: Bye.

Now listen again.

2 What is the woman looking for?

Man: Good morning, madam. Can I help you?

Woman: Oh yes, my daughter left her coat on the bus yesterday. It's dark blue with a wide belt and a large collar, and it's got two big pockets on the front. She left her purse in one of them unfortunately.

Man: I'll see if we've got a coat like that. Just a minute.

Now listen again.

3 Which photograph are they looking at?

Man: I took this on the way up before we reached the forest. You can see the village where we were staying, look. When we got to the top of the mountain, I took lots of photos because there was a wonderful view of the sea from up there. But unfortunately those ones were no good – something went wrong with the camera.

Now listen again.

4 Where is the boy's flat?

Boy: Hi, is Misha there?

Girl: No, sorry he's not. Can I take a message?

Boy: Yes, please. He's coming to see my new flat tomorrow and I need to give him directions. Can you tell him when he gets off the bus, he needs to cross the road and take the first turning on the right, then the second turning on the left. My flat is just before the roundabout on the right-hand side.

Girl: OK. I've got that. I'll tell him.

Now listen again.

5 Who is coming to stay with the girl?

Girl: My aunt's coming to visit us at the weekend. She's bringing my twin cousins – they're six. They were babies last time I saw them, and it was really hard work for all of us because they used to cry a lot then. I'm really looking forward to seeing them again because they live in New York, so I don't see them much. My uncle has to stay behind because he has to work, and Joe, their teenage son, has decided to stay with him, so that's a shame. I won't see them this time.

Now listen again.

6 What was the weather like on Tom's holiday?

Girl: How was your holiday Tom? You had lovely weather, didn't you?

Boy: Well actually, it was much better here. We left here in bright sunshine, but we didn't see the sun again for the whole week. It didn't actually rain, but it was very cloudy.

Girl: What about the hotel?

Boy: Oh, there was a lovely view from our room. The hotel staff said it had rained a lot the week before. So we were lucky.

Now listen again.

7 Where is the desk now?

Boy: You look tired, Alice.

Girl: Oh, I am. I've moved all the furniture around in my bedroom. I used to have my desk behind the door, but I decided to move it.

Boy: So where have you put it?

Girl: I tried it under the big window, but it was too sunny there to study, so I've put it under the little window opposite the door.

Now listen again.

That is the end of Part 1.

Part 2

You will hear a tour guide talking to a group of tourists about a coach trip. For each question, put a tick in the correct box.

You now have 45 seconds to look at the questions for Part 2.

Now we are ready to start. Listen carefully. You will hear the recording twice.

Tour guide: Good morning everyone. I'm your tour guide for today. We've made a change to the trip we usually make on Thursdays. I hope none of you will mind. We're still going to visit the beautiful town of Brampton with its old university, and there'll be time to look round that as usual. But today, because we have a lot of children here this week, we're also going to a wildlife park which a colleague of mine has recommended.

On the way to Brampton, we'll drive through some beautiful countryside. We'll go over the mountain and we'll have a lovely view of the lake from the top. We'll stop there for a few minutes so you can take some photos. In the next valley, we'll have a break for coffee. There's a café near a beautiful waterfall and if any of you want to go for a walk, you can.

We'll get to Brampton at about 11.30. It's a lovely town. We'll start by taking a guided tour of the university, which was built in the seventeenth century. Then there'll be time for all of you to have a look at the shops. Most people come to Brampton nowadays for the shops, but it's the university that made the town famous. If you don't want to look at the shops, I suggest you visit the museum.

After lunch, we'll get back on the coach and go to the wildlife park. We need to stay in the coach while we drive round because we'll see

lions in the park, which can obviously be dangerous. Tell your children not to expect it to be like the zoo – the animals are sometimes hiding in the trees. I know some friends of mine have seen some tigers, but I've never seen them and I'm afraid they no longer have any monkeys, but you may see some giraffes.

We'll leave the wildlife park at half past five. The journey back takes about an hour and a quarter, so we'll return to the hotel at a quarter to seven. There'll just be time for you to change before dinner at a quarter past seven.

Now then, before we get on the bus, if anyone wants to ask any questions I'll try to answer them. I'm going to give each of you an information sheet about the places we're going to visit. Some of you were on yesterday's trip with me and I know you found the information sheet helpful. So, if we just move over here….

Now listen again.

That is the end of Part 2.

Part 3

You will hear someone talking on the radio about a competition. For each question, fill in the missing information in the numbered space.

You now have 20 seconds to look at Part 3.

Now we are ready to start. Listen carefully. You will hear the recording twice.

Radio presenter: Well, that's about it for this month's edition of Book Club. We hope you've enjoyed hearing our discussion this week.

Now it's time for me to tell you about our super new competition. And I have to say, you won't believe the prize we've got for you this month. Would you believe we're giving you the chance to win your own computer. And not just a computer – it comes with a colour printer as well. This is a competition you really have to enter, isn't it? So, what do you need to know? And what do you have to do?

All you have to do is enter our short story competition. It couldn't be easier. We want you to write a short story up to 1,500 words long. The rules are very simple. In fact, they could hardly be simpler. We want lots of entries. What you have to do is sit down and write a short crime story, using your own ideas – and they can be as strange and wonderful as you like, in fact, the stranger, the better. But, and this is important, everything that happens in your story must be in the future. So, just let your imagination fly away and start writing, because this could be your lucky month.

Send your entries to me, Joy Jones, at the usual address. Put your name, address, telephone number and, very important this, so don't forget, your age, at the end of your story. Oh, and I forgot to say, for this competition there's an age limit. You must be under eighteen when you enter. Make sure you post your story in time to reach me by the 8th of March. So good luck, good writing and good reading until next month.

Now listen again.

That is the end of Part 3.

Part 4

Look at the six sentences for this part. You will hear a conversation between a man, Marcus, and a woman, Cora, who work in the same office. Decide if each sentence is correct or incorrect. If it is correct, put a tick in the box under A for YES. If it is not correct, put a tick in the box under B for NO.

You now have 20 seconds to look at the questions for Part 4.

Now we are ready to start. Listen carefully. You will hear the recording twice.

Marcus: Hi there!

Cora: Morning, or should I say afternoon?

Marcus: I'm not late, am I?

Cora: Only a few minutes today. But you're never exactly early, are you?

Marcus: Well, it's the traffic isn't it? There were queues of buses stopping anything from moving up the London Road.

Cora: But that's where you're wrong. It's the cars that make traffic jams because there are so many of them. And most of the time they have just one person in them – like you! At least the buses have more than one person in them. Anyway, I don't know why you don't come to work on your bike. You'd pass all the jams, and you'd be fitter.

Marcus: I just don't accept that. What about the air I'd breathe while I was cycling? I'd get wet in the rain. And I'd arrive at work all hot and sticky.

Cora: But you wouldn't if you allowed enough time to come across the park. It's really quite pleasant riding that way, and it's not much further. And it's cheaper.

Marcus: Yeah, anything would be cheaper than the buses in this town. If they weren't so expensive, more people would catch them. They should make them cheaper, or employers should pay part of people's bus fares. That would cut the traffic and we'd all get to work in much less time.

Cora: And it'd be healthier for everyone, whether they were on a bike or not.

Marcus: If the buses weren't too old and smelly. Some of them are terrible.

Cora: But so are cars and lorries, of course. So, are you getting the bus tomorrow, then?

Marcus: Well, I might consider it, but unfortunately the bus stop's a long way from my flat, so I'd have to get up earlier, and tomorrow's my day off anyway.

Cora: Honestly, I sometimes wonder how you manage to get out of bed in the mornings!

Marcus: Well, I don't have to tomorrow.

Cora: So we'd better get on with some work now.

Marcus: OK, OK.

Now listen again.

That is the end of Part 4.

You now have six minutes to check and copy your answers onto the answer sheet.

That is the end of the test.

Speaking
Part 1

Exercise 2b: Vocabulary and pronunciation

chemistry	biology	physics	environmental science
geography	history	philosophy	music
computing	religion	modern languages	literature

PAPER 2 Listening

There are four parts to the test. You will hear each part twice. For each part of the test there will be time for you to look through the questions and time for you to check your answers.

Write your answers on the question paper. You will have six minutes at the end of the test to copy your answers onto the answer sheet.

Part 1

There are seven questions in this part. For each question, there are three pictures and a short recording. Choose the correct picture and put a tick in the box below it.

Before we start, here is an example.

What will the boy take back to the shop?

Girl: Did you get everything you wanted?

Boy: I did. In fact I only needed to go into one shop. I'd seen a T-shirt in the window and I got the last one in the sale. And some shorts to match. I bought this jacket too but I'm not sure if I like it.

Girl: Oh, it looks great. I'd keep it. But those shorts are a horrible colour. I should change them.

Boy: You're right. They looked different in the shop.

The first picture is correct so there is a tick in box A.

Look at the three pictures for question 1 now.

Now we are ready to start. Listen carefully. You will hear each recording twice.

1 Which is the woman's house?

Woman: You can't miss my house. When you turn into the road, it's on the left. It's next to the house with a huge apple tree in the front garden. Ours has just got a few bushes and flowers. Oh, and there's a bus stop on the other side of the road from us.

Now listen again.

2 Where is the traffic jam?

Man: The police are advising drivers to avoid the city centre this morning if possible. Because the motorway is closed for repairs, there is increased traffic in the city. If you do have to drive into the city centre, turn right at the traffic lights in Kings Road so you avoid the roundabout at the top of Ship Street, where there is a huge queue of cars.

Now listen again.

3 Which wedding present has the man bought?

Woman: I need to buy Julie and Will a wedding present. Do you know what they want?

Man: Well, Julie said they wanted some cups to go with the plates I've got for them. But someone else might get those – you'll need to check with her. What about towels? Everyone always needs lots of those.

Woman: So boring! I'd prefer to buy them a picture or something more interesting.

Man: Well, I bought Julie a picture once and she never put it on the wall. It's difficult choosing for someone else.

Now listen again.

4 How did the man get home?

Man: Oh, I'm glad to be home. I gave up waiting for the bus and decided it would be quicker on foot, but because it was raining so much and there's such a narrow pavement, the cars kept splashing me as they passed. There's never a taxi when you want one.

Now listen again.

5 *What did Simon hurt?*

Woman: You're late home, Simon.

Boy: Sorry. I crashed into John while we were playing basketball at school. I had to push my bike home because I've hurt my knee. John's hurt his hand, lucky thing, so he won't be able to do his history exam tomorrow.

Woman: Let's have a look. At least you didn't break your ankle again like last year.

Now listen again.

6 *Which is the man's mother?*

Man: I'm looking for my mother. She said she'd get here early, so she should be here. You know her, don't you?

Woman: I haven't seen her for years. Is that her, look, with the dark hair and the glasses?

Man: That's not her. Her hair's white now, and she doesn't wear glasses any more. Oh, there she is, coming in now.

Now listen again.

7 *Which poster are they looking at?*

Girl: Can you look at this poster I've done for the concert? It was difficult to get all the information on. Is it clear enough?

Boy: Well, you did the right thing putting all the information at the bottom so people can see it easily. But you've forgotten to put the name of the school at the top. It looks strange with just an empty space there.

Girl: Oh, you're right. I'll add it later. I couldn't decide between a photograph of the school or this drawing of a violin. I think I made the right choice though.

Boy: Yeah, it looks more attractive than a photo.

Now listen again.

That is the end of Part 1.

Part 2

You will hear a successful fashion designer talking about his career. For each question, put a tick in the correct box.

You now have 45 seconds to look at the questions for Part 2.

Now we are ready to start. Listen carefully. You will hear the recording twice.

Fashion designer: I'm quite often asked how I got into fashion. For me, it was something I always wanted to do. However, because my mother was a university teacher and my father a headmaster, they found it hard to accept that fashion could be a serious career. I wasn't bad at school, I mean I was a typical student, passed enough exams and so on, and they could understand I might want to go to art college, but fashion just wasn't a serious subject for them.

Anyway, they said I had to do a year's business course first. I didn't like it at the time, but later, it made a big difference to me. For example, when I started my art college course, I could use a word processor, I knew about managing money, I had an idea of how to talk about business. None of the other students had that. And the other thing I did during that year was to get a part-time job in the office of a small factory making good-quality clothes. The pay was awful, but I learnt a lot there about that end of the industry, so I began to understand what's possible and what isn't. I mean, by watching people, I realised what you can and can't do with different types of cloth, what takes a long time to make on a sewing machine, you know.

Then I did two years at the local art college. I wanted to go to London straight away, but my parents insisted. I think they thought I was too young, I was still only seventeen by then, but in the end it was cost. London is a very expensive place for a student. So I stayed at home until I won a prize for a design which actually gave me a place at a

London college for nine months. There, I was able to make a lot of useful contacts – I was already working for an Italian fashion house three months before I left. I went on to spend three wonderful years in Milan, then I got the job in New York for a year, which was really exciting, but unbelievably stressful. I think probably because I was too far away from my family, more than any actual problems with the work itself. So, I ended up in London, starting my own company, which is stressful in a different way, but really I enjoy it very much.

Now listen again.

That is the end of Part 2.

Part 3

You will hear a tour guide talking to some tourists about a visit to a shopping centre. For each question, fill in the missing information in the numbered space.

You now have 20 seconds to look at Part 3.

Now we are ready to start. Listen carefully. You will hear the recording twice.

Tour guide: Before we go on to look at the cathedral, we're going to spend a couple of hours here in the shopping centre. So get out your wallets and your credit cards. Some of you might want to get some cash first of all. There is a bank. It's on the first floor. You can't miss it – it's next to the cookie shop. Just follow the delicious smell!

If you're looking for particular shops, it might be a good idea to have a map. The newsagent's over there has some which are free. See where I mean? OK?

When you've spent all your money, you'll want to have something to eat. If you want a proper meal, there's a really good restaurant in the main square opposite the fountain. But if you want to spend more time shopping, so just want to have a quick snack there are several places where you can get a sandwich and a drink, but the best one is the snack bar just over there beside the lifts. As well as sandwiches you can get salads and cakes. It's open now, but it does most of its business in the morning and at lunchtime, so it closes at a quarter past two. It's best to get there by about one o'clock anyway or there isn't much choice.

Now, the last thing is very important. We're meeting again at a quarter to three. If you go out of the centre through these doors and turn left, you'll see a large shop selling carpets. The coach will meet us outside the shop. The shop's name is Whitmarsh. Now, do you want to write that down – I'll spell it for you. That's W-H-I-T-M-A-R-S-H. OK? Now, have a good time and I'll see you later.

Now listen again.

That is the end of Part 3.

Part 4

Look at the six sentences for this part. You will hear a conversation between a girl, Alice, and a boy, Sam, about a play their school is doing called Romeo and Juliet. *Decide if each sentence is correct or incorrect. If it is correct, put a tick in the box under A for YES. If it is not correct, put a tick in the box under B for NO.*

You now have 20 seconds to look at the questions for Part 4.

Now we are ready to start. Listen carefully. You will hear the recording twice.

Alice: Hi Sam. What are you doing out here? There's a practice starting in five minutes for the school play. We've decided to do it under the big oak tree in the garden today – it's too hot inside.

Sam: I'm not going to come.

Alice: But you have to come. You're playing Romeo. How can we do *Romeo and Juliet* without Romeo?

Sam: I'm not going to be Romeo any more.

Alice: Oh, don't be silly. Why aren't you? You were so pleased when Miss Hayes chose you. And you're such a good actor, too.

Sam: Well, you might think so, but Miss Hayes doesn't. She says my voice isn't loud enough.

Alice: Oh, that's too bad. I know she asked you to speak louder at the first few practices we had, but you did what she said. You've got a louder voice than most of the other people acting anyway.

Sam: Well, she says she's not going to give me another chance.

Alice: I could go and talk to her. After all, I'm playing Juliet, so it's important I get on with the person who's acting Romeo. I'd prefer it to be you than anyone else.

Sam: It won't help, and she's already asked someone else to be Romeo anyway. She offered me another smaller part, but I don't really want it.

Alice: But it will be such a pity if you're not in the play at all. Why don't you take the part she's offering and maybe you can have a bigger part next time?

Sam: You can't persuade me. I spent such a long time learning Romeo's speeches. I can't start again. I'm going to offer to do the scenery instead. They're still looking for someone to do that.

Alice: So at least I'll see you at the practices. Come on then. I expect everyone's waiting for us.

Sam: I won't come today. I'll see Miss Hayes later and see what she thinks of my idea.

Now listen again.

That is the end of Part 4.

You now have six minutes to check and copy your answers onto the answer sheet.

That is the end of the test.

Test 4

PAPER 2 Listening

There are four parts to the test. You will hear each part twice. For each part of the test there will be time for you to look through the questions and time for you to check your answers.

Write your answers on the question paper. You will have six minutes at the end of the test to copy your answers onto the answer sheet.

Part 1

There are seven questions in this part. For each question, there are three pictures and a short recording. Choose the correct picture and put a tick in the box below it.

Before we start, here is an example.

What will the boy take back to the shop?

Girl: Did you get everything you wanted?

Boy: I did. In fact I only needed to go into one shop. I'd seen a T-shirt in the window and I got the last one in the sale. And some shorts to match. I bought this jacket too but I'm not sure if I like it.

Girl: Oh, it looks great. I'd keep it. But those shorts are a horrible colour. I should change them.

Boy: You're right. They looked different in the shop.

The first picture is correct so there is a tick in box A.

Look at the three pictures for Question 1 now.

Now we are ready to start. Listen carefully. You will hear each recording twice.

---

1 *Which job does the woman do now?*

Woman: All the time I was at school I wanted to be a nurse, but my mother worked in a shop and said it wasn't good to be on your feet all day. She wanted me to be a secretary. I did that for a while after I left college, but I wasn't very keen on it, so I retrained and now I'm doing what I always wanted to.

Now listen again.

2 *Where will they meet?*

Girl: Hi Pip. It's Angie. I'll see you outside the café tonight at seven thirty.

Boy: Oh, but I don't know where it is.

Girl: It's easy to find. It's opposite that new supermarket that's just opened.

Boy: I'm not sure where that is either. I'll wait for you by the bus station, then we can go to the café together. I'll know where the new supermarket is then too.

Now listen again.

3 *Where is the car park?*

Man: The best place to park is near the theatre. When you get to the roundabout, go straight across, then take the second turning on the right. The car park is on the left-hand side.

Now listen again.

4 *Which date is Brian's birthday?*

Man 1: John, did you know it's Brian's birthday next week, his 20th? It's on the 15th.

Man 2: That's Wednesday, isn't it? Is he having a party?

Man 1: Yes, on the 17th at about eight.

Man 2: Oh, next Friday. I hope I get asked.

Now listen again.

5 *Which photo are they looking at?*

Man 1: And who's in this photograph?

Man 2: Yes. That's my brother and his family, but it was taken a few years ago. He only had two children then – he's got three now. The third one was a boy after two girls. I don't see them very often because they live in Australia, but I hope to see them this year.

Now listen again.

6 *Which T-shirt is Beth wearing?*

Girl 1: Do you like the new T-shirt? I got it in the market.

Girl 2: It's great Beth. I bought one there myself the other day. It's got a pattern of black and white squares on it.

Girl 1: Oh, I didn't see those. I bought two, actually – this plain one that I'm wearing and one with some writing across the front. The problem is it's in a foreign language and I don't know what it says.

Girl 2: As long as it looks good, it doesn't matter.

Now listen again.

7 *Where is the man?*

Man: Hello Mary. The train arrived much earlier than I expected. I'm on the platform at the moment. Shall I get a taxi? There shouldn't be a long queue at this time of day ... OK ... I'll go and have a drink in the café while I wait for you.

Now listen again.

That is the end of Part 1.

Part 2

You will hear part of a radio programme called What's On. *For each question, put a tick in the correct box.*

You now have 45 seconds to look at the questions for Part 2.

Now we are ready to start. Listen carefully. You will hear the recording twice.

Martin: Welcome. Jenny and I have got lots to tell you, haven't we Jenny?

Jenny: That's right. This week, on Saturday night, Westfield Radio runs its annual competition.

Martin: What's it for, Jenny?

Jenny: Well, last year it was to find the best dancer, and next year it will be the turn of local actors to enter. But this year we're looking for the best singer in our city. You have to perform alone and we'll provide a musician.

Martin: And what are the rules?

Jenny: Not many. For example, there's no limit on age, whether you're 65 or six it doesn't matter – but you must live within five miles of the city centre. You need to phone your entry before Saturday. We don't accept entries through the post or by fax. And speaking of talent, there's a new theatre group starting every Saturday specially for teenagers.

Martin: And how do people get more information?

Jenny: If you're interested, you need to contact the theatre group's secretary, and I will give you her phone number later. They're going to meet in St Paul's School.

Martin: Right. Well, it's school holidays this week, so what's on offer?

Jenny: OK. To let as many people as possible use the sports hall this week, it will open an hour earlier than usual at 8 a.m. and shut later at 10.30 p.m. instead of nine. If you want to do one of the more popular activities, you should ring and book as usual. The indoor football pitch is always popular and has to be booked in advance.

Martin: But what about the swimming pool?

Jenny: Not quite such good news, I'm afraid. We'd hoped to tell you that the new swimming pool would be ready, but it's not. It will open however before the end of this month, that's about a week later than planned, but good news now – there will be no charge for swimmers for the whole of the first week that it's open. It's the same size as the old one but has much better facilities.

Martin: That's great. Now, Jenny, have you heard of the rock group called Switch?

Jenny: Yup, even I've heard about them, probably because two of their four members were born in Westfield, and all four of them now live here when they're not travelling around the world. This time last year they were four ordinary teenagers and now they're world-famous. Well, they're doing a concert on Saturday evening in the Town Hall, and it will be very popular.

Martin: So get your tickets quickly. Thank you Jenny.

Now listen again.

That is the end of Part 2.

Part 3

You will hear someone talking about the city of Cork. For each question, fill in the missing information in the numbered space.

You now have 20 seconds to look at Part 3.

Now we are ready to start. Listen carefully. You will hear the recording twice.

Tour guide: OK. Welcome, everybody. We're lucky with the weather today. It is unusual for it to be so hot here at this time of year – we're more used to rain, which is why everything's so green. Now, Cork is Ireland's second city and 420,000 people live here. That's much smaller than our capital city, Dublin, which has a population of one million, 58 thousand. The city centre is actually on an island surrounded by the river. When people arrive in the city by car, they often get very confused by all the bridges they keep crossing as they go from one part of the city to another.

As we walk down St Patrick Street, you'll see on one side old buildings going back to the eighteenth and nineteenth centuries. On the other side are mainly modern offices and shops. You may want to come back and spend some time looking at the older buildings and churches we pass. After that, we will visit the famous covered food market. If you want to stop and buy something, I suggest the bread, which they bake several times a day or some fresh fruit. They also sell fresh fish, but it's a bit hot to carry that around today. In the Grand Parade we'll go past some very pretty buildings, and then we'll stop in the café in the art gallery for a drink. This is an excellent place to have lunch if you want to come back another day. We can't visit the university and the public museum on this walk but I recommend that you go there another day. The museum is open every afternoon between two and five except Saturday, and it's also open in the evenings from Monday to Friday. Now, if you're ready, we'll set off.

Now listen again.

That is the end of Part 3.

Part 4

Look at the six sentences for this part. You will hear a conversation between a woman, Kim, and a man, Rob, who live in the same block of flats. Decide if each sentence is correct or incorrect. If it is correct, put a tick in the box under A for YES. If it is not correct, put a tick in the box under B for NO.

You now have 20 seconds to look at the questions for Part 4.

Now we are ready to start. Listen carefully. You will hear the recording twice.

Rob: Were you having a party in your flat last night?

Kim: What? I've got far too much college work to do to have time for parties.

Rob: So what was all that music?

Kim: Well, it helps me to think about my work.

Rob: I can't believe it. It was loud enough for me to be able to listen to it in my flat.

Kim: Oh, was it that loud? Did it disturb you?

Rob: Actually, it sounded quite nice – in the distance. I thought you had invited some friends round. I was thinking, why didn't she ask me and feeling sorry for myself.

Kim: But when I have friends in, I don't play loud music, because then we can't have a proper conversation.

Rob: Yes, I agree. But then I do like something quiet in the background when we're talking. Of course, it's the opposite when I'm trying to study.

Kim: You need complete silence, do you? With me, what happens is that I'm listening to the traffic if it's too quiet.

Rob: No, that doesn't worry me, I can shut that out. But I find if there's music, I'm paying attention to that instead of the work.

Kim: And what part of the day do you work best?

Rob: I don't have much choice, usually it has to be in the evening, although really I'm a morning person. But I have to go into college all day most days.

Kim: I'm useless in the mornings. But I can work right through from the early evening till the next morning if I have to.

Rob: Oh, I could never do that! I always need about three nights to recover if I miss a night's sleep.

Kim: Anyway, let me know if the music keeps you awake.

Rob: I'm sure it won't.

Now listen again.

That is the end of Part 4.

You now have six minutes to check and copy your answers onto the answer sheet.

That is the end of the test.

Test 5

PAPER 2 Listening

There are four parts to the test. You will hear each part twice. For each part of the test there will be time for you to look through the questions and time for you to check your answers.

Write your answers on the question paper. You will have six minutes at the end of the test to copy your answers onto the answer sheet.

Part 1

There are seven questions in this part. For each question, there are three pictures and a short recording. Choose the correct picture and put a tick in the box below it.

Before we start, here is an example.

What will the boy take back to the shop?

Girl: Did you get everything you wanted?

Boy: I did. In fact I only needed to go into one shop. I'd seen a T-shirt in the window and I got the last one in the sale. And some shorts to match. I bought this jacket too but I'm not sure if I like it.

Girl: Oh, it looks great. I'd keep it. But those shorts are a horrible colour. I should change them.

Boy: You're right. They looked different in the shop.

The first picture is correct so there is a tick in box A.

Look at the three pictures for question 1 now.

Now we are ready to start. Listen carefully. You will hear each recording twice.

1 *Which band did the boy watch last night?*

Boy: I saw that band Firestone on television last night. They're your favourite, aren't they?

Girl: They used to be, but they're not the same now they've only got one singer. It was really special when they had two and they sang together.

Boy: But they're still really good. The guitarist and the drummer are both still there, and they're brilliant. I really enjoyed watching them.

Now listen again.

2 *Where is the woman's new flat?*

Man: Where's your new flat, Kate?

Woman: It's at the top of a really tall block – it's one of four blocks of flats which are really close together, but the one I'm in is much taller than the others, so I've got a brilliant view.

Man: What of? Other blocks of flats?

Woman: Well, yes, but I can see trees and green fields in the far distance and the whole of the city. There's a main road outside the front door to the flats, but I can't hear it because I'm so high up.

Now listen again.

3 *Where is the magazine?*

Boy: I bought a magazine about computers yesterday and I can't find it. I left it on the kitchen table. Have you seen it?

Mother: Well, if I see a computer magazine, I usually put it with the others upstairs next to the computer, so you could try there. And you'd better look in that pile of magazines by the bin. I'm going to throw them away.

Boy: Let's see. Yes! I asked you just in time. I won't leave it on the kitchen table next time.

Now listen again.

4 *Which is the boy's teacher?*

Boy: I've just started learning the piano. I've got a really nice teacher. He's called Mr Hall.

Girl: Oh, I know, he taught me when I was quite young. He's got a beard and lots of black hair, hasn't he? I used to be quite frightened of him.

Boy: Well, the Mr Hall who teaches me hasn't got much hair and it's grey, but he does have a beard. And wears glasses.

Girl: But it is the same man, I'm sure. I was only little when he was teaching me.

Now listen again.

5 *What did the man receive in the post?*

Man: Was there any post for me this morning?

Woman: Yes, there was. Two letters and a postcard. Here you are.

Man: One of the letters is for you. I'm expecting a parcel. Did it come?

Woman: Oh yes. I put it over there, look.

Now listen again.

6 *What time is the flight from New York expected?*

Woman: Excuse me, I'm waiting for flight 712 from New York. It was supposed to arrive at nine twenty. It's nine thirty-five now and there's been no announcement of a delay or anything.

Man: I'm sorry, Madam. We've just had a message to say it took off an hour and a half late. Arrival time is now ten fifty-five.

Woman: That's too bad. I've been here since half past eight and it probably won't arrive when you say. I expect I'll be here till midday. That's a whole morning wasted.

Man: I can only apologise, Madam.

Now listen again.

7 *What was the boy doing when the phone rang?*

Girl: What did you do yesterday evening?

Boy: Well, I was supposed to look after my four-year-old cousin while my aunt went to the theatre. But I wanted to watch the match on television, so she found someone else. The annoying thing was that the phone rang halfway through, and I missed the best goal. I'd finished all my homework early, too.

Now listen again.

That is the end of Part 1.

Part 2

You will hear a woman talking to an evening class about carpentry. For each question, put a tick in the correct box.

You now have 45 seconds to look at the questions for Part 2.

Now we are ready to start. Listen carefully. You will hear the recording twice.

Woman: Hi. Well, it's great to see you all. When I suggested this class, they said women don't need a carpentry class. Now, I know that girls in school can do carpentry nowadays if they want to, but when I was at school, it was a boys' subject, and that was that. So, when I got my own flat, I had no idea at all how to put up a shelf even. But when I saw it would cost six months' wages to employ someone to fix my kitchen cupboards, I decided to learn. That was eighteen months ago. I've spent the past couple of months working on a chest of drawers, which I finished last week. I've decided to put it in the sitting room or perhaps the hall, although actually, my original plan was to use it in my bedroom, but now it's finished, it looks so good I don't want to hide it away! So, you see it's not too difficult.

First of all, I want to say a bit about equipment. You will need to buy a few things. Usually it's a good idea to buy the best quality you can afford. Now, that doesn't mean you have to get lots of expensive electric tools. Hand tools are fine. They're slower of course, but you have more control at a slower speed. However, if you aren't very strong, the power of electric tools can be a real help. So you shouldn't feel that's cheating, if that's what you need. Make sure you take good advice on exactly which ones to buy before you spend any money though.

The next point is, don't expect to make anything very big or difficult for the first few months at least. You need to develop your carpentry skills fairly slowly, adding to them with each new thing you make. If you don't, you'll make furniture which doesn't work well, or doesn't look good enough for friends to see, and you won't enjoy what you're doing.

Lastly, you must plan everything you do really carefully. You begin with a list of everything that's going to be necessary, and then think about the order in which you are going to work. So, what I want you to do now is to imagine you want to put up a shelf in the bathroom – and make that list. Then we'll look at the lists together and see what you've forgotten! OK?

Now listen again.

That is the end of Part 2.

Part 3

You will hear someone talking on the radio about a fashion show. For each question, fill in the missing information in the numbered space.

You now have 20 seconds to look at Part 3.

Man: Today we have with us Geraldine Smith, who's going to tell us about this autumn's fashion show. Is it the same as usual, Geraldine?

Woman: Yes, that's right. There are ten art colleges altogether from the area who are taking part. This year the show will be in the sports stadium on the 26th of October. That's a bit later than usual – we usually do it in September – and it will start at seven thirty.

We've done something a bit different this year. We've told the students that they have to make clothes in particular colours – they must all be either grey or blue. So if your favourite colour is red or orange, you won't find it here this year.

The show starts at seven thirty, but before that at six thirty a top hairdresser will give a talk about matching the way you do your hair to look good with the clothes you wear. That will be in the room behind the main hall.

There'll be some stalls around the stadium selling clothes – looking at the list, you'll be able to buy almost anything from sports clothes to winter coats, but there won't be any shoes for sale this year, as we haven't really got room for people to sit down and try them on.

At the end of the evening, we'll announce who has won the prize for the best design. The prize is usually money, but this year we have a computer to give away so I'm sure that will be very useful to whoever wins.

Because we're holding the event at the sports stadium, which is out of town, there'll be two special buses leaving from outside the cinema at six o'clock and seven o'clock.

Entrance tickets are only £2.50 each and they can be reserved by ringing 0965 763298.

Now listen again.

That is the end of Part 3.

Part 4

Look at the six sentences for this part. You will hear a conversation between a boy, Ian, and a girl, Zoë, about a holiday. Decide if each sentence is correct or incorrect. If it is correct, put a tick in the box under A for YES. If it is not correct, put a tick in the box under B for NO.

You now have 20 seconds to look at the questions for Part 4.

Now we are ready to start. Listen carefully. You will hear the recording twice.

Zoë: What are you doing for your holiday this year?

Ian: I might be going to Africa.

Zoë: Wow! How can you do that?

Ian: Well, my uncle and aunt are going to Namibia for a month, and they've asked me to go with them. I have to pay for my air fare, but that's all.

Zoë: You're so lucky. It's a really brilliant place for a trip, I've heard.

Ian: The thing is, I don't know yet whether I'll be able to. I've been saving up, but I don't know whether I'll have enough.

Zoë: Couldn't you borrow from your parents?

Ian: The problem is, they really want me to spend my holiday with them, touring round the United States. They haven't said I can't go to Africa, but they're not going to make it easy for me.

Zoë: That's a real shame.

Ian: Yes, especially as I can go to the States anytime. I've got cousins there, so it'd be easy.

Zoë: Oh, well, it all sounds very exciting. I don't expect I'll get farther than London.

Ian: Surely your family could afford to go abroad if they wanted to?

Zoë: Oh, of course we could. But my dad doesn't really like going away – he says he's out at work all year and he wants a week or two in his own garden. It certainly isn't what I want to do. And my mum isn't keen on planes, so she doesn't mind if we don't go anywhere by air.

Ian: Would they lend you the money to go somewhere, do you think?

Zoë: It would depend who with.

Ian: Well, what about my uncle and aunt's trip? If you came, it'd be even better. And my parents might agree to help me a bit with the cost, if yours help you.

Zoë: But would I be welcome?

Ian: I'm sure they'd love you to come along. Why don't I ask them?

Now listen again.

That is the end of Part 4.

You now have six minutes to check and copy your answers onto the answer sheet.

That is the end of the test.

Test 6

PAPER 2 Listening

There are four parts to the test. You will hear each part twice. For each part of the test there will be time for you to look through the questions and time for you to check your answers.

Write your answers on the question paper. You will have six minutes at the end of the test to copy your answers onto the answer sheet.

Part 1

There are seven questions in this part. For each question, there are three pictures and a short recording. Choose the correct picture and put a tick in the box below it.

Before we start, here is an example.

What will the boy take back to the shop?

Girl: Did you get everything you wanted?

Boy: I did. In fact I only needed to go into one shop. I'd seen a T-shirt in the window and I got the last one in the sale. And some shorts to match. I bought this jacket too but I'm not sure if I like it.

Girl: Oh, it looks great. I'd keep it. But those shorts are a horrible colour. I should change them.

Boy: You're right. They looked different in the shop.

The first picture is correct so there is a tick in box A.

Look at the three pictures for question 1 now.

Now we are ready to start. Listen carefully. You will hear each recording twice.

1 Which instrument is the girl learning now?

Boy: Are you still having violin lessons?

Girl: Well, unfortunately my violin teacher moved away, so I'll start again when I find a new teacher. But I'm teaching myself to play the keyboard. I want to play in my brother's band. He needs someone to play the drums too so if you hear of anyone…

Now listen again.

2 What will they buy for Lucy?

Girl: Shall we get Lucy a book for her birthday? How about one about painting? She's just started some art classes.

Boy: Oh, her mum's got lots of books about art. Why don't we get her a book about sailing – you know she's going on a sailing holiday soon? Or a cookery book? That would be useful.

Girl: But boring. I think my idea is best. She doesn't want to borrow her mum's books all the time.

Boy: OK then.

Now listen again.

3 What will the weather be like on Sunday?

Woman: Here is the weather forecast for the next few days. The fine weather will continue today and tomorrow, but enjoy it because on Sunday it will be cloudy. It won't rain until Monday, and then the rain will only last a few hours. After that, we'll get the fine weather back again.

Now listen again.

4 What did the boy leave in the girl's house?

Girl's voice: I'm sorry I'm not here at the moment. Please leave a message after the tone.

Boy: Oh, hi Sarah. It's Jamie. When you get home, could you have a look and see if I left my wallet in your house? I put it down when I

was showing you that new CD I'd bought. Oh, and by the way I've got your mobile. You asked me to look after it when we were in town, remember? Then I forgot to give it back to you. Ring me back as soon as you can.

Now listen again.

5 What will the boy get from the shop?

Boy: 562900.

Mother: Oh, Sam I'm going to be late home. Could you go to the shop and get something please? I think we'll have an omelette and some salad tonight. We've got eggs and tomatoes, but could you go and buy a lettuce?

Boy: OK. Shall I get some cheese? I like cheese omelette.

Mother: We've got lots in the fridge. But buy some mushrooms to go with it.

Now listen again.

6 Which sport is unavailable today?

Man: Welcome to the activity centre. You have a choice of sports today – indoor or outdoor. There's gymnastics in the hall, and there's an instructor for those of you who haven't done it before. You won't be able to play tennis today – the courts are too wet after all the rain we've had – but we are going to organise a game of volleyball outside today instead.

Now listen again.

7 What is the girl wearing?

Girl: Look what I got in the sales today. What do you think? It suits me, doesn't it?

Boy: It's a nice colour and it goes with your jeans. But aren't the sleeves a bit long?

Girl: I like them like this. It was very cheap anyway.

Now listen again.

That is the end of Part 1.

Part 2

You will hear a radio interview with a teenage boy called Matthew who has invented a game. For each question, put a tick in the correct box.

You now have 45 seconds to look at the questions for Part 2.

Now we are ready to start. Listen carefully. You will hear the recording twice.

Interviewer: Welcome Matthew. You invented a game recently, didn't you?

Matthew: I invented a mini-baseball game a few years ago now, and it's become very popular. I'm fourteen now, but I had the idea when I was 10. It took some time for me to persuade people to take me seriously, so the game didn't actually go on sale until the day after my thirteenth birthday.

Interviewer: And it's made and sold by a small American company?

Matthew: That's right, but when I first tried to find a company to make the game, I didn't have any luck. Some companies didn't reply and the ones who did reply just thought it was a joke because I'm a child. None of them let me show them the game.

Interviewer: What did you do then?

Matthew: When I couldn't get a company to help, my dad went to the bank, but they wouldn't lend us the money. But my parents have a friend who's a really good businessman, and he helped us to make a business plan. Then we talked to my grandmother and my great aunt who are quite rich. They were happy to lend us enough to make the first thousand games. After that, we persuaded a company to make the game for us.

Interviewer: So have you got any more ideas?

Matthew: Yes, I have actually. I've got an idea for a game for younger children. I was watching my sisters playing one day and I got the idea from them. Then I tried it on some other children. The company arranges for me to visit different schools. I ask them what they enjoy and try my ideas on them.

Interviewer: So it's for younger children?

Matthew: Yes. The toy company did some research, and between the ages of five and six, children are interested in animals, colour, food – things to do with their own lives. By the time they're eight, they like the opposite – they prefer games where they can invent things and are more imaginative. Then, between ten and twelve, they enjoy games based on knowledge – quizzes and things like that.

Interviewer: Well, what does the future hold for you Matthew?

Matthew: It's OK inventing games now while I'm young, but when I leave school, I want to do something different. I'd like to learn how to run a business, so that's what I'll study at college. I think actually I'd prefer to work for a company rather than have my own business. You don't have to worry so much then.

Now listen again.

That is the end of Part 2.

Part 3

You will hear a radio announcer giving some information about a cycling holiday with Pathway Holidays. For each question, fill in the missing information in the numbered space.

You now have 20 seconds to look at Part 3.

Now we are ready to start. Listen carefully. You will hear the recording twice.

Announcer: And last today on our holiday programme we have some information about cycling holidays. They're run by Pathway Holidays, and the next one is from Monday 12th June until Saturday 17th June. On this trip, you cycle from Whitehaven in the northwest of England to Sunderland in the northeast. On most days, you cycle around 40 km, the maximum on any day being 50 kms, so over the whole trip you'll cycle about 210 kms.

The trip passes through beautiful countryside. The routes are planned so that you don't have to ride up too many hills. The steepest part is near the end when you get to the highest point of the ride. This is known as Black Hill because of the colour of the rock. After that, it's downhill to the North Sea.

The total cost of the tour is £652 and that includes your hotel, all meals, the transport of your luggage and a guide. This is someone who knows the area and can tell you about it on the route. In fact, the price includes everything except bicycle hire. It's possible to hire a bicycle and you should book one in advance if you want to do that, but they recommend bringing your own bicycle. It's often more comfortable to ride one that you are used to.

Entertainment is provided in the first hotel in Whitehaven – there'll be a musical evening. On Wednesday evening, the hotel you're staying in will organise a quiz, and on the last evening – that's Friday – there'll be a party.

If you'd like more information about the trip, the company advises you to look at their website, and I'll tell you what that is in a minute. We're just going to talk to someone who did this cycling holiday recently...

Now listen again.

That is the end of Part 3.

Part 4

Look at the six sentences for this part. You will hear a conversation between a girl, Jane, and her mother about where Jane will work next month. Decide if each sentence is correct or incorrect. If it is correct, put a tick in the box under A for YES. If it is not correct, put a tick in the box under B for NO.

You now have 20 seconds to look at the questions for Part 4.

Now we are ready to start. Listen carefully. You will hear the recording twice.

Jane: Mum, next month all the people in our class have to spend a week going to work instead of going to school. It's to give us an idea of what we want to do when we leave school. I wondered if I could come to work with you? . . . Are you listening, Mum?

Mother: Yes, I'm listening. Do you think that's a good idea? I'm so busy I wouldn't have time to show you anything. And it's not really very exciting. Let's think of somewhere else you could go.

Jane: But I hear so much about your office. I sometimes feel I've known all the people for years, but I don't even know what they look like.

Mother: But you don't want to be a lawyer. You've always said you want to do something different from Dad and me.

Jane: But I might want to be a lawyer. I want to find out about lots of different jobs – there are so many opportunities nowadays – and then I'll decide what I'm going to do when I leave school.

Mother: What are all your friends going to do during this special week? Are they all going to work with their mums or dads?

Jane: Most of them want to work with children in a primary school for a week, but they already know what that's like. I think it's better to try something you don't know anything about. They're losing a good chance to do something different.

Mother: Well, in that case you don't want to come to work with me – you said I never stop talking about it, so it's not going to be a surprise to you.

Jane: But I want to know what it's really like and what you really do.

Mother: Well, I'm not terribly happy about it. But if it's what you really want and you promise not to complain if you're bored, I'll do it.

Now listen again.

That is the end of Part 4.

You now have six minutes to check and copy your answers onto the answer sheet.

That is the end of the test.

THE SHEFFIELD COLLEGE
CASTLE LEARNING CENTRE